6 Pathways to Leadership & Organizational Success

D1468831

Curt Weeden

Quadrafoil Press
11159 S Riverwood Dr.
Portland, OR 97219

ISBN: 978-0-9743714-2-9

First Quadrafoil Press paperback printing: February 2020
Printed in the U.S.A.

The Quadrafoil Press Speakers Bureau (Capital Media) can bring authors to your live event. For more information about scheduling author Curt Weeden for a speaking appearance, contact Quadrafoil at: info@6pathways.com.

For My Family – and Yours

CONTENTS

Foreword

6 Pathways is an amazing two-for-one book.

First, read the prologue and epilogue. These two chapters detail a breakthrough method for identifying and then prioritizing leadership as well as organizational principles and practices. Thanks to input from 200 nonprofit and private sector executives, the beginning and end of *6 Pathways* describe how to single out those high-priority core values organizations can use to develop strong leadership teams and more effective governing boards.

Next, turn to Chapter One which is the curtain opener to a true story – a memoir that has all the earmarks of a David McCullough historical novel. Author Curt Weeden takes us on a literary ride that stretches from upper-middle class suburbia to New York City's poorest neighborhoods; from the dark cloud of the Vietnam War to CIA operations in South America; from the labor union movement to the business start-up dreams of a pasta maker. On the long road to becoming one of America's most influential philanthropy experts, Curt interacted with U.S. presidents, high-profile celebrities, business moguls, and scurrilous criminals. All left an imprint – sometimes inspirational, sometimes bloody. The adventure tale caught between the opening and closing bookends of *6 Pathways* tells us a lot about America over the past six decades.

Curt and I have worked together for several years co-directing the New Strategies program at Georgetown University's McDonough

School of Business. We have studied hundreds of nonprofit organizations with revenues ranging in size from under $1 million a year to those with billion-dollar annual budgets. A New Strategies Business Advisory Council has provided us with helpful private sector insights from 30 companies all recognized for their corporate responsibility leadership.

Interacting with so many nonprofit and business leaders over the years has left both Curt and me with a lot of questions. Is there a common set of beliefs and behaviors that both business and nonprofit leaders recognize as especially important for organization success? When looking for new hires or making decisions about promoting employees to management positions, what core values should be taken into account? Do organizations function better when leaders have an alignment of beliefs and principles? Or, should an institution (business, nonprofit organization, association, other) embrace leaders who have different value priorities?

6 Pathways helps answer these and numerous other questions. Curt gives us a "Pathways Compass" that helps organizations chart a course by rank ordering a long list of behaviors and beliefs he has chronicled over the years. The Compass is an easy and helpful resource businesses and nonprofit organizations can use to shed light on high-priority values ("A truly enlightening exercise," noted a New York City cultural organization executive whose comment was echoed by many others after being asked to prioritize the Compass's 50 statements). Aside from being an eye opener for those already in leadership roles, Curt's Pathways Compass can be especially valuable to any organization concerned about capacity building – something particularly important to many if not most of the nation's 1.4 million nonprofits.

Over and over, nonprofit executives who attend our Georgetown New Strategies program talk about what they consider to be a vexing challenge. These leaders feel nonprofit boards of directors too often fall short in enhancing the capacity of an organization to meet or exceed current expectations. *6 Pathways* should help address this concern. While in most cases, a board member's core values are in sync with a nonprofit's mission statement, there are unstated differences in views and beliefs about practices and actions needed to carry out that mission. The Pathways Compass helps uncover those underlying differences that sometimes impact decisions board members make – or don't make.

The Pathways Compass is a non-threatening and productive way to extract board member values. The process can be revealing – and can pave the way for a board to reach consensus on key goals and objectives. Here's an example:

A nonprofit asks each member of its board to review and prioritize the Pathway Compass list of 50 principles and practices. One of the half dozen selections most board members put in the "six most important pathways" category is the following: "Visions that are possible are not always probable." A couple of board members strongly disagree. They contend that by over-fixating on probabilities, visions can easily die on the vine. The Compass has uncovered fundamental differences that explain why it is so difficult for board members to reach full consensus on specific program proposals some think have a low probability of success while others criticize those same proposals for not being visionary enough.

Staying with this same example, the Pathways Compass finds *all* board members in agreement that another of the 50 statements ("Pursue purpose and deflect distraction") is high priority for the organization. With the Compass having uncovered common ground, the board sorts out programs and activities that have a probability of success, while at the same time advance a more ambitious vision. These are the initiatives the board unanimously agrees should be *purposely pursued* by the organization (with limited or no distraction).

6 Pathways is likely to bring about systemic changes much the way Curt's first book did when the independent publisher Berrett-Koehler (BK) brought Weeden's *Corporate Social Investing* to market more than two decades ago. BK had (and still has) a reputation for producing some of the best and most influential books in the organization development and institutional leadership resource field. Of all its publications (distributed worldwide in 50 languages), here is what BK says about *Corporate Social Investing:* "… this book has had a far bigger impact than anything we have imagined." This conclusion is not an understatement. Curt's *Corporate Social Investing* has been used by businesses for years to shape strategies for dispensing cash and product donations. Nonprofit organizations have developed new ways to approach corporations based on concepts spelled out in the book.

Fast forward to present day. Along comes *6 Pathways*. It promises to have as much or more impact on business and nonprofit organizations as did Curt's first publication.

While the inside chapters of *6 Pathways* are as interesting and entertaining as any book on the market, it is what Curt gives us in his prologue and epilogue that will endure as an avenue for identifying and developing leaders best suited to build strong, effective organizations.

Bill Novelli
Professor, Georgetown University McDonough School of Business
Author: *Purpose, Passion and Profit: How to Win by Attacking the World's Major Social Problems* (Johns Hopkins University Press – 2020 release)

Note: Georgetown Professor Bill Novelli was CEO of AARP from 2001 – 2009. Earlier, he was president of the Campaign for Tobacco-Free Kids and executive vice president of CARE, the international relief organization. A leader in social marketing and social change, Bill co-founded and was president of Porter Novelli, a global public relations firms (now part of the marketing and communications firm, Omnicom). He co-chairs the Coalition to Transform Advance Care (C-TAC) and sits on several boards including the American Cancer Society.

Introduction

"Memory is a curious machine and strangely capricious."

So wrote Samuel Clemens (Mark Twain) in his short novel, *Three Thousand Years Among the Microbes*. In digging through over a half century of memories in preparation for writing *6 Pathways*, I came to understand Clemens was correct. I discovered some recollections to be undeniably faulty while others truly capricious. I weeded out questionable remembrances and used what was left as cornerstones for this book. For each chapter, I applied a few self-imposed editorial guidelines:

- Men and women referenced with both their first and last names are real people (some still alive; others no longer with us).
- Individuals referenced by just a first name are actual characters – last names have been omitted either because they cannot be recalled or because disclosing their full names would prove either embarrassing or harmful.
- All events and locations mentioned in the book are factual. (However, in a few cases, I have given myself editorial license to modify dates and/or venue details mainly to avoid adding lengthy, irrelevant explanations.)
- Quoted statements are representations of conversations and while words and phrases may be imprecise, they are my attempt to capture content and tone.

Memories are "little threads that hold life's patches of meaning together," is another notable Clemens' quote (from his *Morals and Memory* speech). This simple statement describes what *6 Pathways* strives to do: stitch together memories with observations and revelations that open the door to a better understanding of what life means – or could mean if lessons taught were truly lessons learned. Making the leap from old memories to new pathways that point us toward a more productive personal and professional life required the time and thoughtfulness of many, many nonprofit and business leaders. Their input and support have been invaluable.

- Curt Weeden

Prologue

From Life Lessons to New Pathways

"50?"

The talented editor and educator Norm Goldman (see chapter 6) clearly was having trouble wrapping his mind around 50 "life lessons" plugged into the manuscript he had been asked to review.

"You know, Moses only had 10 points he wanted to make – not 50," Norm reminded me. "And even *he* had trouble getting people's attention."

I was trying to digest Norm's comment when Tom Harvey shot me an email. Tom is a prominent Notre Dame University faculty member and formerly head of Catholic Charities USA (see chapter 14). "Focus on five or six of your list of 50," Tom suggested. "Keep the others as a backdrop. Five or six can have real impact; 50 cannot."

Of the 20 other friends and former colleagues I had asked to review observations of principles and practices I had made over the past 60 years, many voiced a similar refrain. Figure out how to shrink the list to a few high-priority signposts that could be useful to people and organizations serious about charting the best possible course for the future. But how to whittle 50 down to five or six? Which of the many observations would be the most relevant to others – and why?

Thankfully I had access to over 700 senior nonprofit executives with whom I had the privilege of working when they took part in an advanced management education program called "New Strategies." These high-level leaders (most CEOs or executive directors) are responsible for organizations with revenues that range from $1 billion a year to smaller nonprofits operating with less than $10 million per annum. I appealed to 175 of these leaders to take time to study the list of 50 life lessons and single out the five or six most important to them as well as their staffs and organization volunteers (in some cases numbering in the thousands).

Once the return data was tabulated, the results were revealing. See the epilogue for more detailed explanations as to why executives with such wide influence in America selected the following six pathways as important avenues to personal and professional success:

- **In your own way, be insatiably curious.**
- **Intellect, skill, and wisdom are not exclusive to those with a formal education.**
- **Use positive thinking as a lens to look for an opportunity almost always hidden in a problem.**
- **Many errors are starting blocks for improved performance.**
- **Creating can be hard; sustaining can be harder.**
- **A leader's character casts a wide shadow.**

Notably, all 50 life lessons received at least a few "votes" by nonprofit leaders. "I loved them all, so it was hard to choose," wrote Joanna Sebelien, chief resource officer for Harvesters, a prominent food network in Kansas City, Missouri. "It wasn't an easy choice – there are so many great options..." noted Shari Blindt, executive director of Common Hope in St. Paul, Minnesota. "What a challenge!" said Brian McConnell, executive director of the American

Red Cross Finger Lakes Chapter. (For a rank-order overview of the complete list, see page 285-287.)

My blue-ribbon nonprofit selection panel also decisively picked another five "pathways" that fell into a "nearly as relevant" cluster. The runner-up group included:

- **Bad news is best delivered directly and honestly, but with empathy.**
- **A strong delivery with light content is usually more effective than a tepid delivery with strong content.**
- **Talk and promises are easy; deliverables are not.**
- **Hubris may bring attention, but humility will win respect.**
- **Everyone's a salesperson – some better than others.**

Many nonprofit leaders added comments about how one or more of the life lessons impacted their own careers. "I have never stopped being curious and in awe of the great diversity of projects, problems, and solutions," wrote Lisa Ackerman, World Monument Fund chief operating officer, about the top-rated selection. Even those life lessons not considered a high priority by most respondents proved very important to some nonprofit leaders. Paola Vita, the chief advancement officer for New York City Outward Bound Schools, wrote that one life lesson ("*Gray power is America's most unexploited energy source*") is a call to "seek a diversity of perspectives and to look broadly for wisdom."

In reaching out to the nonprofit world, I made a deliberate effort to solicit views from high-level managers active in most corners of the sector: education, health, arts/culture, social services, environment, religion, and disaster response. Feedback came from young and old as well as from decision-makers of all colors who lived and worked in different parts of the country. Still, these were all individuals active in the nonprofit field. Each respondent had opted to circumvent the business and government sectors to work for organizations that had socially important missions and goals. Would their top *6 Pathways* line up with those selected by managers outside the nonprofit world? I decided to find out.

Twenty-five corporate executives I know (and greatly respect) agreed to join a sample group willing to replicate the same sorting process carried out by nonprofit leaders. While smaller than the nonprofit cohort, the business participants were representative of most of the country's largest industry segments: finance, insurance, health care, retail, manufacturing, food/beverage, and entertainment.

When the responses from the business executives were tallied...

The six top choices were exactly the same as those singled out by nonprofit leaders!

While the rank ordering was slightly different between the two responding groups, these half dozen life lessons were judged more important than 44 other options by those in leadership positions in both the nonprofit and for-profit sectors.

A note of clarification: Both survey groups were asked to select five or six life lessons without any requirement to rank those choices by importance or interest (although some executives did so). Through a careful tabulation of results from all respondents, life lessons receiving the largest number of overall "votes" were added to the *6 Pathways* list. Only a few executives picked all six of the highest-ranked options. Most, however, did select at least half the life lessons that surfaced to the top six on the list.

A Pathways Compass

So what do these findings mean?

The small sample certainly can and should be tested with a much larger population of businesses and nonprofit organizations. However, the 200 reactions are definitive enough to warrant putting together a resource called a "Pathways Compass" available to organizations for use in recruiting or evaluating executive-level

leaders. The Compass points the way to those fundamental principles and beliefs that help answer these important questions: Where
does a leader (or prospective leader) stand relative to an organization's basic mission and values? How closely does a leader's choice
of high-priority principles and practices line up with the "top six"
pathway selections made by executives from prominent nonprofit
and business organizations?

Because an individual's pathway choices don't happen to
coincide with the top-tier selections made by other executives
doesn't necessarily mean the person is (or could be) an ineffective or incompetent leader. As pointed out by several of the
200 people who studied the list of 50 pathway options, all had
relevance. The level of importance of each was often determined
by an organization's *raison d'être*. As Steve Hower, an executive
with the health and humanitarian nonprofit Heart to Heart
International, pointed out: "All (50 choices) are very thought-
provoking." The lengthy list of life lessons prompted many to
probe how their own priority principles and values fit with those
of their organization. "Gave me time to pause and reflect," said
Christine Culver, a vice president at the United Performing Arts
Fund in Milwaukee.

Still, with six pathways deemed highly important among successful business and nonprofit senior managers, the Pathways Compass
gives organizations a platform to discuss leadership ideas and
beliefs with current and potential executives. Where choices do not
coincide with the top national rankings, a conversation about the
reason for the variance can be illuminating. For example, if someone assigns a high level of importance to the life lesson that says:
"Outcomes are inches on impact's yardstick" (not one of the six top
pathways), the individual is telling the organization that there is
too much emphasis on short-term achievements (outcomes) rather
than long-term effects (impact). Using the Pathways Compass to
get this concern into the open can itself be very beneficial.

The epilogue at the close of this book details why each of the
six nationally-determined pathway selections can be so important

to an organization and its leadership. But as a lead-up to that closing chapter, many nonprofit and business leaders have pointed out there is a lot of missing information.

"I'm curious to know more about the specific meaning or thoughts behind these life lessons," wrote Mike Wynne, president & CEO of Emerge Community Development in Minneapolis.

Mike wasn't the only one with an inquiring mind. "How in the world did you come up with these observations?" was the most frequently asked question by those reviewing the list of 50.

"Sixty years in the making," I would answer.

"But you need to give us some context," I was told. "Things must have happened in your life that led you to put this list together."

"That they did," I would admit. "That they did." And for those with enough interest and time on their hands, I would tell them the story ...

Chapter 1

Chellel's Market (1958)

In 1958, the epicenter of one of Rhode Island's most desirable suburbs was marked by an upscale grocery market called Chellel's. The store anchored the south side of a small commercial hub trafficked regularly by many of Barrington's 13,000 residents. Barrington was in the white outer rim of commuter communities that encircled Providence, the state's capital city that was turning increasingly brown, black and mottled. No establishment said more about Barrington than Chellel's. Its inventory was high quality and high priced. Its patrons were a cut above shoppers who favored Almacs, the less expensive chain supermarket located only two blocks away. Because Chellel's fronted Barrington's main thoroughfare just at the road's most consequential turn, the store was an oft-referenced landmark. Bear left at Chellel's and County Road would point you out of town in the direction of less-appealing destinations such as Warren and Bristol. Or go straight at Chellel's and travel Rumstick Road into the core of Barrington's affluence. With its prominent location and its unequaled reputation, Chellel's was the town's beacon of prosperity and privilege.

Those who frequently shopped Chellel's had money. It was not uncommon to find an Aston Martin or Porsche Speedster parked aside the store. Shoppers wore Mary Quant or Emilio Pucci as casual clothes. The "regulars" had addresses in a section of Barrington reputed for having the town's highest standard of living. Not everyone in this gilded zone was super-rich; some were marginally well-to-do and owned stylishly modest homes. However, Barrington's extreme elite displayed their status in impressive estates, many of which commanded magnificent views of Narragansett Bay. The most prosperous customers were from the Rumstick and Adams Point sections of town and were well-known to Chellel's staff. For the wealthy, the market was a place to mix shopping with agreeable conversation. Checkout chatter might be about a regatta at the Barrington Yacht Club, perhaps the town's most exclusive society since its founding in the early 1900s. Or about a ladies' golf tournament to be played at the tony and private Rhode Island Country Club, an 18-hole championship course that added a luxurious green carpet to the western edge of the most enviable part of town.

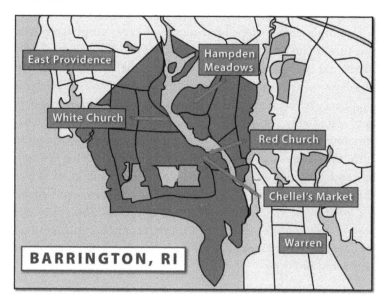

It wasn't only the wealthy who traded at Chellel's; Barrington's fast-growing middle class would sometimes bypass Almacs and willingly overpay Chellel's for tangible goods knowing each purchase came with a bonus: status. On special occasions when fine food was on the table, a host or hostess would deliberately but ever-so offhandedly mention dinner began with a trip to Chellel's. Guests would nod knowingly and return to their dining and drinking made more sumptuous by what they had already suspected. The number of not-so-rich who shopped at Chellel's became the town's economic barometer. When times were good, checkout lines were a fusion of customers from most all of Barrington's neighborhoods. When conditions changed and spooked the middle class away, the store would make the necessary adjustments by cutting expenses (a.k.a. hourly help). For me, this basic, underlying principle of American capitalism would become very personal by mid-summer of 1958.

At the close of my junior year at Barrington High School, I applied for a part-time job at Chellel's, much to the amusement of my parents. They reminded me the store had a reputation for hiring sons and daughters of well-heeled, dedicated customers. The rich wanted their children in the job market not because they needed money but because Chellel's was a kind of finishing school. This was a place where practicing customer relations was a warm-up to oral interviews with Brown, Yale, or Penn. "You'd be better off at Almacs," my father advised me. The chain supermarket was the store of choice for Barrington's common folk which made it, I was told, a far more appropriate work option for someone stuck in my class stratum. I had older friends who held after-school jobs at Almacs. Like all employees, they wore the store's mandatory *I'm Happy to Help You* buttons but quickly complained that happiness of any kind was in short supply. Full-time workers groused about low pay, bad hours and poor working conditions. Even with this insider information, I reluctantly took my father's recommendation and filled out an employment application for Almacs, all the while hoping Chellel's would save me from Barrington's "other" grocery store.

3

For a reason never disclosed, Chellel's did hire me. Maybe a mistake? A fluke? The store surely had to know I lived in a section of Barrington called Hampden Meadows, an apt name for acreage that was mainly farmland until just after the end of the Second World War. During the early 1950s, smaller, relatively affordable houses dotted the once bucolic land east of the Barrington River. Hampden Meadows never had the concentration of wealth as in some other parts of town. But there was no notable poverty either; just an influx of middle-class families drawn to a community that boasted good schools, safe streets, Christian churches, and white people.

Chellel's didn't ask but if I had been pressed for more of my family's history, I might have been candid about how my mother and father gave up their Cranston, Rhode Island rental in exchange for a heavily mortgaged home in Hampden Meadows. I was five when they bought a quarter acre lot just four houses from the Barrington River. If it weren't for a jumble of small, one-time summer bungalows that cluttered the shoreline, the land would have been out of reach for a working-class family of four. My father, a high school dropout, became the architect and general contractor for a two-bedroom house and detached garage. His largely unappreciated talent was the basis for one of many **life lessons** I would learn over the years. **Intellect, skill and wisdom are not exclusive to those with a formal education.** House building was an after-hours project for my father, who had a day job as a warehouse superintendent. Because it took two incomes to make life possible in Barrington, my mother also worked, first as a secretary in the same elementary school I attended after moving to Barrington and later as a bookkeeper for an East Providence asphalt company. Even with both parents employed, saving money to send my younger brother and me to college was more a goal than a reality.

My Chellel's job was the lowliest of positions: a bagger. To me, it didn't matter because I was officially in the labor pool earning my first biweekly paycheck minus deductions. For some of the well-to-do customers who frequented the market, I was a curiosity.

"You're the new boy," fashionably dressed women would comment at the checkout counter. I would respond with a smile. "Someone said you go to Holy Angels," I recall one lady saying with more than a little disdain. Holy Angels was the town's Catholic Church built more than a half century earlier to accommodate a wave of Italians who had migrated to the area to work for the long-defunct Narragansett Brick Company (once called Nayatt Brick). "No ma'am," I answered. "We belong to the White Church." Finding out I was not Catholic and maybe not even Italian brought an immediate look of relief.

Before working at Chellel's, I was aware Barrington was defined, in part, by its churches – more accurately by two churches. Established in the early 1700s, the White Church was one of the town's most celebrated buildings and remains so to this day. Its Congregational parishioners were considered more liberal than the much younger Episcopalian Red Church, located only a mile and a half to the southeast. The two churches were bookends to the town's commercial and government centers all strategically situated along Barrington's main thoroughfare. Holy Angels, on the other hand, was tucked away on a side-street that ran through the town's Italian American neighborhood.

"White" Church   *"Red" Church*

Two weeks into my twenty-hour-a-week schedule at Chellel's, an event of cosmic proportions occurred. I was called to the back of the store where I had a one-on-one meeting with Mr. S, a man whose title "clerk" belied his importance to the store. Mr. S was responsible for Chellel's produce aisle. Nothing was more heralded than the market's long display case filled with flawless vegetables and fruits. Customers constantly gave kudos to the store's butcher, but it was Mr. S who stood alone as Chellel's biggest star. Next to the market's namesake owners, Walter and Raymond Chellel, no one was more respected.

"Assistant produce clerk."

I was stunned. Less than a month on the job and I was being singled out as the back-up to Mr. S? No change in pay but a major uptick in my standing at Barrington's number one store. I asked Mr. S, why me? Why not one of the Rumstick baggers? "You're a hard worker," Mr. S served up an explanation that made no sense. The pace and work ethic among baggers were about the same. I suspected Mr. S wanted a part-time assistant who came from the town's rank and file, not from Barrington's upper echelons.

The next day, I put on an apron and shadowed Mr. S as he created impeccable arrangements using colorful fruits and vibrant greens to catch a shopper's eye. But I quickly learned it wasn't just Mr. S's produce expertise that made his aisle so popular. It was Mr. S himself. Ninety percent of Chellel's customer traffic was female. When Mr. S was on the floor, I noticed women spent a lot of time inspecting casaba melons and Granny Smith apples. They would manufacture questions that gave them an opening to talk to Mr. S who obliged with a comment or two about how impressed he was by a lady's choice of shoes or perfume. Mr. S had an oversupply of male animal magnetism unmatched by anyone I had ever met. He was handsome but not in a Hollywood or *GQ* kind of way. At six feet, Mr. S was trim, had olive-colored skin, and kept his dark hair perfectly groomed. His charisma came mainly from his smile and his eyes. When Mr. S looked at a woman, he caught her gaze and held it, often while seductively stroking a piece of fruit or some type of elongated vegetable. The conversation usually closed with the woman walking away looking flushed and breathing heavily.

There was an irony in the way high-end women were turned on by Mr. S. Although his last name was never used, it was common knowledge he was Italian. While many Chellel's shoppers had a built-in bias toward Italian Americans, the charming Mr. S got a pass. For me, it was another **life lesson: prejudice permits exceptions.** Just because a lady found Mr. S incredibly sexy didn't erase her view that, for the most part, Italians were fundamentally inferior to Americans of a more acceptable ancestry. Over the years, I would find blacks, Hispanics, Jews, Muslims, gays, and others subjected to this kind of thinking. "Yeah, he's a good guy," one might concede and then add: "… but he's not like the rest of them."

Although Mr. S would sidle his way into many a Barrington woman's dreams, in the real world he was an outsider. He lived six miles from the store in Bristol, another small Rhode Island town with an enclave of Italian Americans. Mr. S was insatiably curious about the parts of Barrington that were less known to him. He was very familiar with the unaffordable Rumstick-Nayatt neighborhoods thanks to the monied women who found any excuse to talk to him. He was interested in other fast-growing sections of the community such as Primrose Hill just north of the White Church. However, no area was more intriguing than Hampden Meadows. And no street in that part of town was more alluring than Bowden Avenue which happened to be my address. Years later, I would figure out why Mr. S was so focused on my quiet street. Living only a couple of blocks from my home in a small cape cod cottage hidden behind an absurdly out-of-character eight-foot wooden fence was Nicholas Bianco, a ranking member of the infamous Patriarca Mafia family. The Cosa Nostra organization was once among the most notorious in the nation, raking in vast amounts of money from gambling, prostitution, extortion, truck high-jacking, and loansharking operations.

"Tell me about your neighbors," Mr. S said more than a few times.

I didn't know the Bianco family and could only pass along rumors that Mrs. Bianco started her husband's car each morning. Beyond that bit of stereotypical hearsay, there wasn't much more to report about the mysterious family who kept to themselves behind their barricaded property.

"What about next door?" Mr. S pressed. "Who lives next door to you?"

Bowden Avenue wasn't exactly a hotbed of excitement and I considered ignoring the question. But there was a lot of empty time to fill when cleaning the display case after Chellel's closed for the day. I volunteered what I thought were a few interesting anecdotes.

Walter and Tabby Covell and their two sons, Alex and Chris, were our Bowden Avenue neighbors. Alex was my age and became a long-time friend. Tabby was a sun worshipper who had incredibly tan and eventually very leathery skin. However, it was Walter who was the most colorful character on the block. A graduate of Brown University, he was unquestionably brilliant and unabashedly artistic. During the earliest days of television, Walter dressed in drag and played a character called Mrs. Beeboople on a locally produced children's show. He was a community theater standout and was cast for bit parts in major movies, particularly those filmed in nearby Newport.

Living directly behind our house was the Moniz family. Dad Joe was a traveling salesman married to a super-refined wife more comfortable with classical music than her less culturally-attuned neighbors. Their son, Webb, was smart and aloof. The family moved to Connecticut before my stint at Chellel's, but I kept a distant eye on Webb's career. Not surprisingly, he would go on to graduate with honors from law school but astonishingly would then do a tour in Vietnam as a military officer.

Catty-corner to our home was the Brown residence, a larger home built on an expansive lot. Three towheaded boys (twins and a younger brother) constantly buzzed about the street. Their father, Tom, was a General Electric regional sales manager. He turned local hero one day when he brought home Ronald Reagan, long before the actor became the 40th president of the U.S. Reagan was host of a television production called the *General Electric Theater*. As part of his deal with GE, Reagan was required to visit company plants for 16 weeks of each year (often to deliver as many as 14 speeches a day). When the actor showed up at the Brown's house as one of his mandated stops, it was a sensation.

An immaculately kept house on the Barrington River shoreline belonged to Ed and Betty Materne. It was only a few lots from where I lived but there was no comparison in the size and cost of our properties. One of the Materne children, Doug, was my age and we have also maintained a long-time friendship. Doug's father, Ed, had a well-earned reputation for perfection. He co-founded the West Warwick Screw Products Company that would eventually be passed along to Doug. Ed's pride was his sleek, wooden boat that he kept anchored just offshore from his home. Adjacent to a huge bay window overlooking the river and boat was an enormous indoor saltwater fish tank that itself could be a source of entertainment for an entire afternoon.

"So, you have rich people nearby," Mr. S commented.

I explained the Maternes wouldn't describe themselves as wealthy. But from where my parents found themselves on the economic bell curve, the Maternes were rich indeed. That point of view was made very clear to me by my father as we boarded a skiff to survey a large hole I put in Ed's most cherished possession. I tried to explain how I ran a 12-foot runabout powered by a small Champion horse-powered outboard into the Materne craft. I was towing Doug on a makeshift pair of water skis trying to build up enough speed to get him upright. Too much attention was directed to Doug at the back of the boat and not to where I was heading. As I rowed to the scene of the crime, my father's rage taught me another **life lesson: wounding the rich is more consequential than ravaging the poor.**

I don't know all the details as to how the boat accident incident was resolved. I assume Ed Materne had insurance and if there were a deductible, my father would have at least offered to offset that cost even if he had to do so in installments. The incident did temper another event involving the Maternes not long after the boat fiasco. Doug and his family were perhaps best known for a pet crow kept in a large, screened-in porch at the rear of their house. The bird was called Amos, a politically incorrect name inspired by the radio (and later TV) show, *Amos & Andy*. Unlike the black character featured on the radio whose lower-class characterization was later denounced as being crude and moronic, Amos the crow was exceedingly smart. On occasion, the bird would literally fly the coop and cruise the neighborhood looking for anything that glittered. He would return home many times with stolen goods. Years later after Amos died, the Maternes found a storehouse of jewelry, silverware and shiny trinkets hidden in the eaves of their porch.

It was a fall day when my mother was hanging clothes in our backyard. Out of nowhere, Amos, possibly attracted by a bobby pin or the bright metal spring on a clothespin, swooped from the sky and landed hard on her grey hair. The screams that followed were heard by other neighbors. As upset as my mother was, she held back complaining to Doug's mother, Betty Materne. The hole in the boat was enough to mitigate anything the Maternes or their crow might do short of manslaughter. In retrospect, my mother confessed she should have ratted Amos out. Not long after the clothesline incident, the crow landed on a baby carriage and stole a rattle from a newborn. Fortunately, there were no injuries, but Amos was sentenced to solitary confinement in the Materne porch, which was made escape-proof.

"So, seriously bad things don't happen where you live," Mr. S noted, suggesting his living situation might be vastly different.

I shrugged. I could have countered with another story about Ted and Florence Osmond but no one had heard that tale except my mother. The Osmonds lived in a dilapidated one-bedroom cottage on a side street that ran from my house to the Barrington River. What was once a poorly constructed summer retreat had deteriorated with neglect, its front porch rotted and its tiny front yard taken over by a tangle of weeds. Ted Osmond was grossly overweight and rarely left a tattered armchair in the small and always-dark living room. He didn't have a job and spent his days and nights drinking cheap wine and listening to opera. During the summer months, it was not unusual to hear him bellowing the lyrics to Puccini's *Nessun Dorma*. Ted's wife was a sweet, subservient woman who loved cats. At any time, there were five and possibly even more cats living in the house or under the crawl space.

The cats were a magnet for my brother and me. We would often stop by the house on the way to or from the river. The scene inside would always be the same. Ted Osmond parked in his chair barely able to move because of his enormous belly; Florence fussing with cat food and bowls of water.

It was a hot summer day when I was heading back from an afternoon swim when I stopped by the Osmonds to visit the cats. Oddly, Ted Osmond was out of his chair and standing in the living room. Florence was in the kitchen. There was classical music playing more loudly than usual. The heat and probably too much wine had turned Mr. Osmond's face a deep red. He chuckled something and beckoned me to him, playfully grabbing me around my chest. Then he plunged his fat hand under my swim trunks until he found my penis and testicles. "Feels good, doesn't it?" he asked while laughing even harder. I had no cognizance as to whether what was happening was right or wrong. Sexual abuse and pedophilia were not subjects discussed at home or school. Yet, even so, I sensed this was out of bounds. And so did Florence Osmond.

"Oh, Ted, stop it," she admonished her husband with such gentleness it seemed hardly a rebuke. It was such a minor reprimand I was surprised Mr. Osmond complied. He pulled his hand away and I dashed out the door.

In Barrington, unpleasant and dark events were customarily kept under covers. When Walt and Tabby Covell divorced, the split was hardly discussed. When Avis Hilton, a rarely seen teenage girl who lived at the far end of Bowden Avenue died of an unspoken disease, the brief outpouring of sympathy for the grief-stricken family was quickly relegated to a bad memory. When I told my mother about Mr. Osmond, her shock gave way to a command that my brother and I were *never* to go near "that house" again. We were ordered to walk on the opposite side of the Osmond's narrow street and disregard any of the band of cats wandering the neighborhood. I don't know if my mother or father ever confronted the Osmonds. A few years went by and Ted Osmond was found dead in his armchair, reportedly listening to Mozart's *Marriage of Figaro*. After his obese carcass was hauled out of the rundown house, my mother cooked a pot roast boiled dinner and brought it to Florence Osmond. From that time on, she prepared a meal at least once a week for Mrs. Osmond, who lived at the mercy of other's charity.

I often wondered about my mother's kindness for a woman who was complicit in her husband's mistreatment of me. Florence Osmond was also a victim, my mother once said. The small, mousy lady had such a low opinion of herself, she was easily dominated by her disgusting spouse. So, Mrs. Osmond was given a pardon. Not only did my mother absolve Florence, she joined a few White Church volunteers who offered home care until the day they found Mrs. Osmond's lifeless body surrounded by a battery of yowling cats. This act of exoneration on my mother's part served up still another **life lesson: compassion elevates forgiveness to its highest level.**

Mr. S never was told the Osmond story. I didn't want to take the sheen off the Hampden Meadows picture I had painted. Over the next few weeks, Mr. S wanted to know even more about my somewhat-fabricated, idyllic, Mayberry-like neighborhood. Maybe he's considering moving, I wondered. Then, quite abruptly Mr. S stopped asking questions and shut down small talk of any kind. Why he was acting so differently was puzzling until one late Saturday afternoon when Mr. S served up an unanticipated and unwelcomed explanation.

"You know you're a hard worker, right?" Mr. S asked.

I was moving watercress from the long produce display case and storing the greens in a container for the weekend. I shrugged, waiting for Mr. S to continue.

"The store takes on part-time help when things get busy," he went on. "Then when things slow down, we have to let part-timers go. Even the part-time people who work hard."

A few minutes later, I handed in my Chellel's apron and walked out of the store and never returned. Not once. In just a few months, I had been hired and fired from my first job. Bitter and hurt, I mulled over the reality that hard work was no match for bad luck. It took several more years to expand that observation into another **life lesson: luck trumps everything.** A stroke of bad luck can overwhelm all things living and inert. Good luck, on the other hand, can catapult you over and past life's roadblocks.

Just as misfortune paid me a visit on that unforgettable Saturday, it eventually landed hard on a few of the commercial mainstays that anchored Barrington's shopping center. Almacs went bankrupt in the mid-1990s. The celebrated women's fashion boutique, Cherry & Webb, filed for Chapter 11 in 2000. Starbucks, Verizon, Talbots along with other ubiquitous businesses took over Barrington's most valuable retail storefronts. But nothing marked the town's transition more than the day Chellel's closed its doors. The market that for so long had been one of Barrington's most prominent landmarks gave way to an Ace Hardware store.

Overall, luck has been relatively kind to Barrington. The town remains a coveted place to live even as it has become more inclusive and religiously accepting. When the Barrington Jewish Center opened in 1961 across the street from Chellel's, there were murmurs of concern. The muttering got louder when the town sold Hampden Meadows Elementary School to the Center and the building I once attended as a grade school student was renamed Temple Habonim. But the "Jewish problem" as some called it did not lead to a predicted decline in property values. Quite the contrary.

Over the past fifty years, Roman Catholics have gradually been amalgamated into most of Barrington's social networks.

Walter Chellel, the principal owner of Barrington's most prestigious market, was "outed" as a Catholic even before his death in 1993. Chellel was buried in the town's Santa Maria Del Campo Cemetery, managed by the Catholic Dioceses in Providence, leaving no doubt as to his religious preference. The revelation might have shocked the Chellel's Market clientele years earlier but in the more tolerant Barrington, learning about Chellel's religion hardly raised an eyebrow.

While Barrington has become more religiously open-minded, its racial makeup remains predominantly Caucasian. The town does not discriminate based on the usual black, brown, yellow, and red color lines. Rather Barrington, like so many other affluent communities, uses green to determine who qualifies for residence and who doesn't make the cut. Those with enough cash can buy their way into the community often without regard to race or creed. This reality is the crux of another **life lesson: green is discrimination's color of choice.**

Whether Mr. S ever made the move to Barrington is unknown. If he did, the decision would have been a good one. The town has its blemishes, but it is still a community of choice for many even in the absence of the upscale market called Chellel's.

Chapter 2

Jamiel's Shoe World
(1959-60)

A spiderweb of creeks and tributaries drain into a brackish waterway called the Palmer River that twists through Rehoboth, Massachusetts flowing south into Rhode Island. The Palmer funnels under a small bridge that links Barrington to a neighboring community called Warren. Although the two towns sit side by side, they are as different as the sun and moon. Barrington is twice the size of Warren which sits on six square miles of land. Barrington residents have a median family income two and a half times higher than families living in Warren.

In 1960, my senior year in high school, a huge American Tourister plant commanded the north end of Warren's Water Street. The sprawling manufacturing site was the town's most important economic piston with a thousand employees working day and night shifts. A boat building company called Blount Marine (now Blount Boats) added to Warren's industrial character. Water Street was also home to another Blount operation, a seafood processing center that put clams in Campbell Soup's famous chowder. A waterfront

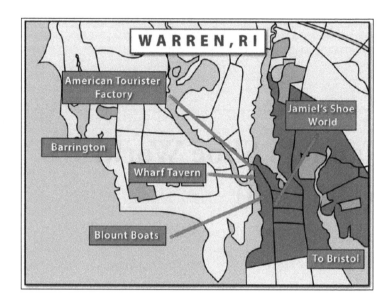

restaurant tucked between Warren's string of riverside factories cel-ebrated its tenth anniversary. Many predicted the Wharf Tavern could never survive given its questionable location. But the restau-rant thrived, becoming a venerable, preferred dining spot even for affluent Barringtonians.

At night, laborers and commercial fishermen trickled into a pair of Water Street bars. Alcohol-fueled fights and an occasional arrest for prostitution gave the road a seedy reputation. A more respect-able part of town was Main Street, Warren's primary thoroughfare dotted with a few mundane storefront shops. Overall, Warren's backwater appearance belied its history as a onetime, prosperous shipping and whaling center. Forgotten by many, the town was the 1764 birthplace of Rhode Island College, a Baptist institution that moved to Providence and morphed into Brown University, one of eight Ivy League schools in the U.S.

For those of us living in Barrington, Warren was a conveni-ent next-door marketplace with an assortment of stores and ser-vices not found in my hometown. Aside from Warren's liquor stores, Delekta's Pharmacy was arguably the most popular shop in Warren. It was a full-service drugstore prominently located on Main Street. About a week after my dream job at Chellel's had been cut short, I was sent to pick up a prescription at Delekta's. My mother had given me permission to drive her used Chevrolet to make the trip and I took full advantage of having a car to ask my current but not-too-serious girlfriend to join me. Once in town, we walked to Delekta's and paid for the two prescriptions. Like many pharmacies in the fifties and sixties, the drug store also had a soda fountain that featured a Rhode Island classic drink called a coffee cabinet. I used some of my meager Chellel's earnings to order the specialty concoction, a blend of ice cream, milk, and coffee syrup. Sharing a cabinet with my girlfriend stirred up a few bittersweet memories.

Warren's Wharf Tavern   *American Tourister Factory*

Shortly after moving to Barrington, my parents found a Warren dentist who practiced in a dark, foreboding second-floor office on Main Street. The dentist was old and so was his equipment. He was also very affordable which for my cost-conscious mother and father was far more important than the man's professional proficiency. Unfortunately for my brother and me, we inherited very bad teeth. That made it necessary to visit the dental office all too often. For us, it was a chamber of horrors mainly because my parents wouldn't or couldn't pay for a local anesthetic to numb the old dentist's torture. Cavities were my most common problem and that meant being brutalized by a cord-based electric drill with a top speed of 3,000 RPMs compared to today's modern, air-driven drills that operate at 200,000 RPMs. The procedure was slow and agonizing, the worn-down drill bit grinding through enamel and striking nerves with punishing jolts.

Trips to the dentist were horrendous but my mother made the experience tolerable by promising each ordeal would end with a coffee cabinet at Delekta's. When the drill went into my mouth, I forced myself to think about the incredibly sweet drink that would be mine if I could only manage to survive.

I poured the last of the coffee cabinet from a silver metal blender cup into a tall milkshake tumbler and shook off my discomfiting dental memories. My increasingly impressed girlfriend finished the drink and then I ordered a one-scoop chocolate cone to cap off our visit to Delekta's. Gorged and happy, we left the drugstore and strolled across Main Street. That's when I spotted a small "help wanted" sign in the window of Warren's sole shoe store.

"This is how you apply for a job?" Joe Jamiel asked a few minutes later. "You walk in here holding hands with a girl and dripping ice cream on my rug. *And you want a job?*"

Joe Jamiel had a bear-like body and an all-business face to match. He was one of 13 Jamiel brothers and sisters whose commercial importance to Warren was undisputed. Jamiels were everywhere. Many family members had fascinating first names such as Bolus, Hirum, Zenobia, and Anissa. Jamiel's Shoe World was attached to a Jamiel-owned hardware store called General Supply. Two blocks away, a pair of Jamiel sisters operated a baby clothing shop. Jamiels sold insurance and ran a court-reporting service. Jamiel's Park replaced a one-time landfill and became a recreation center for the town. The most famous family member was Major General Morphis Jamiel, who after leaving the military became Warren's probate judge.

"Well, I… I just saw the sign in the window…" I stammered.

Joe Jamiel shook his head. "Anybody who has the moxie to walk in here like you just did might have what it takes to sell shoes. When can you start?"

So began my part-time, after-school and weekend job as a shoe salesman. Joe gave me a quick tour of the large storage room in the back of the store where shoe boxes were stacked from floor to ceiling.

Once I learned how to use a foot measuring device, I was told to start selling.

Jamiel's Shoe World carried footwear for men and kids, but the store's most important and most frequent customers were women. From my first hour on the job, ladies became my challenge and often my nemesis. It wasn't unusual for a female shopper to try on a dozen or more pair of shoes only to leave without buying anything. After watching my less-than-impressive salesmanship, Joe pulled me aside.

"What are you doing?" he asked.

"Uh, selling shoes?"

"Bull crap," he shot back. "You're not selling. People come in here not sure what to buy. You aren't helping them. You just throw them shoes hoping something will stick!"

I cringed at the criticism albeit a fairly accurate performance review. Joe followed with more sharp comments and then ordered me to sit in a corner and watch while he waited on three women

19

who had wandered into the store. Joe talked to the ladies, asking them questions, many of which had nothing to do with shoes. In a matter of minutes, he scored two sales. The third woman didn't make a purchase but said she would think about the sling back pump Joe promised to hold for her.

I was enthralled. Before Joe sized a foot, he would size up a customer. He was a kind of retail detective who knew the right questions to ask and quickly found clues in the answers he extracted. The results were amazing.

A couple of weeks later, I was mimicking as much of Joe's technique as I could muster. My track record was far short of what my boss scored on a regular basis, Still, I was averaging about half the "try-ons" per customer as when I started at Shoe World. And my number of sales per hour went up, which clearly impressed my employer.

One afternoon just after we closed for the day, Joe invited me to his backroom office.

"Let me ask you something," he opened. "You think this is about selling shoes?"

Was this Joe's way of teeing up the same bad news Mr. S had delivered that fateful day at Chellel's? I braced myself for what was to come.

"Here's something I want you to remember," Joe continued and threw me another **life lesson: everyone's a salesperson – some better than others.** To Joe, to be human was to sell. Every person is constantly working to convince others to buy goods or services, to persuade someone to buy a concept, an idea. The more effective one is at selling, the more likely one will climb the ladder of success. Whether it's your job or your love life, selling is the key, Joe maintained. The easiest way to irk Joe Jamiel was to say something, anything, derogatory about a salesperson. To do so was to malign that which defines and differentiates mankind.

Jamiel's Shoe World was a classic small business, low-margin retail operation. Each sale produced very little revenue over what Joe paid vendors to stock his store. Shoe World survived on volume, which meant every sale counted. That reality was never more evident than on a Saturday when Joe and his wife Lily took their usual hour-long lunch break. The only time during the week when the store was not staffed by either one or both of the two Jamiels was for sixty minutes on Saturdays. That schedule was apparently no secret to a burly, poorly dressed man who walked into the store carrying a shoe box. Many of Jamiel's male customers were rugged types looking to get a deal on steel-toe boots. So, although the man had an unmistakable taint of sweat and beer, he was not that out of the ordinary. After taking a few steps, the disheveled man tripped over a chair and sent a stack of about-to-be restocked wingtip oxfords flying in different directions. He landed hard on his hands and knees out of sight behind a display case. In seconds, the man was upright having retrieved his box and looking apologetic for the mishap. My coworker was busy fitting a small child with a pair of mary janes, which meant I was stuck with collecting and rematching the jumble of polished black oxfords.

"I got this here return," the man interrupted me as I began picking up shoes.

"Ok," I said, putting the clean-up on hold. "Do you have a receipt?"

"No, Joe said I don't need one," the man replied. "Joe told me to bring 'em back if I didn't wear 'em outside. They don't fit right."

The man shoved his box into my belly. I popped the cover and checked the Florsheim's that looked as new as the shoes littered all over the floor. The label on the box exterior was smudged, making it impossible to check the inventory number but the price was obvious: $15.95. These were pricey shoes. A pair of men's oxfords in 1960 averaged $13.

"I don't know if I can do this without a receipt," I explained. "You might have to come back when Joe's here."

"Trust me," the man rallied back. "Joe's a friend. It ain't gonna be a problem."

"Yeah, but ..." I resisted.

"Look," the man was sweating profusely, an aftereffect of his fall, I assumed. "I don't feel good. I don't wanna get sick right here in the store. Joe's a friend. Just tell him I brought the shoes back. He'll know. Trust me. Trust me. It's all fine."

There was more talk, the words coming fast, many punctuated with warnings about vomiting and passing out. I gave in to the pressure and withdrew $15.95 from Jamiel's cash register. The man shoved the money into a torn jacket pocket and quick-stepped out the door.

Joe and Lilly returned from lunch the same time I finished rounding up the oxfords and coming to a disturbing realization: I was a pair short. When Joe found the missing Florsheims neatly positioned in the $15.95 box, I broke into a cold sweat.

"What's this?" His eyes turned to lasers and they pointed right at me.

Until that afternoon, I had never seen Joe Jamiel lose his cool. My stupidity ignited a fury so extreme and out of character, it sent my coworker scurrying to the bathroom at the back of the store.

"He ... he fell behind the display," I stammered. "I couldn't see what he was doing." Another look at Joe and I knew an explanation was pointless. He was seething, probably already having calculated how many sales it would take to cover the nearly $16 that had walked out the door thanks to my brainlessness.

"Some bum walks in here and you throw money at him?" Joe yelled.

"I'm really sorry, Joe," I blubbered. "Maybe you could take it out of my pay. Really, I want to pay you back. Let me work it off." I had mixed feelings about making the offer. At $1 per hour – the going minimum wage at the time – I would be selling shoes for free over the next week or more. On the other hand, if giving up the money meant defusing Joe's anger, it might be one of the best investments I could make.

"I leave for an hour and look what happens!" Joe kept on screaming.

"Well, he said he knew you," I said. "He told me to trust him."

"*Trust him?*" Joe erupted again. "*Trust?*"

Probably because I was upset and nervous, I began babbling about my English teacher's discourse on the meaning of trust the day before. Our teacher was in love with proverbs and she had singled out her favorite, a Russian saying she made us memorize: *Doveryai no poveryai.*

"Trust but verify," I mumbled, offering up the proverb's English translation. The words came across as totally nonsensical given Joe's meltdown. But I couldn't conjure up anything better.

"What?" Joe shouted.

"Our teacher – she talked about how trust is okay as long as it can be verified."

Joe blinked in disbelief. I was using a Russian proverb to explain away why I had been taken as a fool. After a few moments of silence, Joe came back at me with a growl.

"Here's a message for your teacher," he said and then barked out another **life lesson: verify first; trust later.**

I would recollect Joe's editing of the Russian proverb many years later when Ronald Reagan signed the Intermediate-Range Nuclear Treaty. In 1987, Reagan would tell Mikhail Gorbachev the U.S. would trust Russia if the treaty's terms could continuously be verified. Had the president asked Joe Jamiel for advice, the Shoe World proprietor would have told Reagan he had it ass-backward. Don't trust until all the treaty provisions have been fully verified.

Getting scammed didn't cost me my Shoe World job and my pay wasn't docked. I donated a few hours overtime to clean the storefront windows and the back bathroom. Joe's anger subsided to a lingering irritation and then to a subdued realization that he bore some of the responsibility for what had happened. Leaving the business in the hands of a teenager – even for an hour – wasn't the smartest management decision he had ever made.

I worked at Jamiel's throughout the summer following my high school graduation. My last day was a hot August afternoon. Before leaving Shoe World, I thanked Joe for what he taught me – not just about selling shoes or the perils of being hoodwinked but also about life in general. I learned running a small business required knowing at least something about a lot of things: marketing, purchasing, taxes, payroll, supply chain administration, human resources, and more. Later in life I would spend time with faculty members at some of the best business schools in the country. None of them had Joe Jamiel's all-round business acumen.

Leaving Shoe World for the last time, I took a roundabout route back to Barrington. I detoured through some of Warren's less-traveled streets just to lock in a memory of this small town's unusual mix of industry, residential neighborhoods, shops, restaurants, and taverns. Warren even had a small movie house. I drove past the Lyric Theatre, the Saturday morning go-to place for younger kids who would crowd the iconic building on Miller Street to watch cartoons and serial cliffhangers like *Commando Cody, Flash Gordon,* or *Hopalong Cassidy.* The Lyric would eventually succumb to time and technology with TV becoming the Saturday morning entertainment medium of choice for children (or perhaps more accurately, their parents). The Lyric would be swept up in Warren's transformation, first converted to an antique shop and later a gift store.

I drove the length of Water Street stopping in front of Blount Marine to watch welders working on a ferry soon to be added to New York City's Circle Line fleet. Blount would ultimately produce five of the six ferries used by that tourism company to transport passengers to and from the Statue of Liberty. Luther Blount's company was as remarkable as the founder himself. His shipyard built more than 300 watercraft ranging from tugboats to fishing trawlers. Blount would continue working in the marine construction field until his death in 2006. Obituaries described the 90-year-old Blount as a "crusty New England shipbuilder." But he was also something else: a careful and effective philanthropist.

During his lifetime, Blount donated millions to different causes. In addition to the $1 million he donated to Warren to preserve public access to the town's waterfront, most of his charitable support went to projects and programs that were even more targeted. He had a strong interest in aquaculture, which he backed up with several major grants. Roger Williams University, located in the next-door community of Bristol, developed the Luther Blount Shellfish Hatchery and Oyster Restoration Center. Blount donated a cruise ship valued at $6.5 million for oceanographic use. Blount's approach to philanthropy surfaced later in my life as a delayed but important **life lesson: let who and what you know best serve as a compass for your charity.** Much of my career would be spent working with grant-makers and recipients of donations of both money and time. The judgment and practices of the old "crusty New England shipbuilder" turned out to be beacons I would use over and over to guide both donors as well as those nonprofits looking for support.

I circled back to Warren's Main Street and made a final pass by Shoe World. Had Joe Jamiel the power to see the future, he would learn his classic mom-and-pop store would survive another half century. It would be handed over to son Francis Jamiel, a Brown University graduate and football player known to most in town as "Tut." The store would succumb to big box competition in 2012, and four years later Tut would fall victim to cancer.

Shoe World's final years would come on the heels of a much more publicized and tragic Jamiel family event. The store adjacent to Joe Jamiel's business was General Supply hardware owned and operated by Joe's brother, Amon. In 1978, Amon would be found murdered in the shower of his Warren home, shot six times in the head and four times in the abdomen. No weapon would be found and the crime scene not properly secured by police. The killing would remain an unsolved mystery even eight years later when the youngest of Amon's three sons would be indicted for the crime. An unauthorized leak of subpoena details would force a grand jury to dismiss the case.

Time and circumstance would erode the Jamiel dynasty just as Warren gradually would undergo a remarkable transformation. It was unfathomable to consider the town could or would turn into a super-gentrified municipality. Yet that's exactly where Warren was headed. The huge American Tourister plant would go dark but then undergo a $30 million makeover with apartments and retail space replacing luggage assembly lines. Galleries and specialty shops would be sprinkled throughout the main part of town. Warren was on a path to become so trendy some would call it "the Brooklyn of Providence."

I crossed the small Palmer River bridge into Barrington, my rearview mirror catching an image of Warren I would not see again for some time to come. In four years, I would make a return visit to the town in a very different capacity. Coming back to this small, under-appreciated village would be a pleasure.

Chapter 3

Northeastern University (1960-65)

T o call 1960 a transformative year would be an under-statement. The United States sent three special forces teams to Vietnam as one of the first steps in what would become a nightmarish maelstrom. The Organization of Petroleum Exporting Countries (OPEC) was launched with few imagining what a global powerhouse the cartel would turn out to be. And the age of Camelot dawned with John F. Kennedy defeating incumbent Richard Nixon in the closest presidential election in U.S. history.

On the November day when Massachusetts learned a native son would be heading to the White House, I found myself caught up in the most exuberant celebration in the nation. Boston became party central not just for the city's Irish Catholics but for nearly everyone in "Bean Town." The excitement reached a fever pitch among the city's small army of college students, most of whom were ardent Kennedy fans. Boston bars opened their doors and beer flowed like a river. Drinking age rules went out the window and for the first time, I drank to excess and ended the night with my head in a Northeastern University dorm room toilet.

My decision to enroll in a college known primarily as a commuter school with a penchant for engineering students was based on three harsh realities: too little money; no connections; a shortage of brains. Northeastern lacked the cachet of big-hitting schools where some of Barrington's well-to-do or super-bright high school students ended up: Harvard, Yale, Penn, Brown. However, Northeastern had a few qualities that made the university a prime candidate for me. First, it was affordable. Second, the school's main point of difference in the higher education world rested on its "cooperative education" option that enabled students to work as well as study. And third, this was a school driven to claw its way up the national rankings of the country's over 5,000 institutes of higher learning (something it has been able to do with remarkable success over the past few decades).

Cobbling together my meager earnings from Chellel's, Jamiel's and a couple other high school jobs along with money my parents had been able to set aside, my first Northeastern year was funded. After that, I would be relying on money from a college "co-op" job and part-time employment to be squeezed in while taking classes. Of course, there was the option of taking a student loan but I came from a long line of New Englanders who fended off borrowing except for a home mortgage, a car, or (God forbid) an unexpected illness.

A king-sized downside to Northeastern's co-op program was spending an extra year in school. It took five years instead of four to snag a bachelor's degree with the extra time needed to fit in requisite on-the-job experience. As it turned out, the one additional year was incredibly valuable to me, although it would take a lot of reflection to come to that understanding.

Mechanical, civil, chemical, and electrical engineering were favorite majors for many at Northeastern. Not for me. Math was far from my strong suit which relegated me to one of the university's

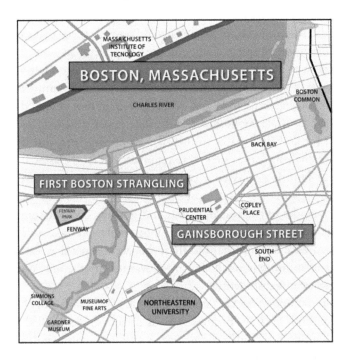

less reputed academic programs. Without much thought, I declared myself an English major, mostly as a placeholder until I could figure out a more practical course of study.

Before and during my college years, my mother never missed an opportunity to give me career counseling. She thought I should either be a teacher or work for the U.S. Postal Service. "You're good with children," she would tell me. "But if you don't want to work with kids, you can get a really secure job working for the post office." Having married a man who had to cope with three major, stress-inducing job changes, my mother wanted a more certain future for her two boys. She got her wish with my younger brother who was mathematically inclined. He would end up at Worcester Polytech, easily graduate with an engineering degree and quickly get recruited by the Raytheon Corporation. I was the son who gave my mother, quite literally, an ulcer. Aside from being a teacher or a letter carrier, there didn't seem to be any avenue I could possibly travel that would lead me anywhere except a schoolhouse or a post office.

After a relatively uneventful freshman year, college life took a hard turn in 1961. Northeastern had a limited supply of university-owned housing units and most were reserved for first-year students and co-eds. Male sophomores and other upper classmen had to search for and find places to live. For co-op students, this was a notable challenge since they were required to attend classes at the college's Huntington Avenue campus for a semester then leave for their assigned co-op jobs (most often located outside Boston) for the remainder of the academic year and possibly over the summer as well. Semester-long, four or five-month rentals in the city's Back Bay area were not only hard to find, they were expensive. Packing young men into one small apartment was usually the only option for cash-strapped students.

Gainsborough Street is a small avenue lined with four-story brick buildings not far from Boston's famous urban parkland called The Fens. During my Northeastern stint, a string of roommates and I lived in three different Gainsborough apartments. For one semester, the son of a Jewish butcher kept us stocked with chorizo, liverwurst, prosciutto, and pepperoni. A business major from a family-operated taxi service in Western Massachusetts joined us for a year. Another business major spent a semester living in one of our Gainsborough apartments but died from natural causes the next. My most memorable roommate was also from the Western part of Massachusetts – "Hob" Harris.

"The Pru"

Time has fogged any memory of how and when Bob Harris acquired his sobriquet. Nearly everyone in my circle of college friends acquired a nickname. For no explainable reason, mine was "Larry" which was an improvement over "Weed," my high school and later-in-life label. Harris's punchy moniker matched his looks and personality. While average in height and build, Hob had a take-charge way of carrying himself that made his presence loom large. He wasn't cocky to the point of being obnoxious and in fact was usually very affable. But if anyone challenged him the wrong way, he was quick to push back. Hob was also an extraordinarily hard worker always coupling a part-time job with his studies. He was not overtly religious, but his family's devout commitment to the Lutheran church clearly had an influence on his own beliefs.

In June 1962, Hob and I found a seedy bar on Commonwealth Avenue, where the atmosphere was grim and beer a bargain. After a couple of rounds, we overheard a pair of Mohawk Indian iron-workers talking about a near-miss accident on one of the top floors of a mid-town skyscraper still two years away from completion. Dubbed "The Pru" by locals, the 52-story Prudential Tower was to be the symbol of a rejuvenated Boston. Native Americans known for their fearlessness when it came to working hundreds of feet in the air were the most celebrated workers responsible for building the upper section of the tower.

"What is it about you Indians?" Hob asked, not long after we invited ourselves to join the two Mohawks. "You're different. You can work 700 feet above ground without blinking an eye. That's not normal."

This was a typical "Hob moment." He was incredibly inquisitive and had a knack for asking questions that could easily ignite a bar fight. But the way Hob connected with people rarely led to anything but a fascinating conversation. He taught me another **life lesson: in your own way, be insatiably curious.** Hob Harris was overtly interested in what others had to say. Collecting verbal responses was how he satisfied that curiosity. Others might turn to books and data files in a search for answers but not Hob. He was a master at tugging information out of people without being at all obnoxious or annoying.

Before the night ended, we were treated to a free course on the connection between Native Americans and the construction industry. According to our drinking mates, not all Indians had an equal capacity to handle heights. The five tribes of the Iroquois nation were the source of the most prized aerial workers and one of those tribes, the Mohawks, was the best of the best. Our two new friends said they had a lot of employment offers but signed up to work on the Pru because there was status in building a tower attracting attention both inside and outside the U.S. When completed, the structure would be the tallest high-rise in the world outside of New York City. That record would be shattered by the 110-story Sears Tower (now Willis Tower) that opened in the mid-1970s. Until then and even after, the Pru was Boston's pride.

After a few hours and more than a few beers, Hob and I weaved our way back to Gainsborough Street. It was around 8 p.m. and across the street from our apartment building, we spotted two police cars and an unmarked van. A tough-looking man dressed in a dark suit darted across the avenue and ordered us to stop.

"You know who lives there?" the man pointed to the opposite side of the avenue while at the same time showing us a badge.

"Nope," Hob replied. People on Gainsborough lived cheek to jowl but there was not a lot of neighbor interplay.

"Where were you tonight?" the man asked just as a uniformed cop showed up and flipped open a small spiral pad.

"We're students," I said nervously. Hob and I were both 21 and legally allowed to drink. But we were clearly tipsy. I had visions of a long night in one of Boston's infamous drunk tanks. "Just had a couple of beers and heading back to our place." I jerked my head toward the fourth floor of our walk-up.

"Ever hear the name Anna Slesers?"

Hob and I looked at one another. We shook our heads.

The man studied our faces carefully. "This officer will be asking you a few more questions. He's going to want to know exactly where you were and for how long. You're going to tell him how we can reach you any time day or night. You get that? If we want to talk to you, make sure you show up. Understand?"

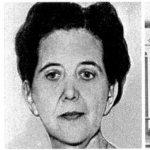

Boston Strangler Victim #1   *Suffolk Downs*

The rugged man trudged back to the other side of Gainsborough. Hob went into his usual inquisitive mode and convinced the uniformed cop to volunteer information that probably should have been kept confidential. Police had responded to a call from the son of a 55-year-old Latvian woman who had been strangled with a sash ripped from her bathrobe. Anna Slesers was a divorcee who worked as a seamstress and lived alone. Apparently, Hob and I were the first to be questioned just after Boston's finest arrived on the scene. No one knew at the time, but Slesers would be the first of 13 women to be murdered over the next 19 months. It was the start of a killing spree by a man the media branded "The Boston Strangler."

Having achieved a kind of accidental fame for being connected to one of America's most publicized whodunits, Hob and I followed the case carefully. As the body count mounted, much of Boston and surrounding suburbs went into panic mode. The strangler's victims were female ranging from 19 to 85, white and black. Women were told to lock doors and windows, demand identification from anyone coming to the door, walk in pairs or groups. Be wary of strangers, even those dressed as a woman or clergyman.

There was palpable relief when police announced the capture of the alleged strangler in March 1965. Albert DeSalvo, a maintenance worker, claimed he was the killer but would later recant his confession. In 1973, DeSalvo was stabbed to death as he slept in his prison cell, leaving many to wonder if he murdered anyone. When DeSalvo's body was exhumed in 2001, his DNA did not match evidence taken from the body of a woman thought to be the strangler's last victim. That discovery has stoked an ongoing debate over DeSalvo's guilt or innocence.

The same year the strangler began terrorizing Boston, Hob and I distracted ourselves by teaming up with a new roommate, Norm Merlet, to launch a venture that led to another **life lesson: enough is rarely enough.** Merlet was tagged "Kid" because he was the youngest of our roommates. Along with Hob, Kid was a horse racing fanatic. He followed the thoroughbred circuit regularly and on paper could pick winners with uncanny accuracy. At Hob's suggestion, the three of us set up a non-incorporated business appropriately called Tri-Ass. We lured 20 investors to chip in $3 apiece tempting them with a very strong probability they would double their money in a day. We deducted $5 apiece from the investment pool for subway fares, hot dogs and, of course, beer. With $45 left to wager, we took the train from North Station to Suffolk Downs.

The trek to the East Boston track took less than an hour. As we passed Logan Airport, Hob and the Kid studied the better's bible, the *Daily Racing Form,* and agreed on picks for nine races. We arrived at Suffolk Downs, a 30-year-old, mile-long dirt oval, just ahead of the first bugle "Call to Post." Two hours later, Tri-Ass had turned its $45 investment pool into $225, a goodly amount of money considering the average income in the U.S. at the time was under $120 a week. From the moment we had arrived at the track, Hob and the Kid insisted the three-to-one entry running in the last race of the day was the main reason why we were at Suffolk Downs. The horse was a guaranteed winner. "Bet it all," Hob said, and the Kid agreed enthusiastically. Tempted by the prospect of a *very* big windfall, I cast another "go for it" vote. Had logic prevailed, we would have wagered $100 and protected the rest. Instead, we bet the ranch. The nag charged out of the starting gate and was ahead at the turn but ran out of steam long before the finish line. The race was a symbolic harbinger of what would happen to Suffolk Downs itself. The track's attendance boomed when it first opened in 1935 but inched lower even as a series of different owners tried but failed to bring it back to life. In 2017, Suffolk Downs would be sold for $155 million, destined to become a mixed-use residential and commercial development.

We returned home that day with a really good story that came with a very bad ending. Short of the last race, we had all the cash we needed to enrich ourselves and reward our investors. The urge to grab even more won out and as I would find later in life, this same Suffolk Downs phenomenon would crop up over and over. "Enough" was a concept that alluded most people. No matter how much one had of anything, there was always more to get.

"You ought to run for class president." Hob's suggestion came out of the blue not long after our horse-racing scheme ended up on the rocks.

"Me? Why?"

'Why not? Your high school buddy was voted in as president last year," Hob reminded me. He was right. Al Martone was Barrington, Rhode Island's answer to the sexiest man alive. He was handsome to the core, an A-team basketball player, an honor roll student, and all-round nice guy. There hadn't been a girl in our high school who wouldn't have shaved her locks to have just one date with Martone. When he picked Northeastern as his college of choice, there was more than a little head scratching as to why the most popular student in Barrington wouldn't have found a spot in a more prominent university. But Al was as smart as he was good looking. He went on to graduate from Northeastern with a chemical engineering degree, got an MBA from Babson College (first in his class) and leveraged his education to develop technical products for Exxon, General Electric, and a few other industrial behemoths. He would end his career running and selling a highly successful printing business.

"Martone could be a *GQ* model," I told Hob. "There's not a co-ed in America who wouldn't vote for him. I'm a string bean with glasses."

Hob agreed I wasn't exactly Omar Sharif but if we played down my looks, winning wasn't out of the question. However, the likelihood of two students from the small town of Barrington scoring back-to-back presidencies was more of a stretch. Still, with Hob as the catalyst, a group of friends and supporters miraculously put me over the top after a few weeks of on-campus campaigning.

"Just lay low," a faculty advisor said shortly after my victory.

"Excuse me?"

"Being class president is 99 percent ceremonial," the advisor explained. "Show up for a few photos, go to an awards dinner, and stick with your studies."

I was incredulous. This was it? After hosting a frog-jumping contest and handing out peanut brittle to hundreds of would-be voters, I was destined to just fade away?

"Don't rattle the cage," the advisor told me. "You're class president. What more do you want? It will look good on your resume."

The experience was another **life lesson: check the prize before running the race.** Had the university encouraged me to leverage the position, I might have helped the school in some small way. After all, Northeastern was on the cusp of a major transition. Founded in 1898 with classes first held at a downtown YMCA, the university had already come a long way and had a vision of joining the ranks of the nation's most respected private institutions. A class president could have mobilized thousands of students to become walking billboards to expedite the expansion. But that didn't happen. I did what I was told and drifted back into the pack. The experience was so meaningless I didn't reference my term of office on my resume, much to the surprise of the few faculty members who even knew there was such a position as class president. I had spent a lot of time and energy chasing a pointless goal. From here on, I would be more diligent in checking the value of the prize before beginning the chase.

During my freshman and sophomore years, there was no let-up in my mother's persistent push to get me into the teaching profession or into the nearest post office. "A teaching certificate wouldn't hurt," she said. "I checked – a couple of courses and student teaching is all it will take."

I explained how I had loaded my English major with journalism electives and was looking to the media world for future employment. My mother wasn't buying it. So, I caved and tweaked my academic plan and not long after found myself student teaching at Foxborough High School 20 miles south of Boston.

In the 1960s, Foxborough was a small community with only a few history buffs remembering the town was once home to the Union Straw Works, the world's largest straw hat factory. That manufacturing facility had burned to the ground in the early 20th century leaving the suburb a rather innocuous halfway stop between Providence and Boston. Unbeknownst to me and probably every Foxborough citizen at the time, the town was destined to become a household name for football fans across America.

Foxborough, Massachusetts   *Gillette Stadium*

During the early 1960s, Foxborough High School mirrored the town's general demographics. Of the community's 10,000-plus residents, 97 percent were white. Average household income was 30 percent higher than the rest of the nation. Education was a high priority for taxpaying parents which made it no surprise that nine out of 10 students went to college. The high school's light-filled, perfectly maintained classrooms were surrounded by football, baseball, lacrosse, and soccer fields. A public school Shangri-La.

My Foxborough teaching mentor was a diminutive, white-haired lady named Mrs. Hart who epitomized the teacher we all wish we had. This small woman not only had a colossus-sized brain, she was consistently caring and supportive to everyone, not just students. Among other duties, Mrs. Hart taught junior and senior advanced English classes that she decided should be my student-teaching training ground. From day one, it was an exhausting intellectual challenge trying to keep pace with teenagers who were only a few years younger than I and a lot smarter. I spent nights studying Beowulf, George Eliot, and Ezra Pound *Cliffs Notes* in a desperate attempt to stay ahead of the pack.

There was a lot to learn while at Foxborough. One important revelation led to another **life lesson: the classroom is democracy's nursery.** While parents, relatives, clergy, friends, and the media may shape the thinking and behavior of young people, teachers have an extraordinary opportunity to foster critical thinking. And that can be a democracy's secret sauce. In a republic where much of the future hinges on the voting inclinations of individuals, helping students learn how to discern the difference between fact and fabrication, between substance and empty promises can be a stage-setter for the future. Mrs. Hart and many other Foxborough educators had teaching styles that coaxed students to be informed and analytical. For some high school seniors, that meant higher SAT scores. The bigger payoff was a more thoughtful electorate. Conclusion: we need a lot more Mrs. Harts.

My final day at Foxborough High ended with a low-key farewell party. Afterward, I drove north to Boston, passing the time with thoughts about how I needed to thank my mother for championing teaching as a career option. Not far from the Foxborough town line, I cruised by the Bay State Raceway. The harness racetrack was well known to horse enthusiasts drawing as many as 10,000 patrons on some evenings. At the time, I had no way of knowing Bay State would slowly fall on hard times and succumb to a wrecking ball in

2000. Taking its place would be a gargantuan 66,000-seat facility eventually to be called Gillette Stadium (naming rights would be bought by Gillette's owner, Procter & Gamble – a 15-year deal at $8 million a year). Foxborough would become home for the either loved or hated New England Patriots, a powerhouse team destined to set a record by making 10 Super Bowl appearances.

With student teaching behind me, I returned to my Gainsborough Street apartment which had become too much of a "good time central." Friday and Saturday nights attracted throngs, some drawn by a 15-gallon keg of Pabst Blue Ribbon, others by a large black rabbit we rescued from a Northeastern research lab and housed in the apartment's non-working fireplace. Sunday mornings would often begin with our drawing straws, the loser forced to clean vomit from the stairway leading to our walk-up. As we got older and a little wiser, the weekends turned tamer. Hob worked longer hours at a local Brigham's ice cream parlor, one of many such iconic storefront outlets scattered throughout Massachusetts and other parts of New England. The future wouldn't be kind to Brigham's. Bad management would push the chain into a slow decline, the company finally declaring bankruptcy in 2009. Its skeletal remains would be purchased by the American dairy corporation, HP Hood.

Like Hob, I took hourly-rate jobs throughout my time at Northeastern. In the winters, I wore a Metropolitan Transit Authority vest and shoveled snow from the MTA's above-ground tracks. I had a short career as a night watchman before finding work as a bartender at the Back Bay Harvard Club on Commonwealth Avenue. Dressed in a club-provided sport coat and tie, I manned a portable bar rolled into any of several smoke-filled private rooms where I would usually find up to six men hunched over a table playing high-stakes poker. The instructions were clear: stand, don't sit, at the rear of the bar and serve only when asked. Behind the array of top-shelf liquors and bottles of pre-mixed martinis, I watched piles of chips worth a thousand dollars or more change hands. At a time when Hob, Kid and I had to scramble to find 54 cents for a dozen eggs, this was an astounding sight. Each night ended with club managers looking the other way while I gorged myself on leftover port wine-infused cheese spread and crackers washed down with ginger ale or tonic water. My lower back ached from standing in one place for hours but a full stomach was a reward for the discomfort.

While the Harvard Club experience helped me grasp what "wealth disparity" really meant, it wasn't my most memorable job. Working as a parking lot attendant took that prize mainly because of an event that happened 1,800 miles away on a November afternoon in 1963. At around 2 pm, I was herding cars into a large open lot not far from Northeastern's main campus. A young woman pulled her Chevy into an open space. Her car radio blasted Elvis Presley's *Return to Sender* but midway through the song, the music was interrupted by a news bulletin. The woman jumped from her car.

"Kennedy's been shot! *The president's been shot!*"

An hour later, another bulletin: John F. Kennedy was dead. Drivers stumbled back to the parking lot. Some were openly crying; all looked shell shocked. The university cancelled most classes and area businesses shut their doors. Cars drained out of the lot in a slow, mournful procession much the way the luster of Camelot faded on that tragic November day.

While different part-time jobs and a full class load kept me busy, I managed to squeeze in a few hours a week to drill with the campus Army Reserve Officers Training Corps (ROTC). A persuasive recruiter convinced me to sign up late in my freshman year. Doing a couple years in the army after college as a commissioned officer was a *far* better option than getting caught in the draft, he said. The draft had been enacted 20 years earlier and would continue until 1973 when the U.S. armed forces would turn all-volunteer. But in the 1960s, the draft caused ceaseless uncertainty and anxiety for males ages 19 to 26 except for those in college. Higher education was a temporary shelter for many including me.

"Once you graduate, you'll be a second lieutenant," the recruiter said. "And when there's no war going on, being a second lieutenant is a walk in the park."

Maybe the recruiter knew more than he was packing into his sales pitch. But like the rest of America, probably not. There actually was a war going on even though Washington told us we were only involved on the margins. Americans were "advisors" helping South Vietnam push back insurgents from the north. Furthermore, the military added, the conflict in Southeast Asia was near an end, thanks to U.S. assistance. The Viet Cong were "getting whipped," General Samuel Williams assured America in an interview with *Time-Life* magazine. At the close of 1960, there were 900 military personnel in Vietnam, all classified as advisors. Five Americans had been killed during the year.

The promised "walk in the park" began to fade as early as 1961. Major media publications and outlets openly questioned the military strategy behind U.S involvement in Indochina. The growing debate had no impact on those of us in ROTC. We were locked into the army by contract. So, to make the best of my time while in the reserves, I decided to join the Northeastern ROTC marching band. I played the saxophone and clarinet (poorly) and for an unexplained reason, was invited to join two dozen far more skilled band members. In 1963, I had worked my way up to drum major, probably promoted to that position just to get me away from any kind of musical instrument. The band perfected a half dozen John Philip Sousa selections and we were invited to march in an occasional patriotic parade. Band life was relatively easy, and I wondered if I could keep this arrangement going when marshalled into active duty. That plan changed after a sidebar conversation with a platoon sergeant.

"You know what you band people do in combat?" the sergeant asked.

"Play music?"

"Wrong," he said. "You're expendable. So, you probe for landmines."

Using a long titanium shaft that ironically looked something like an orchestra conductor's baton, band members hunted for buried landmines. With that information now in the open, I

41

Northeastern University

decided to specialize in something other than music after earning my commission.

By mid-year 1964, South Vietnam was in political chaos – and I was on my way to basic training at Fort Devens, a rambling, 5,000-acre facility only an hour and a half drive from Boston. During several weeks of "basic," not much was said about Vietnam. However, there were mock Vietnamese villages constructed in corners of the sprawling fort. These training sites were tea leaves foretelling the road ahead for the country's armed forces.

The first weeks of basic were miserable, with non-commissioned officers given free rein to debase men who had yet to earn their lieutenant bars. After a month, the experience turned fascinating. Most in my platoon stopped fighting the urge to push back on orders. We became compliant and did what we were told. Because there was so little thinking to be done, basic was – in an odd way – refreshing. Of course, there were interludes where training was either unpleasant, frightening or both. I was a member of a three-man team charged with carrying, firing, and maintaining a temperamental M60 machine gun. In the dark of night with dummy but realistic mortar fire on all sides, I would feed ammunition to a gunner who fired up to 500 rounds per minute in the direction of the fabricated Vietnamese village. We quickly understood the deadly potential of this 23-pound weapon. We also recognized how incredibly easy it would be to chalk up a lot of collateral damage.

After basic, I returned to campus for my final year of college. The U.S. presidential election was in full swing with Lyndon Johnson poised to defeat war advocate Barry Goldwater. Vietnam was the central campaign issue and as such, it put a spotlight on the growing quagmire in Southeast Asia. The U.S.-backed South Vietnamese government was labeled by some in the State Department as incapable of carrying on the affairs of the country. If the war were to continue, it was on track to become an American-led and American-owned conflict.

I continued my ROTC band activities while at the same time catching up on Vietnam developments. This wasn't a fight against communism, I concluded. It was a Washington decision to prop up a totally broken regime that was distrusted or despised by most all of Vietnam. Out of my ROTC uniform, I joined students who assembled on campus to ask the obvious questions: What was our mission in Vietnam? Did Washington understand the likely consequences of an escalated war? Unlike Berkeley, Columbia, and other universities throughout the nation, Northeastern was not a mecca for student protests. When the campus quadrangle was jammed with sign-carrying young people in the fall of 1964, the depth of concern in the country was becoming obvious.

While my reservations about Vietnam weighed heavily, I was bound by agreement with the U.S. Army to stay the course. Then something completely unexpected happened. Late in 1964, the army quietly acknowledged there was a glitch in the reserve officer system. All current ROTC participants had to re-sign their commission agreements. If you didn't sign, you were out.

"Just need your signature and a date," a first lieutenant said after I was called into the campus ROTC office. A grizzly staff sergeant shoved the contract toward me.

"Can I think about this?" I asked.

43

"You don't think," the sergeant reminded me. "You do."

"But what if I don't sign?"

The sergeant glared at me. "I'll make it my life's work to get you drafted into the most miserable unit in this man's army."

The lieutenant interceded. "Look, you're a journalist, right?" He opened a file folder and flipped through a few sheets of photocopied paper.

Calling me a journalist was a stretch, at best. My Northeastern co-op job was working for a weekly newspaper. I had written a couple of feature articles that had gotten some regional attention. But I certainly was not Pulitzer Prize material.

"You've got it made," the lieutenant said. "With your background, you probably will never do time outside the U.S. My guess is you're heading to the Department of Defense."

"Defense Department?"

The lieutenant nodded. "DOD publishes *Stars and Stripes* and they handle the press on what's going on in Vietnam."

I had seen a few of those releases. The military churned out a steady stream of updates faxed to most media outlets around the nation. The information was selective, focusing on whatever small bright spots could be found in Vietnam. Increasingly, the Associated Press, United Press International, and the largest mainstream newspapers were doing their own reporting, often ignoring the sanitized military releases.

"I don't think I want to do that, sir," I said to the lieutenant. "I mean I don't know if I'm the right person to make a case for what's going on in Vietnam."

"You don't *want to do that?*" yelled the sergeant. "Just sign the damn paper!"

I begged for 24 hours to think about what I should do. The lieutenant handed me the re-enrollment form and ordered me to have it on his desk – signed and dated – by noon the next day. Even before I stepped out of the ROTC office, a decision had been made. I would rather be a conscript folded in with thousands of other drafted Army grunts than be part of a propaganda machine promoting a U.S. policy that seemed terribly ill-conceived.

The next day, I put the unsigned form in an envelope with a cover note. When I arrived at the office, the lieutenant and sergeant were not there to berate me. I dropped the envelope on the lieutenant's desk and unceremoniously ended my association with ROTC.

I was conflicted about my 1964 ROTC decision and I remain so to this day. Because of a bizarre hiccup in the military system that mandated reserve officer cadets recommit to the army, I exercised the option of taking an exit ramp. What was my main motivation for making this call? Was it a reaction to Washington's ineptitude in assessing what was really going on in Southeast Asia? Or was this an act of cowardice? Was this my way of protesting short-sighted U.S. policy-making? Or was this rolling the dice hoping I might somehow escape the draft? Possibly an act of rationalization, I have come to accept this **life lesson: there is honor in duty and service if conscience is uncompromised.** The military taught me the logic and necessity of the command chain. In most cases, complying with orders coming from whatever authority layer just above you is essential to an organization structured like the military. But compliance must have limits. There is no honor in committing atrocities even if ordered to do so. There is no honor in wantonly harming noncombatants. It is not dishonorable to reject participating in a war that lacks purpose and, in many ways, is unconscionable. I remind myself constantly that duty and service are not exclusive to the military. There are other ways that lead to honorable citizenship. Helping America's million nonprofit organizations address our nation's needs and minimize conditions that lead to war has been my conscience-driven career choice. The decision to travel that path had its starting point when I separated myself from Northeastern's ROTC program.

The Vietnam War fractured many lives. Most affected were the family and friends of the more than 58,000 U.S. soldiers killed during the conflict. Of the 2.5 million service personnel sent to Vietnam, over 300,000 were wounded. Those who returned physically unscathed were left to mentally and emotionally ponder how their country had been willing to sacrifice so much only to renew relations 20 years later with the Communist-led Socialist Republic of Vietnam. I realized this bewilderment could reach a level of anguish when I had a long lunchtime conversation with Chris Kjeldsen, a Johnson & Johnson vice president and former Marine who saw action in Vietnam. I befriended Chris while I was a J&J consultant. Chris was one of the most even-tempered and nicest people I ever met. On this day, though, he became unusually animated about J&J's just-announced decision to do business in Vietnam. A couple of years earlier, President Clinton lifted the two decade-old trade embargo with the country. Corporations started flooding in. "What was the point?" Chris asked. "I watched men die. And for what?" Chris, age 59, succumbed to a long illness in 2003. Had he lived until 2016, he would have been even more perplexed. Two-way trade between Vietnam and the U.S. climbed to $52 billion per annum. Vietnam would become our country's 16th largest trading partner.

Another victim of the Vietnam war was my friendship with Hob. Unlike me, Hob entered the Army as a second lieutenant immediately after graduating from Northeastern. He served with distinction in Vietnam and after leaving the military became a successful New Jersey businessman. The war hardened him. Our relationship ended many years later when he and his wife visited my family. Hob was uncomfortable with my slightly-left-of-center orientation. He politely expressed his own opinions which were much more to the right. The night ended with an apology from his wife. "Don't mind him," she said. "He thinks there's a communist under every bed." I can't fault Hob for his point of view. Had I experienced Vietnam the way he did, my own mindset might be vastly different.

In the spring of 1965, I graduated from Northeastern – miraculously with honors and thanks to an array of jobs over the years, no

Professor Everett Marston   *Evening Institute for Younger Men*

debt. My grade point average had been boosted by strong marks in courses where instructors had a remarkable capacity to turn subject matter into highly relevant contemporary information. One such instructor was Professor Everett Marston. A long-time faculty member at the university, Marston was part historian and part author/playwright. The professor wrote several short stories, plays and novels. One of his nonfiction books, *Origin and Development of Northeastern University,* chronicles the evolution of my alma mater from its start as Boston's Evening Institute for Younger Men (1898) to its emerging national prominence in 1960. Marston died in 1970. He didn't live long enough to witness Northeastern's continued evolution.

Professor Marston would frequently end a class with a quote, usually from his literary hero, the four-time Pulitzer Prize winner Eugene O'Neill (*Long Day's Journey into Night, The Iceman Cometh, Desire Under the Elms*). On occasion, he would excerpt a line or two from another of his favored playwrights, authors or poets. After one lecture, he left the class with this William Butler Yeats quote:

Education is not the filling of a pail, but the lighting of a fire.

By blending learning with experience, Northeastern has been a torch that has ignited many a career. And the university itself has become a kind of firestorm in the higher education world. Northeastern is now recognized as the national leader in experiential learning and cooperative education. It has been a steady climb to the top for this great school and I am grateful for having been on board for part of its journey.

Chapter 4

Phoenix-Times Publishing Company (1961-65)

"Quarter pound spaghetti, one meatball, and a medium bucket of steamers."

The waitress scratched the order on the back of a napkin. "You want it to go?"

"Yeah, working late again."

The woman nodded and tossed the napkin through a wall opening that gave customers a full view of Tweets' inner workings. Two men in white T-shirts hunkered over pots of boiling pasta and simmering softshell clams everyone in Rhode Island called steamers.

Tweets was a one-story, brick restaurant foodies called a dive and people like me worshiped as nirvana. Anthony "Tweet" Balzano wasn't big on ambience but huge on portions. Plus, the prices were always right. Under a buck for a whole pound of spaghetti with red clam sauce. And sometimes, you even got a free meatball.

As great as Tweets was, I had discovered a while ago it was not an ideal venue for date night.

"Oh, my god!" my girlfriend of the month had said much earlier in the year. She watched aghast as Tweet strolled out of the kitchen into the dining area with our order. He carried a platter of steamers in one hand, pasta in the other, and a loaf of Italian bread stuck under his armpit.

"I can't eat that!" my girlfriend staring wide-eyed at the bread and Tweet's sweat-stained shirt. "*I won't eat that!*"

I shrugged, said I understood and proceeded to dip the surprisingly salty Italian bread into the container of melted butter that

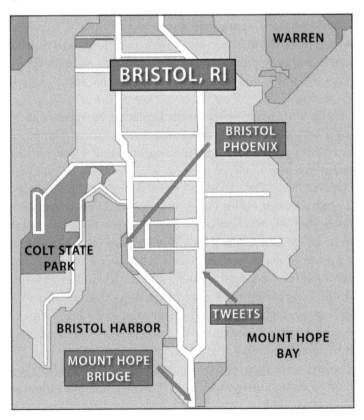

always accompanied a serving of steamers. Our relationship ended shortly thereafter.

It took four minutes to drive from one side of Bristol, Rhode Island to the other. Tweets' food was still hot when I parked a block from Thames and Bradford Streets and an old man in a pressman's cap screamed: "*The front page just got pied!*"

I put my Tweets' take-out on the metal desk that was sometimes mine and sometimes the parking place for another *Bristol Phoenix* intern. I hustled into what the printing trade called the "backshop" and saw lead slugs strewn over the floor planks. For sure, I would be eating cold food tonight.

The *Phoenix* was a weekly paper that had been Bristol's source of local news and happenings for over a century. The publication was delivered to homes and newsstands on Thursdays, which meant it had to be printed on Wednesday nights. So, midweek was always stressful and much more so when a crisis struck. Like on this evening.

Along with many other small-circulation newspapers in the early 1960s, the *Phoenix* was a letterpress operation. The process started with people like me pounding out copy which was then handed to a lone Linotype operator who converted text on paper to type on metal. On a good day, the operator could process about 30 words a minute on his Linotype keyboard. The machine would spit out thin pieces of lead called slugs that were lined up in a long row or galley. One of the shop workers would ink the galley, toss on a sheet of paper, and roll out a galley proof. Reporters were responsible for checking the proof for errors. If mistakes were spotted, the Linotype operator would have to produce another set of lead slugs as a replacement for the faulty part of the galley. This was something to be avoided since Mr. Linotype was a sullen individual who detested do-overs.

Galleys were then sorted and reassembled along with photo blocks to create a newspaper page. This jigsaw combination was put together inside a metal frame known as a chase. There was no bottom to a chase and all the bits and pieces of the page were kept in place by a quoin – a wedge-like device that used pressure to keep things in order.

"I'm not doing this again," Mr. Linotype snarled, looking at the mess on the floor. The accident had happened when a press operator dropped a chase as it was being moved from a metal, wheel-mounted table onto the bed of the flatbed press. When a chase falls apart and slugs of type go flying, it is a catastrophe called a "pie" that strikes terror in every printer's heart. There are two remedies to the problem. The first is to find each lead slug and try to reconstruct the page. This jigsaw method can be very time-consuming and often ends in failure because of damaged or missing slugs. The other option is to have Mr. Linotype redo everything from scratch.

"I want new galleys!" Roz Boswell yelled at Mr. Linotype.

There were glares back and forth. "It's gonna be overtime," Linotype snapped.

"Shut up and just do it!" shouted Roz.

Bristol Phoenix Office   *Linotype Machine*

Roswell Bosworth Jr. was a tough, no-nonsense type whose gruff commands where honed during his time in the Army Air Force. Although just in his mid-thirties, he was an authoritarian figure who probably would have preferred the title Mr. Bosworth. But he was the son of Roswell Bosworth Senior who had been the editor and publisher of the *Phoenix* since 1928. So, the "mister" title was reserved for the elder Bosworth. That left the son with the handle "Ros" which everyone mouthed as "Roz."

I don't know how Northeastern University convinced the Bosworths to take on a second-year college student as a co-op worker. What I did learn was that this was the paper's first experience with a work-study program and the jury was out as to whether it would be worthwhile. My first month at the Phoenix-Times Publishing Company – the holding corporation for both the *Bristol Phoenix* and a more recent start-up, the *Barrington Times,* launched in 1958 – was part coffee boy and part apprentice. I had taken introductory journalism courses at the university but this real-life exposure was nothing like academia. I was a paid intern which meant the salary was low and the hours long.

"Tomorrow night – cover the school board meeting," Roz issued the unexpected order while flipping through display ads that would run in the next issues of the *Phoenix.*

"Me?" I was stunned.

"Yeah, you," Roz confirmed. "You're supposed to be a reporter, right? So, report." He looked up from his cluttered desk. "And wear a suit and tie."

The next night, I went from underling to journalist. There was nothing special about the school board meeting. The 10 paragraphs I put together the next morning were even more ho-hum. Still, Roz seemed satisfied.

"You know how to work a Graflex?" Roz asked already knowing the answer.

"Not really."

"Jimmy will show you," Roz noted. "Then I want you on call for accidents. If Jimmy can't take the shot, you show up. Got it?"

I didn't *get it.* And I didn't *get* Jimmy. A week into my *Phoenix* job, I learned *Jimmy* wasn't really Jimmy. The Bristol-born high school dropout had a real name but because he was a mirror image of the boy reporter who worked at the *Daily Planet* with Clark Kent (a.k.a. Superman), *Jimmy* was his inherited new name. Jimmy wasn't highly educated but knew his way around cameras and most anything mechanical. When the old press stopped working, which was frequently, an emergency call went out to Jimmy. He wasn't always a fix-it genius, but he worked miracles on several occasions.

"This here's a Graflex 4 by 5," Jimmy began my photography orientation. "I use it and so do the cop stringers."

Jimmy explained the *Phoenix* had a deal with a couple Bristol police officers. They were usually first on the scene of most catastrophic events. If the *Phoenix* used one or more of their photos, Roz paid them in under-the-counter cash. Jimmy handled more mundane shoots, including high school sports events which were his favorite.

"Word is the Graflex is on its way out," Jimmy continued. "There's 35 mm cameras startin' to be used. But as far as I'm concerned, nothing's gonna replace this here press camera."

Jimmy fondled the Graflex for a few seconds and then somewhat reluctantly handed me the camera. For two days, I practiced adjusting the accordion-like bellows and taking flash photos with one replaceable bulb after another. Then the *Phoenix* got a call about a serious one-car accident on Metacom Avenue, a main drag that ran the length of Bristol. A drunk driver plowed an old Ford into a pole not far from Tweets. It was Jimmy's day off and the two photo-taking cops were handling another traffic incident at the north end of town. Roz pointed to the Graflex and head waved me out the door. I arrived on the scene a half hour after rescue workers had extricated the driver from a twisted pile of metal and glass. A Bristol patrolman I had never met was supervising the removal of the wreckage. A quick conversation with the cop and he had no problem with my taking a few pictures as long as he could be shown pointing to the blood-splattered front seat of the mangled car. The next issue of *Phoenix* featured a front-page, lower-fold photograph of the cop looking at the remains of the Ford as if it were a big-game trophy. Later, the cop called to thank me for turning him into a local celebrity and then added.: "If there's anything I can do for you …" It was another **life lesson: favors foster reciprocity.** The

Graflex Press Camera   *Mount Hope Bridge*

new patrolman friend would repay me with many favors over the next few years, the first coming only a couple of weeks after my car wreck photo.

"Jumper on Mount Hope Bridge!" Roz shouted at me a week after my debut with the car wreck photo. He had just fielded a call from the Bristol Police Department. "This one's yours. I want a money shot especially if he goes over. Hear me? Don't screw it up."

It was late morning and Jimmy was in the backshop working on the finicky press. Both photo-cops weren't available for any *Phoenix* work until after dinner. That left me. I grabbed the Graflex and made a short drive to the two-lane, scenic bridge that hooked Bristol to Portsmouth.

"The *Journal* is on its way," my patrolman pal whispered when I showed up at the bridge's toll booth. The cop had pulled his car sideways across the road blocking all access to the bridge. "The *Journal* guy's an idiot – I'm not a fan. I can stall him for maybe five minutes. If you get lucky and the jumper takes a dive, you got yourself an exclusive."

The *Providence Journal* was the state's daily and main news source. To scoop the *Journal* might make Roswell Bosworth Junior crack a smile. That would be a rarity. I jogged halfway across the 1,200-foot suspension bridge, heading toward a gaggle of uniformed officers standing in a semi-circle around a shirtless man who looked to be in his 40s. The jumper stood outside the bridge guardrail, his feet braced against a steel beam.

"This one's definitely going," one cop said to another. "Seen enough of these to know what's gonna happen."

Another uniformed cop turned to me. "Better get that camera ready."

I lifted the Graflex and pointed in the direction of the distraught man. He was in perfect frame, arms stretched out behind him, hands clutching the metal guardrail.

"Snap it when I tell you," the cop-in-the-know said. The jumper cocked his head in my direction. He was wide-eyed with fear and despair. It was the most gut-churning expression I had ever seen. Then the jumper released his grip and yanked his arms to his side.

"*NOW!*" two cops yelled at once as the man fell forward, his body ramrod straight as it began a horrifying descent toward the choppy Mount Hope Bay 130 feet below.

The cops jostled their way to the guardrail just as the jumper hit the water with a soft thud. Then they all turned to me.

"You … you didn't take the shot," one said, looking incredulous as he spoke.

"Why? What's wrong with you? When does somebody like you *ever* get a chance like that?"

I wanted to explain I had never seen anyone about to die; to tell the cops that what I saw in my viewfinder just before the man jumped was terrifying. Someone in such agony shouldn't have his last few seconds of life on film, I thought. But to confess to being soft-hearted to a group of men so accustomed to pain and misery would not go well for me. So, I shrugged and headed back to the foot of the bridge where a *Providence Journal* reporter was arguing with my Bristol cop-friend.

I returned to the *Phoenix* office. Roz was waiting at the front door. "I was too late," I lied before he could say a word. Roz studied my face. More than likely, he knew I wasn't telling the truth. But for sure, he knew I looked upset. "All right," he said, choosing not to launch an interrogation. "Get back to work."

I returned to my desk and tried putting together a few paragraphs about plans for the town's signature event – the nationally heralded Fourth of July parade that had been held in Bristol since 1785. Even mundane writing was difficult given that I had just watched a man jump to his death. I had heard the Mount Hope Bridge had been the last stop for a lot of people since it opened in 1929. It would be the endpoint for many more over the years to come. Teachers. An assistant school principal. A priest. Men. Women. The old bridge was both beautiful and monstrous at the same time. For most, it was the passageway between two historic communities; for others, it was an escape from life.

"Some say the bridge is cursed," said Roswell Bosworth Sr. who was seated in a corner office not far from my desk. "It was built by a private company. Five days after it opened, Wall Street crashed. The company went bankrupt a few years later."

There was no one in Bristol and possibly anywhere else who was a better student of New England history than Mr. Bosworth. He wrote a column that appeared in every issue of the *Phoenix*. His editorial *nom de plume* was "The Scribe." A pen and ink sketch of a distinguished-looking man smoking a pipe caught Mr. Bosworth's image perfectly. As hardnosed and irascible as Roz could be, his father was even-tempered to the point of being gentle. Some of my favorite *Phoenix* moments were listening to the old man recollect the past.

Coggeshall Museum & Farm   *Herreshoff Marine Museum*

"There's good evidence that our first Thanksgiving didn't happen in Plymouth, Massachusetts," Mr. Bosworth informed me on one early November day. He was writing a column about Hegler's Turkey Ranch, a 22-acre farm located across Mount Hope Bay in Tiverton. "It was most likely right here in Bristol. This is where the Pokanoket Tribe of the Wampanoag Nation camped for the summer and fall."

Mr. Bosworth was not only Bristol's most prominent historian, he was also the town's most avid cheerleader. He was quick to write or tell locals and visitors alike to visit the 48-acre Coggeshall Farm to find out what life was like centuries ago; or take a few minutes to check out the America's Cup Hall of Fame at the Herreshoff Marine Museum. The long-time *Phoenix* publisher was also candid – sometimes brutally so – about Bristol's dark past when it played a role in the nation's slave trade. One of the town's most wealthy and notorious citizens was George deWolf, known for transporting rum from his Bristol distillery to Africa where his ships were then loaded with slaves bound for the West Indies and elsewhere.

Mr. Bosworth was a great believer in the power of understanding the past. He left me with another **life lesson: time boils away fabrication and exaggeration to leave a residue called truth.**

As much as Mr. Bosworth loved looking back, his son Roz was all about the present and near future. Had he not been wedded to small-town community newspapers, he would have been an investigative journalist as doggedly perseverant as Bob Woodward and Carl Bernstein.

"You and Jimmy," Roz shouted at me. "Get in here."

We marched to a quiet corner in the rear of the backshop.

"There's something I want you to do and you're going to make sure you don't get caught doing it," Roz informed us.

Jimmy and I looked at one another. If nothing else, Roz had our attention.

"Frank Balzano," Roz growled. "He's using town employees to do work on his property. I need proof about what's going on."

Balzano was the town highway superintendent and tight with some members of Bristol's town council. He had a reputation for being arrogant and hot-tempered. The *Phoenix* had run stories in the past about Balzano, stories that included quotes from other town officials who criticized the man's "strong will" and his language that one councilman said could be a "verbal holocaust."

An hour later, Jimmy and I were slithering through waist-high grass and weeds that had taken over a vacant lot next to Frank Balzano's modest three-bedroom house. Phase one of our quickly hatched plan was for the two of us to crawl through the field getting as close as possible to Balzano's yard. Four men and a backhoe – all probably paid for by the Town of Bristol – were grading a strip of land that looked like it was about to turn into an asphalt or concrete driveway. The plan's second phase was for Jimmy and me to take turns popping up over the high grass, each of us snapping a few shots of the work brigade and then quickly squirming our way back to a side road where our get-away car was parked.

"Perfect picture," Jimmy bragged after using the Graflex to take the first photo. "Your turn," he said and handed me the camera.

"Anyone looking this way?" I asked.

"Nah," Jimmy assured me. "Nobody's paying attention to this here empty lot."

I stood up, aimed the Graflex and found a stubby man standing dead center in my viewfinder. The worker had walked to the field for a bathroom break. He was relieving himself no more than 20 yards from where I was now standing. I lowered the camera and gasped. The man zipped up, shouted something, and pointed at me. I reached down, grabbed Jimmy by the collar, and both of us raced across the field.

"You told me nobody was looking!" I screamed at Jimmy. "*You told me nobody was looking!*"

"Geez, the guy had to pee," Jimmy said. "Bad luck, is what it is."

Jimmy had no idea as to just how bad the luck would turn out to be.

Not long after our return to the *Phoenix* office, Jimmy's single shot of the work crew building Balzano's driveway was developed. It was a beauty. Without divulging our narrow escape, we handed Roz the explicit print expecting a lot of praise and even a bonus. Instead, Roz took the photo, studied it carefully and shoved it into the bottom drawer of his desk.

"Thanks," Roz muttered. And that was it. The *Phoenix* never ran the picture but I knew it was a high-caliber piece of ammunition Roz could and probably would use when the time was right.

A week went by and I was back to my routine reporting work. Roz sent me to cover a regular meeting of the town council. Replacement equipment for the fire department, a zoning exemption, report from the Fourth of July planning committee – nothing out of the ordinary. The meeting ended shortly before 10 p.m. I was leaving town hall when someone I didn't know asked if I had a couple of minutes to talk to one of the councilmen. He led me into an empty corridor that ran along the back of the council meeting room.

"Wait here," the man instructed and quickly retraced his steps to the corridor entrance. Along the way, he nodded to a dark side room. A door cracked open and Frank Balzano stormed toward me.

"I should break every bone in your body" Frank screamed while at the same time punching his forearm into my neck and lifting me off my feet. "You think I don't know what you did? If I *ever* see you anywhere near my house, I'll kick your skinny ass from here to Providence."

The profanity-laced shouting went on for another couple of minutes. Frank's sidekick who drew me into the corridor stood watch to ward off any witnesses. Balzano ended the confrontation with a hard shove that sent me to the floor. He and his accomplice marched out of the building leaving me in a crumpled pile.

Minutes later, a janitor appeared at the opposite end of the corridor. "What are you doing here?" he asked, surprised to find anyone still in the building.

59

I stood up, straightened my rumpled tie and said: "That's the same question I've been asking myself."

After a sleepless night, I met Jimmy at the *Phoenix* office in the morning. I warned him to be on the lookout for Balzano but we both agreed the workman who spotted me probably didn't get a good view of my accomplice. More than likely Jimmy was safe. Next, I found Roz in the backshop and reported what happened.

"Maybe I should go to the police," I proposed. "There's this cop I know ..."

"Did Balzano cut you?" Roz interrupted.

"No."

"You have any broken bones?"

"No."

"Then drop it," Roz said. "It won't happen again."

"But..."

"It won't happen again."

And it didn't. I left two days later for my next semester at Northeastern. It would be months before I returned to Bristol and when I did, things had changed. Big time.

During my time away from the *Phoenix,* Frank Balzano resigned. Whether the photo stuck in Roz Bosworth's desk drawer had any-thing to do with the resignation remains a mystery. I was told Frank was still living in his Bristol home accessed by an impressive, recently paved driveway. My goal was to steer clear of Balzano since he might blame me for his recent misfortune. Although I never saw Frank again, Jimmy told me he thought Tweet Balzano was Frank's cousin. Dining at my favorite restaurant would be too much of a risk, I decided. Tweets would forever be off limits. One poisoned meatball and I would be finished.

Before I could settle in behind my old *Phoenix* desk, Roz waved me into the backshop. "You're being promoted," he said with abso-lutely no fanfare.

"What?"

"News editor."

"What?" I was barely 22 years old and already a news editor? I was an up-and-coming Arthur Ochs Sulzberger!

"Of the *Warren Times*," Roz went on.

"What?"

"The *Warren Times*," Roz repeated.

"Oh."

The *Warren Times* was a Bosworth start-up first published in 1961. The goal was to make the new paper as successful as *The Barrington Times* and the historic *Bristol Phoenix*. But Warren was a smaller and less affluent market. The paper was struggling for a foothold and its future unclear. It occurred to me my assignment as news editor of the *Warren Times* was not a lot different than being named first mate of the Titanic.

The next day, I showed up at a small storefront office only a couple of blocks from Jamiel's Shoe World. *Warren Times* was stenciled on the front door. I was greeted by Lucille, a tall, thin woman who made an instant impression as being warm and gracious. Not so nice was Bob, whose job was to sell display ad space. Bob was in his late 40's, overly slick and fast-talking.

Three weeks into my new assignment, a middle-aged woman walked into the office with copy for a one-inch classified ad. Lucille normally handled this kind of routine transaction but when Bob saw the woman, he quickly took over. Bob and the customer laughed and carried on until noontime when Lucille left for lunch announcing she would be making a stop at St. Thomas the Apostle – Warren's popular Catholic church. As soon as Lucille was out of the office, Bob whispered: "Do me a favor. Close the office for a half hour. Just stand outside."

"What … what are you talking about?"

"Just do it," Bob insisted and hurried back to the woman.

I did what I was told. I hung a *CLOSED* sign on the door and for thirty minutes stood stewing outside the office. Bob and his lady friend had giggled their way into the *Times'* bathroom, the only portioned-off part of the office. When they reappeared, Bob knocked on the front window and gave me a thumbs up. The woman was smoothing her skirt and straightening her hair.

"Whew, that's what I needed," Bob exclaimed.

"It's not going to happen again," I replied, surprising myself with how much authority I injected into the comment.

"Excuse me?"

"You want to play around? Well, that's your business. But don't use the office."

Bob glared at me. "Let's get a few things straight. I'm twice your age. So, don't tell me what to do. And in case you forgot, you're not in charge. I get paid by the boys in Bristol. So, I'll be doing whatever I want in this office."

"Nope," I said calmly. "You won't."

The mid-day confrontation triggered a tense stand-off between Bob and me with Lucille caught in the middle. Over the next three weeks, I avoided Bob as much as possible. At any moment, I expected him to test me in some way to make it clear he was the alpha male in the office. Instead, Bob jumped ship for what he claimed was a better paying sales job in East Providence. My time with Bob was unpleasant but instructive. He taught me there were occasions when taking a stand was essential even if that stirred up uncomfortable consequences.

I was getting close to graduation day at Northeastern and the end of my final co-op tour of duty at the Phoenix-Times Publishing Company. While briefing a reporter who would be taking my place as the *Warren Times* news editor, Roz Bosworth called. He summoned me back to the *Bristol Phoenix* office.

"We want you here full-time," Roz said, "You graduate in June and start back at the *Phoenix* in July."

The offer was completely unexpected. While there had been a few verbal "attaboy" compliments over the years, Roz had never served up a formal performance review.

"I don't know, Roz," I replied. "I have an offer from New York University that comes with some financial aid and a graduate student deferment."

Roz nodded in a way that told me he was anticipating my response. "I can get you into a University of Rhode Island grad program. You won't get drafted. Get your master's degree at night and get paid a salary working here."

I was grateful for Roz's confidence and the generous offer. But it wasn't clear that working for a community newspaper group was the right career path for me. Plus, the incident on the Mount Hope Bridge and the encounter with Frank Balzano made me wonder about my journalistic competency. I told Roz I would think about the proposal and get back to him the next day. But even before our conversation ended, Roz knew I would be heading to New York City.

My last day at the Phoenix-Times Publishing Company closed with a slow drive through the back streets of Bristol, a town I had come to know well and appreciate even more. It was just after five when I cruised past Tweets Restaurant. The parking lot was already dotted with cars. Tweets would go on forever, I thought. But I was wrong. Faced with $100,000 in unpaid taxes, the Balzano family would shutter the restaurant in 2014.

Change would reconfigure Bristol in other ways over the years to come. The old toll booths that guarded the entrance to the Mount Hope Bridge would be removed in 1998 – the 30-cent per car toll not enough to meet payroll for booth operators. Roger Williams College moved from an innocuous downtown Providence address to Ferrycliffe, formerly an 80-acre dairy farm perched on prime Bristol waterfront property overlooking Mount Hope Bay. The college would add 50 more acres after it earned its university status in 1992. With over 5,000 students and more than 3,500 employees, it would radically alter the town's character.

Some things didn't change, of course. Bristol's Fourth of July parade would continue to uphold its claim as the oldest "military, civic and fireman's" patriotic event in the nation. The Mount Hope Bridge would remain the last-ditch stop for the distraught. In a three-year period, Mount Hope and two other regional bridges would record 29 suicides. And the *Bristol Phoenix* would do what it had done since 1837 – publish a quality weekly paper.

Roswell "The Scribe" Bosworth Sr. would live out a dignified life. His son, Roz Junior, would die at age 90 and be celebrated by many as "the dean of Rhode Island community newspapers." The *Warren Times* (eventually called the *Warren Times-Gazette*) would be bundled with the *Phoenix, Barrington Times,* and five other weeklies all produced by a revamped Phoenix-Times Publishing Company to be called East Bay Newspapers. New technologies would spell the end for the backshop's old flatbed press. Printing would be outsourced to much higher-tech shops in Massachusetts and later to Newport, Rhode Island.

Three generations later, the *Phoenix* and its sister papers remain family-owned. East Bay Newspapers operate out of the same Bradford Street building where the Bosworths taught me a lot about journalism and even more about life.

Chapter 5

City Teachers Association (1965-66)

I n so many ways, 1965 was a year of change. Race riots erupted in the Watts section of Los Angeles while in stark contrast, the federal Voting Rights Act was signed into law guaranteeing African Americans the right to vote. For the first time, a government-mandated health warning was stamped on each pack of cigarettes sold in the U.S. The "Great Northeast Blackout" cut off electricity to 30 million people in seven states. *Doctor Zhivago* debuted diverting the public's attention to a story about an early twentieth century Russian Revolution and away from the foreboding news

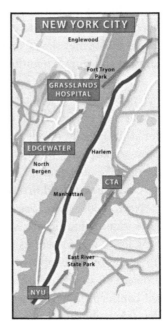

about a contemporary revolution going very badly in Vietnam. And in August, I married a woman I had dated during most of my college years.

The marriage had a hopeful beginning but 13 years later fell apart. We began as a couple very much on the same track, both practicing a strong work ethic and doing what we could to right at least some of the world's wrongs. For me, the focus on fixing things outside the marriage became more absorbing than the marriage itself. The experience exposed many of my shortcomings and led to another important **life lesson: marriage is a kind of interpersonal battery, powered up at the start; likely to weaken or die if not periodically recharged.** Looking back, I treated marriage (along with too many other life events) as a consulting assignment. The task was doing everything necessary to get to the altar. Once vows were exchanged the deal was finished. Time to move on to the next opportunity or challenge. I wasn't immune to marital messaging on TV/radio and in magazines/newspapers ("Seven Ways to Keep Your Marriage Alive," "How to Stay Connected to Your Partner"). However, the advice never really resonated and consequently, a partnership so promising in the mid-sixties slowly unraveled but not before it produced an unusual and truly extraordinary group of children.

Firstborn was a son who would come to reject money, material goods and social status as determinants of success. Bright (University of California Berkeley graduate) and handsome, he could have easily traveled a more conventional path. Instead, he chose a minimalist life, not yielding to the lure of chasing a dollar for the sake of acquiring "stuff." Not an easy path to follow but to his credit, he has held firmly to his beliefs.

Next, a daughter was adopted into the family. An African American infant, she was labeled "difficult to place" by the State of New Jersey given a serious shortage of homes for children of color. It remains inconceivable why placement could possibly have been a problem for an infant with such a vivacious personality. Spirited and self-confident, our new daughter quickly assimilated, so much so that skin color differences became irrelevant. "Although it's obvious

I'm black living in a family with two white parents, I never felt adopted," she would say later as an adult. But outside the household, discrimination was a reality particularly for someone raised in a largely Caucasian world. Our daughter used her positive attitude and perseverance to navigate through and around racial disparities. She would ultimately enroll in a special program at Spellman College and then earn a bachelor's degree at Howard University, perhaps the most prominent of all 100 historically black colleges in the U.S.

The third arrival was another biological son whose even temper was matched by his overall good nature. He would leverage his education (University California undergrad, University Wisconsin graduate degree) to achieve domestic and international professional success. Then he took a sharp turn and applied his creative skills to designing and constructing eco-friendly buildings winning awards for his "green designs." More importantly, he would become the kind of father to his children I wish I had been to mine.

Fourth to the family was a second adopted child. After months of being passed through the foster care system's revolving door, she immediately connected with her newfound siblings. Like her older sister, she, too, was African American. Kind and sensitive, she had many endearing qualities. But it was her remarkable love for any and all animals that was obvious to everyone. With incredible determination and grit, she worked her way up and over numerous barriers to land a top job in one of the most celebrated dog breeding kennels in the world. Not immune to racial discrimination, her disposition – sometimes tough but most often exceedingly gentle – won over most people regardless of their attitudes about color, ethnicity or gender.

A fifth child joined the clan when I remarried in 1980. Younger in years and smaller in stature, she was in every way the little sister who would show incalculable courage when she was in her early teens. Diagnosed with advanced Hodgkin's disease, most of her high school years were spent in and out of the hospital. Her bout with cancer changed her life in many ways. While a strong

67

candidate for a college engineering program, she chose instead to enter the health care profession, graduating from Villanova's School of Nursing and earning a graduate degree from the Medical University of South Carolina.

When all together, this blended collection of five very different children turned heads. Black and white, male and female, tall and short – this was not an ordinary family unit. In spite of – or perhaps partly because of – a broken marriage, each of the children would become remarkably strong in their own way. This is not to suggest that in the eyes of these children a failed marriage was more positive than negative. Divorce rarely makes it easier for children to travel a path to adulthood.

Married life began in Edgewater, a small New Jersey borough located about three miles south of the George Washington Bridge. From one window in a tiny walk-up apartment, a narrow opening between taller buildings offered an elongated view of the Hudson River. Edgewater was still in its early stages of aggressive residential development. During the early 1900s, the town was a manufacturing hub. Plants produced chemicals, dyes, oils, and sugars – there was even a Ford Motor assembly facility in Edgewater. Just before the Depression, nearly 9,000 workers were employed by different industries all with an Edgewater address. As the 20th century progressed, the town's industrial prominence faded. Factories were demolished and replaced with apartment buildings and condos. Over the years, the residential population would more than double, people drawn to the town by its waterfront location and mostly by its relatively easy access to Manhattan.

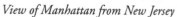

View of Manhattan from New Jersey   *The A Train*

My commute to New York University from Edgewater was not difficult but long. After a short bus ride over the George Washington Bridge, I would transfer to New York's famous A Train. The subway express would shoot the length of Manhattan to the West 4th Street station in Greenwich Village. Weather permitting, the walk to the NYU building adjacent to Washington Square Park was always interesting given the motley crowd that usually gathered around the square's popular arch. My graduate school focus was on organization design with an emphasis on how K-12 public education could be restructured to deliver a better "end product." I immersed myself in books authored by the leading organization thinkers of the time – Amitai Etzioni, Warren Bennis, and others (popularized experts such as Peter Drucker and Jim Collins had yet to make their appearance).

Once into the rhythm of grad school, I managed to juggle my schedule and moved most classes to late afternoon and evening. That left days open for gainful employment that I discovered was an absolute necessity for me. Finding a job was less about bringing more money into the household and more about assuaging a male ego. My wife was working as a public-school teacher and my NYU costs were minimal. So, if we maintained a spartan lifestyle, we could probably have made ends meet. Still, I was uncomfortable not being a financial contributor, so I began a search for part-time employment. NYU steered me toward New York City's substitute teaching pool where per-diem pay was high and for good reason. The city could have sent me to any of its 1,800 schools but the need for subs was greatest in an historic section of New York called Harlem.

My New York City substitute teaching career was short. Even so, it ranks as among the most notable failures of my life. While I owned a teaching certificate, the only frontline experience I had was in Foxborough, Massachusetts's super high-performing high school. I was ill-equipped to deal with forty or more deeply disadvantaged teenagers whom I usually found shoehorned into whatever badly deteriorated classroom was designated as my responsibility for the day. In Harlem, a substitute was not a teacher. A successful substitute was more a warden who knew how to keep peace. Within minutes of an opening bell, an ineffective substitute like me was at risk of falling prey to the pack and when that happened, an administrator had to be summoned to restore order to a totally out-of-control classroom.

My substitute assignments put me in classes where students were all black and brown, many speaking English as a second language, and a large number reluctantly biding time until they could legally escape the requirements for a formal education. As one way to keep order, I manufactured exercises that tapped into real-life issues and aspirations of young people long ago relegated to the underclass. "Write down what you think you will be doing in five years," I said and handed out sheets of lined paper. "Then turn your paper over and write what would you *want* to be doing in five years?" Once finished, the papers were collected and except for a few outliers, the class openly talked about what they had written.

There was almost always a *huge* gap between what young people wished for and what they considered was their prescribed destiny. Wishes were not unlike those of any adolescent – fame and fortune. Usually basketball or music. But expectations were different (listed in rank order): making money on the street (meaning drugs and sex), not going to juvie or jail, not getting shot, just getting by.

For years, I kept dozens of those handwritten sheets of paper in my briefcase. When my NYU classmates would get esoteric about education reform, I would pull out the sheets of paper as a disconcerting reality check. Years ago, I misplaced those papers and some of my Harlem memories began to fade. Then, in 2009, the film *Precious* was released. The movie about an overweight, illiterate, and abused teen living in Harlem and struggling in school as well as life brought everything back. After watching the film, I stood in the theater corridor and broke into uncontrollable tears. This young woman (played wonderfully by Gabourey Sidibe) was the student I left behind; the child I was incapable of helping either as a teacher or mentor.

Later in my career, in the early 1990s, my Harlem experience came into play when working on an early childhood project. The health care giant Johnson & Johnson hired me to come up with ways to bolster the nation's Head Start program. For me, this was a high-priority assignment since Harlem had taught me another **life lesson: to get to a good place begin the journey pointed in the right direction.** Making course

Precious (Gabourey Sidibe)

adjustments for teenagers who had been on a damaging trajectory since birth was a daunting challenge. But what if, at a very early age, children were put on a path more likely to get them to a positive and productive place when they reached adulthood? This was a question I posed to Dr. Alfred (Al) Osborne, Jr. who at the time was a professor at UCLA's Anderson School of Management (he would later become interim dean). It was the beginning of a long-term friendship and a 14-year project called the Head Start – Johnson & Johnson Management Fellows Program administered by UCLA's Anderson School.

Al Osborne was (and continues to be) one of the nation's most respected experts in the fields of entrepreneurship and organizational innovation. He used those skills to help Head Start directors learn and apply business concepts to structure their programs and produce the best possible results from sometimes-skeptical public and private funders. Head Start has long had its share of critics who reference studies showing pre-kindergarten gains attributed to the program disappear by the second or third grade. The phenomenon is called the "Head Start fade" and has been held high as an argument against investing government funds for a benefit that evaporates in two or three years. But other studies have made a compelling case for Head Start. Nobel Prize-winning economist James Heckman has gone on record reminding the public that Head Start children attend more years of schooling, earn higher incomes, live healthier, and engage less in criminal behavior. Researchers also report other long-term effects linked to Head Start which to me are even more compelling: kids in the program exhibit more self-control and greater self-esteem.

"You're spending too much time in the weeds," one of my NYU classmates told me. I had dragged myself to a lecture on *Critical Thinking and Creative Problem Solving* after seven demoralizing hours in Harlem. "Get out the classroom and start thinking how to change the system."

"What are you talking about?"

"Look, why are you in graduate school?" he asked. "You're studying organizational development, for godsakes. Not classroom methodology 101."

"I can't organize one class, never mind a school system," I lamented.

"You're trying to change from the bottom up. Think systemic. Top down."

"How do I do that?"

"I don't know," he shrugged and yanked a notice tacked to a job placement board. "Here, try this."

Communications Coordinator – City Teachers Association, a National Education Association affiliate.

The next day, I called about the job. The day after that, I was sitting in a gloomy third-floor office staring at a short man in his fifties with dyed brown hair.

"Call me Al," he said. "I don't like mister or sir. Just Al."

"Ok."

"You know what we do here?" Al asked. He spoke with a slight slur that I wrongly assumed was a speech impediment.

I had researched the City Teachers Association and knew what it was *supposed* to do. Years earlier, the National Education Association had battled with another union, the United Federation of Teachers (UFT), for the right to represent educators under a newly adopted collective bargaining law. Over 61 percent of teachers in New York City voted for the UFT, backed by the AFL-CIO, to be their bargaining agent which left NEA's affiliate, the New York State Teachers Association, out in the cold. The City Teachers Association – or CTA – was a lingering reminder to New York's nearly 50,000 teachers that the NEA was still around if they wanted to connect with a more "professional" organization.

"We care more about education quality than the UFT," Al insisted. "We think the kids should come first."

"Ok."

"That's what separates us from the regular union."

"Ok."

"Not that we don't want teachers to get better pay and working conditions."

"Ok."

Al ran a yellow pencil through his hair which was slicked back with too much pomade. "We put out press releases and op-eds on how teachers make a difference. That kind of thing. You interested?"

It wasn't the opportunity of a lifetime but yes, I was interested. I showed Al a few *Bristol Phoenix* articles and said I could probably deliver what he needed. Al agreed. If I wanted the job it was mine.

It would be a contract deal with no benefits. If things didn't work out, we would go our separate ways with no complaints.

"Need you to start real soon," Al shook my hand. "Like the day after tomorrow."

"Ok."

CTA was a two-office rental with a small common area just big enough for a pair of secretarial desks. The office was housed in a drab multistory building only a few blocks from Times Square, which in 1966 was appropriately labeled a "cesspool" crowded with sex shops, peep shows, and drug addicts. The heart of Manhattan would remain a seedy sore spot until 1994 when the newly elected mayor, Rudy Giuliani, would order a cleanup.

Two days later, a small elevator that could accommodate no more than four people bucked and jerked its way to the third floor. I exited and walked to a frosted glass door stenciled with an eye-level sign: *CTA – City Teachers Association*. My first day on the job and I was welcomed warmly by a woman in her thirties whom Al introduced as his secretary, "Missy." A pretty blonde named Mary Jane who looked like she belonged in junior high school said hello. Later that afternoon Mary Jane, whom Al announced would be my assistant, gave me an abbreviated story of her young life. She lived with her divorced mother on the upper East Side. This was her "very first job" since graduating from a private school where tuition was more than a showroom-new Maserati.

After wading through a stack of National Education Association (NEA) background materials, Al invited me to an early lunch. He led the way to a small ground floor restaurant where the wait staff greeted him like their most important patron which, as I quickly learned, is exactly what he was. We were seated at "Al's table" and without placing an order, two Bombay Sapphire martinis showed up. "Cheers and welcome aboard," Al toasted and proceeded to down the first of three cocktails. My boss insisted I keep pace but after two drinks, I politely declined another. Over salads and fresh-baked brioche bread, Al interrogated me about my past but offered no information about his professional or personal life. I would never get to know much about Al except for one stark reality – he was a drunk. The walk back to the CTA office was not easy for me. I was not an experienced heavy drinker and the alcohol made me woozy. I was taken aback at how Al's gait was steady and controlled.

Weeks went by and except for a few days when Al would be summoned to Albany or Washington to meet with NEA officials, lunch was always the same. These were business meetings, Al noted, which suggested he was writing off our liquid meals as legitimate expenses. I lied about a stomach issue that kept me from down-ing more than a single alcoholic beverage. But even one mid-day martini made it difficult to get through the afternoon at CTA and NYU classes in the evening.

"Next Monday afternoon," Al said at one of our lunch sessions. He tilted his gin-filled glass toward me. "I need you to stand in for me. At a debate at Fordham University."

"Debate?"

"Yeah, not a big deal."

"What kind of debate?"

There was a lull and then the answer: "With Al Shanker."

"Al ... Al Shanker!"

"Yeah, but it's a nothing event," Al assured me. "Don't worry."

"Al Shanker!" I yelped. "Are you crazy? Sending me to debate Al Shanker?"

Shanker, the son of Jewish immigrants from Poland, was the current UFT president and was already reputed to be one of the most aggressive and skillful labor leaders in the country. Disregarding provisions that prohibited teachers from striking, Shanker had rallied nearly 6,000 educators to take up picket signs in 1960. Soon after, the city reluctantly agreed to a collective bargaining process for teachers. That led to a pitched battle between the UFT and NEA to determine which organization would represent teachers at the bargaining table. With financial help from the AFL-CIO, Shanker's union won. UFT took the city but NEA used its small CTA staff to peck away at Shanker and company.

Albert Shanker   Contenders in the National Battle to Represent Teachers

I continued my argument that sending me to Fordham was a *really* bad idea. But it was useless; there was no escaping the debate. The event was scheduled for 3 p.m. at Fordham at its main Bronx campus. Any appearance after noon was not on the calendar for Al unless CTA was to be represented by an inebriated executive director who had trouble piecing together a coherent sentence.

It was an anxious weekend leading up to the Monday confrontation with an icon of the labor movement. I took the B train to Fordham Heights and walked to the renowned Jesuit university. A professor guided me to an auditorium jammed with a standing-room crowd. My mouth went dry. But then a miracle – this wasn't a debate. I was told Shanker was going to talk for about 20 minutes, take a few questions and leave. I would be on stage after he was gone. With no seats open, I stood and listened in awe as the UFT president gave an animated speech that wowed the audience with lines like:

"It's dangerous to let a lot of ideas out of the bag, some of which – I admit – may be bad. But there's something more dangerous and that's not having any new ideas at all."

Days after listening to Shanker, I realized there was not a lot of substance in what he had to say. But the *way* he punched out his message led me to another **life lesson: a strong delivery with light content is usually more effective than a tepid delivery with strong content.** This take-away was not always easy for me to follow when preparing remarks for future paid speaking engagements. My inclination was to jam facts and figures into a speech. But Shanker (and others like him) taught me audiences have a limited capacity to absorb detailed information. Better to hammer home a couple of key points with as much entertainment-like energy as possible.

After Shanker exited the stage, the podium was mine. Before I said a word, most of the auditorium emptied out. I was left with a handful of students who patiently waited until I finished my 20 minutes and then asked if CTA was hiring part-time workers.

The next day, Al wanted a lunchtime report on the Fordham event. I grabbed a notepad and reminded Mary Jane to lock the office door until we returned. Mary Jane was doing a solo for the day because Missy was on vacation. As usual, lunch took two hours with three martinis for Al and one for me. After my capsule account of the Shanker non-debate, we walked next door and took the rickety elevator to the third floor. The doors opened and we were face-to-face with two uniformed New York City police officers. A third cop in plain clothes and a badge on his belt was inside the CTA office talking to Mary Jane and an older woman who looked like Mary Jane with wrinkles.

"You the employer?" the non-uniformed officer asked Al.

"Yeah, but what's going on here?"

"*What's going on?*" the wrinkled lady shouted. "You're out to lunch and you leave my daughter in this... in this awful place alone?"

Al turned to Mary Jane who was in spasms from her uncontrollable crying. "You were supposed to keep the door locked," he said.

"*She did keep it locked!*" yelled the woman, obviously Mary Jane's mother.

Al and I traded confused looks. "Well then, what happened?"

"*What happened?*" the mother screamed. "I'll tell you what happened. Somebody stuck his... his *thing* through the mail hole."

Everyone's eyes turned to the waist-high brass mail slot complete with a spring-loaded interior plate that had been installed in the frosted glass door. Many office doors in older Manhattan buildings were similarly equipped.

Al shook his head trying to clear the Bombay Sapphire cobwebs. "You mean, a man put his..."

"Yes!" the mother shrieked. "While my daughter was alone in this godforsaken office! In the middle of the day, a pervert put *it* through the opening."

The plainclothes cop tapped a spiral pad with a ballpoint pen and tried hard to look serious. "We just need a little more information," he said to Mary Jane. "Could you give us a description. Size? Color? Distinguishing marks?"

Mary Jane's wrinkled mother grabbed her daughter and bulldozed her way to the elevator. The two uniformed officers couldn't hold back their laughter.

"I told my daughter not to work in Midtown on the West Side," the mother snarled. "She lives on the East Side! Uptown on the East Side! She doesn't belong here. She will *not* be back." Mary Jane continued to sob as the elevator doors slid shut. She probably didn't hear one of the cops call out, "Hey, Miss, was there a stamp on it?"

I would never see Mary Jane or her mother again.

The incident rattled Al who suggested we shut down early and get a drink. I declined explaining I had a presentation to make to one of my NYU classes. Al waved me off and promised to start a search tomorrow for Mary Jane's replacement.

I was back in our Edgewater apartment around 11 p.m., exhausted by the events of the long day. Sleep came fast but at 2 a.m., the phone rang.

"Mr. Weeden?" a gruff voice asked.

"Yes."

"This is Grasslands Hospital in Westchester County."

"Grasslands?" I knew nothing about the hospital.

"Your employer told us to call you."

"What?"

"He was in a car accident. He's being treated by our trauma team."

"A car accident!" I said, suddenly no longer feeling sleep deprived. I didn't even know Al owned a car. "Is he ok?"

"Not really. But he insists on checking himself out. He wants you to drive here and pick him up."

"Me? Are you sure you're calling the right person?"

"We're sure." The voice gave me driving instructions to Valhalla, New York. At 3 a.m. I was on the road and took the nearly empty Palisades Parkway heading north toward White Plains and then on to Grasslands, formerly a U.S. Army hospital but later handed over to Westchester County. The hospital was huge but clearly dated. Fast forward another decade and it would be shuttered to make way for a huge regional trauma center to be renamed the Westchester Medical University Hospital.

Grasslands Hospital – Valhalla, New York

"Uh, Al?" I sputtered when an emergency room nurse helped my boss to a seat across from a discharge administrator. Al was barely recognizable. His face had a half dozen stitched up lacerations. A baseball-sized lump disfigured his right cheek, partially closing one eye. Al's white shirt was discolored with blood and what looked to be a tincture of iodine.

"We're not recommending him for release," the no-nonsense discharge lady said and pushed four sheets of paper toward me. "Sign these. Once you take him, we're not liable or responsible for any further medical event."

"Well, why is he being discharged?"

"His request," she answered. "We can't hold him against his will. We could if one of our techs hadn't screwed up his blood test. He should be in a drunk tank."

"What happened – the accident, I mean?"

"Hit a tree head on," the lady replied. "Single car. A rental, I think. There's a copy of the preliminary police report with the papers you'll need to take with you. The cops are holding his license until the results come back from a second blood test. If he was DUI, he'll probably be toast."

I glanced at Al. "He doesn't look good. What if something happens while we're on the road?"

"It's on you. If it was me, I would get him to another emergency room. He's got a concussion and some internal injuries. No bones broken which is a miracle given what he did to his car."

An orderly wheelchaired Al to the emergency room entrance. I opened the passenger side of my car and pushed Al inside. "Where should I take you?" I asked.

Al mumbled an address in Queens. I began the longest one-hour drive of my life. It was 4:30 a.m. when I pulled onto the Hutchinson River Parkway, the morning rush yet to begin. Ten miles later, Al vomited blood and puke. "Pull over!" he gurgled.

I found a narrow shoulder and stopped. Al opened the passenger door and rolled out of the car onto the pavement. I turned the engine off and ran around the back of the vehicle. Al was unconscious. I pulled him into a sitting position, and he came to. With some effort, I got him back into the front seat.

"I'm taking you to an emergency room," I said. Just before stopping, I had seen a road sign for the Sound Shore Medical Center in New Rochelle.

"*No!*" Al shouted. "Take me to my mother's house in Queens."

"Your mother's house? Why your mother's house?"

Al dry heaved and said: "It's where I live."

Another 45 minutes and I pulled in front of a small but tidy row house in the Forest Hills section of Queens. I helped Al out of the car and up six stairs to the front entrance. Somehow, Al managed to pull a set of keys from his pants pocket, unlocked the door, and stumbled into a dark foyer.

"That's all," he mumbled and waved me off. The door closed. I would never see Al again.

I drove back to Edgewater and after a shower and a clean set of clothes, I took a bus and subway to midtown Manhattan. I was in the CTA office at 9 a.m. sharp. Al's secretary, Missy, was already at her desk looking very worried. She had just fielded a call from the New York State Teachers Association (NYSTA), the

NEA affiliate that on paper had responsibility for CTA's New York City activities.

"They told me about Al's accident," Missy said. "They're sending someone here later this morning."

Missy tried calling Al's home phone several times but there was no answer. She was dialing again when a man named John knocked on CTA's office door.

"We made a decision about CTA that has nothing to do with Al's accident," John said after introducing himself as an NYSTA officer. "We're going to close down the operation."

Missy gasped but I looked nonplussed. Paying for a staff and office in a city where UFT ruled the roost had never seemed to me to be a good investment.

"What about Al?" I asked.

"We'll follow up," John replied in a tone of voice that told me he didn't want to elaborate.

Both Missy and I would be getting a severance package, John stated. He asked us both to stay with CTA for at least another week to help with packing files and handling other office-closing chores.

John had already spoken to a lower Manhattan law firm about interviewing Missy for an admin job. A glimmer of relief cut through her gloomy facial expression.

"There's a posting for a communications professional at an NEA affiliate in New Jersey," John said. "New Jersey Education Association. Ever hear of NJEA?"

Just in passing, I answered. John recommended I arrange to meet with the organization and that he would put in a good word if needed. He handed me an index card with NJEA's Trenton address and phone number.

Over the next couple of weeks, I tried to reach Al. He either wouldn't or couldn't accept my calls. Upon reflection, I was bothered by my relationship with a man whom I knew was a troubled alcoholic even before his car accident. I had willingly become his lunchtime drinking partner, which only exacerbated his addiction. Could I have coaxed Al into taking a walk in Central Park instead of downing three martinis? Maybe it would have been impossible to alter the ways of a lonely alcoholic living in his mother's house. The point is – I never tried.

In 2006, long after CTA disappeared, NEA's New York affiliate and a UFT-inspired state union called the United Teachers of New York would stop fighting and get married. Called the New York State United Teachers (NYSUT), the organization would become a powerhouse representing 600,000 teachers and paraprofessionals. Of the NYSUT's 900 affiliates, one was then and continues to be the heavyweight: New York City's 140,000-member UFT.

Chapter 6

New Jersey Education Association (1966-72)

"They threw a table and a chair over the balcony!" the motel manager screamed and pointed to Hayden "Bud" Messner and John Molloy. The two were leaning against a second-floor railing, each clutching a beer can and laughing hysterically.

"How do you know it was them?" another NJEA field representative challenged the manager.

"I *know!*" the man screamed. "I'm calling the cops!"

"Wait a minute," the rep said calmly and reached for his wallet. "Let's not blow this out of proportion. We'll pay the damages and quiet things down."

The manager shook his head and muttered, "I should-a known you union people would cause problems."

The rep shook his head. "We're not a union."

"Yeah, right," the manager huffed. "And that's not a table and chair floating in my damn pool."

It was one of the few occasions when I was on the front line with NJEA's foot soldiers. My assignment was to log quotes from grateful teachers whose salaries were about to get a boost thanks to a just-negotiated contract. Molly and Messner had teamed with a small group of local association leaders to push a reluctant school board to accept an agreement earlier in the day. Now it was celebration time capping off weeks of bargaining.

I had joined NJEA's communications team nearly two years earlier and was, among other things, the assistant editor of a tabloid sent monthly to thousands of teachers statewide. The newspaper concentrated mainly on labor-related developments impacting educators in New Jersey's nearly 600 operating school districts.

It was the fall of 1968 and the start of a new era for Garden State teachers. In September, the New Jersey legislature had overridden a governor's veto to give public employees (including educators) the right to set up and join "exclusive bargaining units." Most teachers were already members of local NJEA organizations, so creating a network of bargaining units was not difficult to do. NJEA quickly beefed up its task force of full-time and part-time negotiators. Now, a multitude of contracts were in the process of being negotiated. If bargaining stalled or school boards became especially resistant, the call went out for NJEA's heavy artillery which included super-tough field reps like Messner or Molloy.

"Acting like a bunch of frat kids!" the motel manager grumbled and retreated to his office but not before shaking a fist at Messner and Molloy. The two battle-hardened representatives were in their mid-thirties, physically big and behaviorally boisterous. In some ways, they were caricatures of union organizers who were not hesitant to throw their weight around and occasionally went off the rails. In other respects, they were experienced, effective negotiators who could close a deal even when contract talks between teachers and school boards seemed to be at an impasse.

Messner and Molloy were standouts in an NJEA division some called Bertolino's Battalion – a group of field operatives under the command of an upbeat, charismatic operations leader named Jack Bertolino. Unlike Messner and Molloy, many battalion members were not flamboyant types but one-time teachers who provided serious counsel to local NJEA affiliates engaged in contract talks. Although the battalion was on call to provide New Jersey teachers with all the services and support of a union, the reps did not consider themselves organized labor agents. Instead, NJEA underscored the point time and again that it wasn't a union – it was a professional association. According to NJEA, the distinction meant those in Bertolino's Battalion were not in the same league as Jimmy Hoffa or other notorious unionists. Still, most of the public shared the same point of view as the unhappy motel manager – the only difference between the battalion and a straight-up union was semantics.

The few years I spent with NJEA were instructive on many fronts. While working at the association, I train-commuted to New York to continue my graduate studies at NYU. After being handed a master's degree, I decided to continue graduate work thinking I might go the long haul and land a doctorate specializing in organization development. Academia served up an oversized helping of institutional design theory. But it was NJEA that offered on-the-ground exposure to the inner workings of one of the most powerful institutions in New Jersey. The association afforded me many valuable insights with one that would prove especially relevant in the years ahead: organizations that rely on discretionary support (dues or contributions) from individuals must constantly be on their "A" game. It takes exceptional marketing, communications, service delivery, and stewardship skills to convince individuals to pay for something not deemed a requirement or necessity. Of course, if an organization could come up with a way of collecting dues on a *non-voluntary* basis, then life would become much easier. And that is exactly what America's unions managed to do – at least for a while.

In places where a union was designated an "exclusive bargaining agent" not everyone bought into the union cause. There were those who refused to pay union dues. Even so, these individuals benefited from the union's efforts to win compensation increases and improved working conditions often necessitating long and expensive interactions with legislators. Organized labor made a convincing case that this wasn't kosher and, as a result, unions won the right to collect what were termed "fair share contributions." Critics had another name for the practice: "forced union dues." For teachers who opted out of joining a union or professional association, this meant their pay would be docked for what equated to union membership (at a slightly reduced rate than full membership).

This fair share arrangement was particularly helpful to NJEA and other like organizations. It wasn't necessary to convert every teacher in a school district to become a dues-paying participant – usually just a majority would do the trick. This revenue advantage was a boon to unions active in the public sector until the U.S. Supreme Court changed the rules of the game in 2018.

An Illinois state worker named Mark Janus would challenge the "fair share" practice and his complaint would slowly work its way up the judicial ladder. When the Janus case would finally get its day in the nation's top court, justices would overturn 40 years of precedent by stating it would no longer be legal to compel all workers to cover collective bargaining costs.

Long before the Janus ruling, unions still had to recruit a majority of teachers to support a bargaining unit and that was no easy task. The price tag for an NJEA membership averaged around 1% of a teacher's annual salary – not a huge outlay of money but for educators who were not highly paid, taking even a small financial hit was a big deal. When Bertolino's Battalion delivered a handsome contract, the return on an NJEA member's investment was obvious. But between contract negotiations, benefits were less apparent. That's when messaging and special events were used as a constant reminder that NJEA was a valuable resource.

A consistently promoted story line for NJEA was how the association was able to pressure state legislators to change laws, regulations, and funding decisions that affected every school district in New Jersey. Part of my job was to feed educators an ongoing news stream reminding them their professional association fees were underwriting what many considered the most powerful lobbying effort in the state. Communicating NJEA's legislative achievements wasn't always easy because the organization's executive director and chief lobbyist did not relish much personal media attention. Dr. Frederick Hipp ("call me Fred," he insisted) was an imposing figure with an always-agreeable temperament. Far from a fist-pounding, cigar-smoking deal maker, Fred was a gentleman who got things done without a lot of fanfare. Along with his government affairs director, Lewis Applegate, the two demonstrated how it was possible to work with lawmakers to shape public policy without resorting to tactics and antics that might make for colorful news stories but would too often needlessly get in the way of making the best possible decisions. They both also won accolades for helping the state secure support for other non-NJEA ventures such as what is now the New Jersey State Museum. These two "class acts" were the antithesis to far too many loud-mouthed, say-and-promise anything lobbyists who regularly flocked to Trenton. Fred and Lew taught me still another **life lesson: those who have no regard for respect and dignity should not be respected or dignified.**

N.J. State Capitol Building   *NJEA Headquarters*

Of course, there were occasions when tensions were high between NJEA and state officials. But decorum didn't disappear during those heated times. This atmosphere of civility made it much easier for people with different views, even those with hurt feelings, to regroup and move on.

Fred Hipp would continue to lead NJEA until 1978 ending a 32-year stint as one of the state's most influential citizens. "Among the most powerful people in New Jersey," the *New York Times* would note in an article about Hipp. "He moved a nice association of schoolteachers to a tough union of 78,000 members who usually get what they want in Trenton and most other places."

NJEA's continuous flow of print media helped the association stay linked to thousands of association members. But the glue that really affixed the organization to New Jersey teachers was the annual NJEA convention. Held each fall in Atlantic City, it was (and continues to be) one of the largest professional events in the nation. State law required schools to close for two days which gave tens of thousands of teachers – along with retired educators and college students – the opportunity to travel to the city's massive convention center. Promoted as an important professional development opportunity, the convention was not without its critics. "A huge party," some lawmakers complained. Others pointed out that a *lot* of teachers never made it to Atlantic City at all but rather used the time off as a vacation.

NJEA Convention – Atlantic City   *F. Lee Bailey*

Although attendance was not 100 percent, more than 50,000 convention-goers usually jammed Atlantic City for the event. The toll road leading into the city would typically report a 46 percent hike in its collections. Plenary sessions drew huge crowds especially when the attraction was a big-name speaker. One notable who drew a sizeable audience was a then 33-year-old lawyer named F. Lee Bailey. The criminal defense attorney had achieved stardom when he successfully convinced the U.S. Supreme Court that neurosurgeon Sam Sheppard had been denied due process when tried for the murder of his wife, Marilyn. Sheppard had spent 10 years in jail until Bailey took over the case and won a "not guilty" verdict on appeal. The high-profile case not only made Bailey the lawyer-of-choice for many but also an in-demand speaker.

"Pick him up at the A.C. Airport and when he's finished, bring him back," I was told by one of the convention coordinators. "Use the Caddy. And chat him up on the way in so he'll remember there are a bunch of teachers in the hall."

I found the rented Cadillac in a reserved parking spot outside the convention center. Why I was the designated driver ordered to chauffer a celebrity was never made clear. But I did what I was told and drove 13 miles to the small but busy Atlantic City Airport. A half hour later, Bailey walked out of the terminal with a scowl on his face and a strikingly beautiful woman at his side. I introduced myself, helped both passengers into the rear of the car and headed toward the Atlantic City Parkway.

"Thank you very much for putting this event on your schedule, Mr. Bailey," I opened and checked the rearview mirror as I spoke. "I thought it might be helpful if I told you a little about who will be in the audience ..."

Bailey winced and jerked his head toward the woman. She leaned forward, her mouth a couple of inches from my ear.

"You know how many of these speeches Mr. Bailey is doing this week?" she asked.

"I ... I don't ..."

"Seven," she interrupted. "Two today. One this afternoon in New Jersey and another in Boston tonight."

"Oh, that's quite a schedule," I said while at the same time calculating Bailey's weekly take in speaker fees.

"And you know what the last thing Mr. Bailey wants to hear right now?" she whispered.

"No."

"Your voice. So, shut up and drive."

Not another word was exchanged during a 20-minute trip that seemed to drag on for 20 hours. After I pulled to a stop at the convention center, Bailey was escorted to Boardwalk Hall, a massive venue with seating for 14,000. An hour passed and after a few preliminaries, he was introduced to polite applause and instantly morphed into a completely different human being. For 40 minutes, he enthralled the crowd with a powerful speech Bailey called "Justice and the Press." He was animated and passionate as he belted out one personal anecdote after another and ended by crediting teachers for everything he had been able to accomplish in life. The standing ovation was deafening.

The drive back to the airport was as uncomfortable as the trip to the convention center. Nothing was said. Not a word. Bailey and the woman got out of the car and marched into the terminal. No "thank you" or "goodbye." I pulled into a vehicle waiting area and caught a glimpse of the two boarding an executive jet. As it lifted off and circled north toward Boston, I was left with another **life lesson: caution – manufactured public images can mask arrogance and disrespect.** Bailey's practiced performance impressed many but once he was off stage, his arrogance and disrespect defined the man. In the years ahead, I would meet movie stars, sports icons, and U.S. presidents. My Bailey experience taught me public reputation sometimes was a crust that hid far more important human qualities both good and bad.

Bailey's NJEA appearance came at the front-end of a whirlwind legal career. He would go on to make headlines by playing a leading role in some of the nation's most controversial cases. Bailey would represent Patti Hearst, the newspaper heiress kidnapped by – and conscripted into – the Symbionese Liberation Army. It would not be one of his most stellar achievements (Hearst would be sentenced to seven years in prison for her role in a bank robbery). Still, his notoriety would make him a go-to defense attorney which explains why he would take on perhaps his most famous case: the O.J. Simpson murder trial. It would be Bailey's cross-examination skill that some would contend was the main reason Simpson was acquitted.

Eventually, Bailey's hubris would get him into trouble. Florida would find him guilty of attorney misconduct and disbar him. By reciprocity, he would be prevented from practicing law in Massachusetts. Bailey would then move to Maine, apply for a law license only to have that application denied. A majority of the state's board of bar examiners would conclude Bailey did not have the "requisite honesty and integrity" to practice law.

Unlike Bailey, most of the featured speakers at each convention were prominent educators or policy makers who used the event to push their ideas for education reform. There were also dozens of smaller sessions where presenters discussed different teaching techniques and methodologies. It was at one of these breakout meetings where I bumped into a South Jersey middle school teacher.

"I was told you wrote that cute story about Lucy!" the woman said, checking my name tag.

"Lucy?"

"The elephant," she chirped. "Remember? *Lucy leaks?*"

How could I forget. I had knocked out a short feature about how one of New Jersey's lesser-known landmarks was falling into disrepair. Lucy was a 65-foot-high wooden elephant that stood tall in the oceanfront town of Margate not that far from Atlantic City. It had been built in the 1880s to lure tourists and promote land sales. According to some, it was the oldest roadside tourist attraction in America. The "Lucy Leaks" lead I had used turned into the butt of many a joke.

Lucy the Elephant – Oldest roadside attraction in America

"It *does* leak and they need to fix it!" the woman said emphatically. "The kids love Lucy. Even my exchange student from Norway thought the elephant was amazing!"

"Oh, you have an exchange student?" I asked, trying to shift topics from an old wooden structure that at one time was the eleventh tallest statue in the country.

"Yes. She's an AFS student from Norway."

"AFS?

"American Field Service," the woman explained. "Maybe you could do an article on the organization. Oh, in fact, they just hired a new and very young CEO."

I mentally filed the information under "interesting but not particularly relevant." It wouldn't be long before I would come to realize my filing system was all wrong.

While the NJEA Convention with all its professional development offerings helped distinguish the association from a common trade union, the organization also produced a monthly magazine that aspired to achieve the same goal. Vastly different than the tabloid I helped churn out, the *NJEA Review* was a slick publication with articles that ranged from how to schedule a student tour of the state capitol building to ways community colleges could enrich K-12 education. *Review* editor Norm Goldman also reported to my boss, Marvin Reed. Goldman and Reed were notably different than those recruited as Bertolino's Battalion members. Deeply concerned about education quality and with an eye for strong graphics and editorial content, Goldman produced first-rate editions ten times a year (the *Review* wasn't printed in July and August). The former factory-town teacher had not only been a NJEA affiliate president but also had handled public relations for his school district. Goldman's multi-faceted talent was tapped in full by Reed who set the professional tone for the organization.

Reed was a Rutgers University grad (Phi Beta Kappa) and had a mostly serious demeanor that made him look as brainy as he really was. He had been with NJEA for 12 years when I first met him. I found him to be as astute about Jersey politics as classroom practices. An avid reader and a fan of both opera and theater, Reed seemed at times a contrast to the often rough and ready tribe of contract-negotiating field reps. If all NJEA employees were put on a bell curve, Messner and Molloy would be on one side, Marvin Reed on the opposite. The Association's top man, Fred Hipp, was astutely aware of Reed's intelligence. The two would meet regularly, often daily, to discuss legislative options as well

Marvin Reed   *NJEA's Monthly Magazine*

as state and national events that had an impact on New Jersey schools.

Reed was also a kind and tolerant supervisor. During my NJEA tenure, I made my share of mistakes but was never castigated. Quite the contrary. It was Marv who left me with a very helpful **life lesson: many errors are actually starting blocks for improved performance.** He was a master at recognizing how to extract something positive out of what most of us would consider a negative. To hm, a shortcoming was a platform for new learning. Reed was not only masterful in carrying out his communications responsibilities, he was an outstanding role model for the kind of high-quality teacher NJEA wanted to attract and retain throughout the State of New Jersey.

"Bill Hayward's moving to California," Marvin informed me one morning.

I wasn't sure how to react. Hayward was NJEA's radio & TV producer. Plus, he was the champion behind a move to bring college professors into the association. Bill's departure would leave a deep hole.

"You interested in doing the radio and TV?" Reed asked.

"Me?"

"Not the higher education work – someone else will handle that," Reed went on. "You'll do *Speaking of Schools* and a little television. Someone else will take over the newspaper."

"Marv, I don't have a clue about …"

"Hayward's a decent teacher," Reed interjected. "You have a month to learn the ropes."

Hayward *was* a good teacher and a talented host and producer of a daily radio feature aired on 40 stations in and around New Jersey. Each *Speaking of Schools* segment was only five minutes long and available as a public service "drop" stations could insert into their weekday programming any time day or night. NJEA in conjunction with the New Jersey Parent & Teachers Association would bundle five shows on a single tape that would be shipped weekly to each station. Most *Speaking of Schools* episodes included interviews with innovative teachers talking about creative ways to connect with kids. On occasion, Hayward would track down minor celebrities who would gladly contribute five minutes waxing about how teachers changed their lives. "Get a personality on air when you can," Hayward told me. "You know, anybody who's got name recognition. Stations love that."

As soon as I was handed the *Speaking of Schools* microphone, I took Bill's advice to heart. I put out cold calls to performers, authors, and athletes whose schedules had them making a stop somewhere in New Jersey. Surprisingly, some were not only responsive but were informative and entertaining guests. No one was more enjoyable than Jim Bouton, the major league pitcher who was on the road promoting his successful and controversial book, *Ball Four*. Bouton's chronicle of his days (and nights) with the New York Yankees, Seattle Pilots (now the Milwaukee Brewers) and Houston Astros was an eye opener, so much so that the major league commissioner called it detrimental to the sport. *Time* magazine had a different opinion citing *Ball Four* as one of the 100 greatest non-fiction books of all time.

Bouton wasn't a rock star, but he was in great demand. He certainly didn't need to carve out time to do a five-minute interview on a show that some stations aired after midnight. Yet Bouton *did* take the time, a relaxed two hours talking about the periodic glitz and prolonged grind that came with a pro ball contract. He was the antithesis of F. Lee Bailey. "Hey, I'm just a ball player who can write a little," he said. "Not that big a deal." Bouton left me with a helpful **life lesson: hubris may bring attention but humility will win respect.** Over the years to come, I would meet many famous people. Humility would consistently be the quality that would most impress me. Among the most well-known and truly humble notables I would encounter was President Jimmy Carter. After an hour talking about fly fishing and his favorite charity (Habitat for Humanity), his lack of ego was extraordinary. Critics might despise Carter's politics, but if they spent time with the man, his humility was so profound it would be impossible not to respect him.

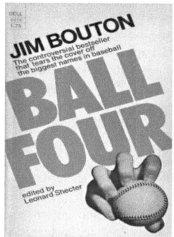

One of 100 best non-fiction books   New Jersey's public television network

For NJEA, radio was how the organization reached out beyond the education community to the public at large. There were no commercial TV outlets in New Jersey and while public television had a foothold in New Jersey through WNET, a Newark-based operation, most of the broadcast content was pointed at New York City. Lawmakers concluded that what the state needed was a public TV station that was truly all about New Jersey. So, in the spring of 1971, WNJT was born. Fresh out of the gate, the station was starving for locally-produced shows which explains why a call went out to me asking if NJEA couldn't bring a little *Speaking of Schools* content to a one-hour special about education in the Garden State. Called *The Magic of Making It Happen*, it was my one and only on-screen appearance. This was the first color broadcast for WNJT and was one of the earliest productions to use "blue screen" technology (now more commonly a "green screen") called a traveling matte to create special "magical" effects. My performance was far from Emmy-worthy but the show still managed to get more attention than many expected because of its reliance on technological wizardry.

A few days after *Magic* aired, my phone rang.

"We've been retained by an organization in New York City to fill an executive-level job," a male voice on the other end of the phone informed me. "You're the guy on the TV show, right?"

"Yeah, but ..."

"A couple of people have recommended you for this opportunity."

"They have?" I had never been head-hunted before. Furthermore, I was stunned anyone had tuned into a show about New Jersey schools broadcast on a still very obscure TV channel.

"The American Field Service, AFS," the voice went on. "Ever hear of it?"

The Lucy the Elephant teacher with the AFS exchange student from Norway. It had to have been her who had floated my name.

"We want to do an in-person interview," said the voice. "Next week. This job needs to be filled fast."

"Look, I'm doing fine here at NJEA..."

"Really?" the voice interrupted. "Let me ask you something. What's your career track there? You report to a guy who's going to stay put for a long time. You've got nowhere to go except to some other lateral job. Upward movement for you is nothing more than a dream. Ever think about that?"

The voice had done his homework. Marvin Reed was likely to be a NJEA fixture for many more years. And yes, I had thought about that. I also had thought *a lot* about the unforgettable day I told the Army I was out. Instead of doing battle in the jungles of

Vietnam, I told myself to find another and hopefully better way to make a difference. Helping to elevate the social, professional, and economic status of teachers was important. But how much was I really contributing to that effort? Not a lot, I had concluded.

"Know what we're talking about here?" the voice asked. "You start at a director level at a very respectable international organization. Ninety percent chance you'll be a vice president within five years. So, don't let this one fly by, my friend."

I didn't.

After digging deep into the history of the American Field Service, I discovered it was an organization more suited to the promise I had made to myself after taking an exit ramp from the U.S. Army. In exchange for not fighting or advocating for what I considered a pointless war, I was to invest my time and limited talent to helping prevent future armed conflict. Given that goal, AFS seemed to be a far better option than continuing with NJEA. The American Field Service had its origins in France when the American Colony of Paris put together an "ambulance," the French term for a temporary military hospital. During the First and Second World Wars, AFS volunteers provided medical services including operating fleets of ambulances used to haul wounded soldiers and civilians to treatment facilities. Exposed to the bloody brutality of conflict (over 100 million military personnel and civilians died during the two wars), AFS created an international scholarship program in 1946. The goal was to help young people understand and respect intercultural differences with the hope such insights might lessen mankind's inclination to kill and maim one another. I pulled together enough background information about AFS to reach a decision:

While NJEA was doing important things for teachers, it was time to move on.

Later that month, I met with Marvin Reed and broke the news. Marv said he understood. We worked out an exit plan and not long after, I was sitting at a desk in a midtown Manhattan office.

The NJEA I left behind would grow into an organized labor colossus enlisting over 200,000 teachers, retired educators, cafeteria workers, and school bus drivers as members. Regional offices would spring up in 22 locations around the state. Even after his death at age 83, Fred Hipp would be credited for most of NJEA's growth and influence. He would be memorialized with the launch of the Frederick L. Hipp Foundation for Excellence in Education. That foundation would annually award grants to "school employees to expand their visions of excellence in our classrooms and schools."

Marvin Reed would retire from NJEA after 31 years of service. But he was hardly the type to hit a golf ball or take up backgammon. In 1990, he would become mayor of one of New Jersey's most prestigious communities: Princeton Borough.

Chapter 7

American Field Service (1972-76)

I was in a time warp. Seated across from me was a 30-year-old consultant just named president of a very old organization – one that dated back to the First World War. Pictures of uniformed men driving modified Model-T ambulances hung on the wall of the wood-paneled office on East 43rd Street. The grainy photos made Dr. Steve Rhinesmith look even younger than he was.

"So, here's the bad news," Steve said without so much as an iota of panic. "We're financially underwater. I'm talking hundreds of thousands of dollars."

I swallowed hard. When I made the decision to leave NJEA and accept a job as director of communications for AFS International Scholarships, I knew the organization had some minor funding challenges. Now I was being told the place was hemorrhaging money.

"Oh, and there's more," Steve added. "We don't see things getting better in the short term. We've got a worldwide oil crisis that's not looking good. Then there's the dollar devaluation…"

"Steve," I broke in. "I just bought a house! I'm moved my family to North Jersey and I'm …"

"Not to worry," Steve broke in. "This is all fixable."

That's when I understood why the AFS board of directors hired this untested son of a Methodist minister to turn around a financially fragile organization. This was the most confident human being I had ever met. Just listening to him turned my trepidation into an assumption that maybe AFS wasn't really going to go under.

"How bad?" I asked.

"Well, the general reserve fund is gone. And some of the endowment was invaded so we could pay a few bills."

"Oh, my god," I moaned and my anxiety roared back. I pictured my three-bedroom, heavily mortgaged house in Springfield, New Jersey. It wasn't much to look at, but my wife and kids had settled into the working-class neighborhood. And although my commute was a long bus ride to the Port Authority terminal followed by a mile walk to and from the East Side of Manhattan, I had developed a friendship with a few bus mates that made the trip more than tolerable. My fast-paced hike from one side of Manhattan to the other gave me a daily chance to suck in New York's energy which I had grown to love. Was the whole deal about to blow apart?

Steve laughed as he was inclined to do in even the most stressful situations. "Relax! We still have cash and there's more in the endowment if things really go south. We'll tweak our program fees and cut some costs. It will be fine."

And eventually things were fine, although the journey to a better place wasn't always smooth. AFS had to navigate one financial pothole after the next. But the unflappable Dr. Rhinesmith (he earned his Ph.D. from the University of Pittsburgh Graduate School of Public and International Affairs) never lost his cool. To him, each bump in the road was a challenge that always had an answer. His upbeat demeanor and his uncompromising confidence left me with another **life lesson: use positive thinking as a lens to look for an opportunity almost always hidden in a problem.**

AFS International Scholarships   *Dr. Stephen Rhinesmith*

When Steve took over AFS in 1971 and then hired me, AFS was a youth exchange organization active in dozens of countries around the world. By giving teenagers intercultural learning opportunities, AFS contended that an interchange of knowledge and experience would "create a more just and peaceful world." This scholarship-based, trading places concept was a far cry from how the organization got its start nearly a half century earlier.

AFS began as the American Ambulance Field Service in 1915. It operated during the early years of World War I under the command of the French Army. American volunteers transported wounded soldiers back and forth from the front lines of bloody battles waged at Verdun, Champagne, and other parts of France. As the war progressed and the U.S. became embroiled in the conflict, the organization was absorbed into the federalized U.S. Army Ambulance Service, a huge operation that included over 2,500 volunteers.

Between the two World Wars, AFS became a slimmed-down organization that developed a scholarship program for U.S. and French graduate students. Its first foray into the scholarship field was short-lived. With the outbreak of the next global conflict, AFS returned to its ambulance service roots and sent volunteers first to France and then to assist the British Armies in North Africa, Italy, India, and eventually Germany.

In 1947, AFS was retooled into a student exchange program with young people brought to the U.S. from 10 countries (most in Europe). The program continued to expand and when Rhinesmith was handed the reins, over 4,000 AFS scholars from more than 50 countries were trading places each year. While the organization had no shortage of exchange students and host families, it was coming up light on cash. In 1974, the AFS board treasurer put it this way: "for every dollar AFS collected in student family fees, it paid out $2.30 to meet costs."

"So, here's the plan," Steve said as he scanned the small meeting room that faced the spectacular Ford Foundation headquarters on the opposite side of 43rd Street. Rhinesmith had called together several senior staff members to an unusual closed-door meeting. We knew this was going to be a serious conversation. Seated next to Steve was Bill Orrick, a former private school headmaster who was the organization's elder and most highly respected statesman. To his side, Santo (Sandy) Mistretta, a just-hired finance and administration vice president. Alice Gerlach was the only woman present but arguably the most important staff member since she had responsibility for the small army of young counselors and placement field representatives who dealt directly with AFS students and their families. Two consultants had been asked to join the meeting: Dr. Reed Whittle, an organization development specialist who had earned his stripes at MIT's Sloan School of Management and the University of Chicago; and Charlie Bergman, a Harvard alumnus who billed himself a fundraising authority because of his connections mostly to his old college classmates. There was one other attendee at the meeting: me.

"We're going to cut staff," Steve announced. Alice Gerlach looked like she had been stabbed in the eye. Whatever blood AFS was about to spill would be coming mostly from her department.

"Is this absolutely necessary?" Alice asked.

"It is," Steve replied. "We need to do this to bring expenses in line with revenue. But there's another reason. Dr. Whittle and I have taken a hard look at how we're structured – how we're operating. There are a lot of inefficiencies we need to fix. Even if we weren't getting hammered financially, it's time to retool."

Bill Orrick folded his hands and looked at Rhinesmith. "My guess is you're talking about firing a lot of dedicated young people who are going to be devastated."

Steve nodded. There was no arguing Orrick's point. AFS had dozens of employees working in placement and student counseling roles, coordinating programs in different parts of the world and shouldering burdensome administrative duties. Ages ranged mainly from the mid-twenties to early thirties. Some were Peace Corps alumni and some (like Steve Rhinesmith) had themselves been AFS exchange students. Many had to wrestle with thorny problems inherent in most exchange programs. A teenager contracts a potentially fatal illness 3,000 miles from home. A host family father gets too friendly with a Nordic under-aged girl. A kid gets locked up for pot possession. Bigtime challenges put on the shoulders of young people paid low-end nonprofit wages.

"Who's going to deliver the bad news?" Alice Gerlach asked, her unhappy tone making it clear she wasn't about to be the messenger. "This is on me," said Steve. "Let's get everyone together this Friday."

Full staff gatherings were not common at AFS and even before Rhinesmith called the assembly to order, rumors about "workforce reduction" were being whispered in every corner of the building. When the staff finally crammed together on a Friday afternoon, anxiety was palpable. Photographs of war-weary World War I AFS ambulance drivers covered one wall of the room. The AFS old-timers seemed to be giving Steve uncertain looks as he began to talk. Was Rhinesmith a young reorganization genius or a madman about to bury AFS? After the hour-long meeting ended, the answer was clear.

Rhinesmith did not sugar-coat the bad news: 75 jobs were being eliminated. Then he softened the blow by explaining 60 new jobs would soon be added, with each position more sharply focused on the organization's most important priorities. The unlucky staffers who were getting pink slips could apply for these new openings. No guarantees – but at least there was a glimmer of hope for some in the room. Steve's calm, caring presentation led to an amazing response. Most of those who would no longer be working at AFS thanked Rhinesmith for making what they knew was a hard decision. To them, the organization's survival was paramount. Steve had read his staff's deep concern for AFS perfectly. Watching his presentation that day left me with another **life lesson: bad news is best delivered directly and honestly, but with empathy.**

Pruning personnel in New York was just the first phase of a wider AFS makeover. Cutting costs and increasing participant fees in locations outside the United States was the next order of business. Rhinesmith dispatched his senior staff to all corners of the globe as part of this streamlining effort. Reed Whittle and I were put on a Pan Am flight to London, the first of a series of stops in Western Europe. Although Pan Am was already experiencing deep losses (the airline would keep flying until its collapse in 1991), it did its best to convince customers there wasn't a cloud in the sky. One tactic used to keep passengers feeling good about Pan Am was to interrupt the trip periodically with a few give-away contests. The top prize was a bottle of Dom Perignon.

"Are you ready?" the flight attendant called out and held the precious bottle above her head. "If any passenger on board is wearing mismatched socks, this champagne is yours!"

Without saying a word to one another, Reed and I each pulled off a shoe and removed a sock. We traded hosiery, put our shoes back on, and hit the call button.

"Can you believe it?" the flight attendant yelped. "We have *two* winners." She walked to the back of the plane and winked. "A bit of a scam, fellas," she said. "But I love it."

The Pan Am experience was the start of one of my closest friendships. Reed was incredibly smart and had astounding recall. He would speed-read one or two books a week, with a preference for nonfiction American and world history. It was on a return flight from Europe when Reed asked what brought me to AFS.

"Truthfully?" I gave the question several seconds of thought before answering. "Conscience more than anything."

"Meaning what?"

I told Reed about my decision to leave the Army ROTC program after four years in the reserve and 10 weeks of basic training.

"The Army gave you a way out and you took it," Reed said. "So, what's the problem?"

"Still wondering if I should have given the military my full pound of flesh."

Reed shrugged. "Fighting a war in Vietnam we had no business fighting in the first place?" He along with every other adult American had read the *New York Times* release of the Pentagon Papers in 1971.

"More like being assigned to the Department of Defense to promote the war," I said.

"Even worse," Reed responded. "So, let me get this straight. You take a perfectly legitimate exit ramp from the Army but that's not sitting well. Instead of looking for work on Madison Avenue or Wall Street, you do the nonprofit thing serving your country in a never-ending search for peace and harmony."

"A little cynical," I shrugged. "But something like that. What about you? Why AFS?"

Reed said he was using the organization as a kind of laboratory – a place where he could test certain organizational ideas and assumptions. Plus, he liked working with Steve Rhinesmith, whom he found intelligent and open to trying new ideas. But Reed made it clear AFS was far from a long-term career option. He had a fatalistic view of the world and while he agreed intercultural exchanges were enlightening to some, any aspiration AFS had about creating a peaceful world was folly.

"Human conflict is as inevitable as death," Reed contended.

"Meaning what?" I asked. "Like the war in Vietnam was inevitable?"

"Maybe. Whether it was or wasn't, we didn't need to jump in the ring. There are plenty of wars around and always will be. We should learn to pick and choose more carefully."

I thought about what Reed was saying. "There are consequences of sitting on the sidelines, you know," I pointed out.

"There are short-and long-term consequences to anything you do or don't do – no exceptions. In Vietnam, we racked up a big body count to put a chokehold on communism. It was a stupid goal. But it really doesn't matter who wins or loses. I'll bet you a dinner at Le Cirque we'll be buying rice and selling cars in Vietnam within 15 years."

Dr. Whittle never had to pick up the tab at Le Cirque (then one of the top restaurants in New York) because the Vietnam story unfolded just as he predicted.

A few days after Reed and I returned to New York from Europe, Steve Rhinesmith summoned me to his office. "Let's go ahead with the Helen Hayes thing."

The "thing" was the production of 30- and 60-second public service announcements that would star Helen Hayes, known to most as "the first lady of the American Theatre." Ms. Hayes had been recruited as an AFS spokesperson by Ward Chamberlin, an AFS board member who was one of the founders of PBS and NPR, and Bud Taylor, an entertainment lawyer whose wife, Sunny, was also on the board. My job was to script the PSAs and pull together a film crew to handle the shoot at our midtown headquarters.

"Listen, I have another idea," Steve added before I could leave the room. "Helen Hayes has a new movie coming out. A kids' film she shot for Disney. What if we could host the premiere here in New York? Great fundraiser, right? See if Bud or Ward can talk her into going the extra mile with us."

First Lady of the   *AFS Benefit Premiere*   *English Mastiff*
American Theatre

It turned out to be an easy "ask." Helen Hayes and Disney agreed to open *One of Our Dinosaurs Is Missing* as an East Coast evening benefit for AFS. Ms. Hayes also volunteered to do a three-minute AFS promo film we would show as an introduction to the Disney feature. A woman who handled Ms. Hayes schedule blocked out a full morning when the public service announcements and the short promo would be shot at AFS headquarters.

A couple of weeks later, on an early spring day, a film crew converted an AFS meeting room into a makeshift movie set complete with tripod mounted cameras, backlights, diffusers, a boom mic, and a row of easel pads turned cue cards. My PSA and promo scripts were handprinted in large letters on 20 by 28-inch flipchart sheets. Ms. Hayes would simply read the words. The plan was to use a few shots of her speaking and edit most of her narration as a voiceover to go along with footage already taken of AFS students in different countries. Quick and easy. What could possibly go wrong?

At 10 a.m., a late-model but unassuming station wagon turned onto 43rd Street. From a second-floor office window, I caught a glimpse of a middle-aged woman behind the wheel of the car. Ms. Hayes was seated in the back. As the car made a slow approach to the front of the AFS building, a college kid guided a huge dog (an English mastiff, I was told later) to the curb directly in front of the building's entrance. The car cruised slowly forward as the animal squatted.

"I've never seen anything like that!" exclaimed one of the film crew members who was standing next to me by the window. She pointed to an enormous pile of excrement covering the curb and part of the street gutter.

"Oh, my god!" I groaned and ran out of the building.

Too late.

The station wagon driver had been scanning the buildings on 43rd Street looking for the correct address. She probably saw the dog but not the brown pile on the side of the road. The car squished over some of the manure and rolled to a stop with the back door directly over the poop. Helen Hayes, one of the few people on earth to ever win an Oscar, Emmy, and a Tony Award; Helen Hayes, the recipient of the Presidential Medal of Freedom, the nation's highest civilian honor; Helen Hayes, perhaps the most dignified and distinguished member of the acting profession; Helen Hayes, the woman who stepped out of the station wagon into a still-warm, stinking heap. Her left foot was buried so deep I couldn't see her ankle.

The station wagon driver shut off the engine, circled the front of the car and gasped. Helen Hayes and everyone around her stood frozen. I was now only a few feet away and could find no words. A half dozen AFS staffers appeared, their mouths stretched open at the sight.

"Perhaps someone could direct me to the lady's room," Ms. Hayes finally broke the awkward silence. The station wagon driver whom we later learned was also the constant companion to the film and theater star escorted her to a bathroom where the two disappeared for twenty minutes.

"I think we exhausted your supply of paper towels," Ms. Hayes said with a smile as she walked out of the restroom and headed to the temporary film set. After a lighting and sound check, the cameras rolled. The first take was a 60-second PSA that was anything but inspiring. We did a playback and it sounded like a sales pitch for a sugar-coated cereal that might air on a Saturday morning kids' show.

"You know that wasn't any good, right?" Ms. Hayes said and stared at me.

"Well, I ..."

"You're the director, aren't you?" she asked.

I blinked. "Yes, ma'am. I guess I am."

"Then *direct me,* damn it!" she ordered.

I wiped the sweat from my forehead and took a deep breath. "Well, the people we most want to reach are parents, not kids. I think if you spoke on camera like you were talking to a mom and dad who might host an exchange student..."

"That's *exactly* what I need you to tell me," Ms. Hayes said and left me with an important **life lesson: manage talent by directing talent.** The experience left an enduring imprint. Going forward in my career, I would manage a lot of people. All had some level of talent. A few were superstars, so exceptional they spurned being told what to do. But my brief time with Ms. Hayes made it clear that talent unguided could easily head down the wrong path so as to be easily wasted. Regardless of how little or how much talent subordinates might have, they need clear, specific direction.

The morning shoot ended on a high note with Helen Hayes graciously thanking me and the film crew for our work. She walked to the headquarters exit, shaking hands and giving autographs to several AFS employees who had lined up to meet the theatrical legend. No one seemed to be the least bit put off by the offensive miasma coming from her left shoe.

The PSAs were quickly edited. We convinced the Ad Council to list them as a priority campaign option (a kind of "Good Housekeeping Seal of Approval" in the advertising industry). The spots ran nationwide on different TV stations usually plugged in as fillers and often not shown until the wee hours of the morning. Still, the ads prompted a response from numerous families who wanted to know more about what AFS had to offer.

One of Our Dinosaurs Is Missing opened on a hot July night just after Independence Day. The New York premiere was a private showing in a small Broadway theater. Seats were filled with AFS major donors, board members, and several New York City dignitaries. The guest of honor was Helen Hayes who was seated in a section reserved for several veteran actors and actresses all in the same age bracket as the 70-something First Lady of the American Theatre. It was a successful evening on many fronts including donations received from the more well-to-to attendees.

I was far from an experienced development or fundraising expert. But AFS was a training ground where I learned the fundamentals about charitable giving. The *Dinosaur* function was a perfect example of a relatively low-cost, high-return special event. Big dollars were contributed by guests invited by AFS board members who taught me the value of naming well

The Ford Foundation   *AFS Headquarters*

connected individuals as directors. The fundraising consultant Charlie Bergman, who could drop more big names into a single sentence than anyone in New York, added little value. He left me with another **life lesson: talk and promises are easy; deliverables are not.** With little help from Charlie, AFS was shoring up its fundraising capabilities. We launched a magazine called *Our World* along with a newspaper that got AFS connected with past student participants (called "returnees") and host families. A carefully developed and monitored individual donor base began producing good results. We still fell short in raising money from corporations but especially vexing was the lack of grants from large private foundations – like the one I could see from my office window.

On the other side of 43rd Street was one of the most striking buildings in Manhattan. The Ford Foundation (set up by Edsel and Henry Ford in 1936) was housed in a 12-story steel and glass showcase that boxed in a spectacular interior atrium, a perfectly maintained mini-forest open to the public. At the time, the foundation had assets of $2 billion making it the largest grant-making institution in the nation (nearly four times larger than the next charitable giving giant, the Andrew Mellon Foundation). I made friends with a couple of foundation program officers and we occasionally got together for a coffee break or lunch.

"Private foundations are required by tax law to give away a certain percentage of their assets each year," one of the Ford people said while working on a bagel and cream cheese. "But that requirement is pretty loose."

"What do you mean?" I asked.

"The tax man allows a foundation to count its operating costs as part of the payout provision. Before any nonprofit gets a grant, the foundation covers its own salaries ..."

"And other costs like paying for that palace where you hang out," I said and cocked my head in the direction of the foundation headquarters.

"Exactly."

We talked more about the inner-workings of family and independent foundations. The two program officers told me there were not many large-scale foundations in the U.S. Yet there were thousands of smaller foundations often run by family members.

"Foundation donations only add up to around 15% of total charitable giving in the U.S.," the program officer stated. "Corporations? They're a whole lot less generous."

"Really?" I was surprised by what I heard.

"Businesses are super cheap – their donations add up to around 5% of all contributions collected each year," my foundation pal said. "Think about it. There are over four million companies just in the U.S. Get them more involved in philanthropy and the whole game gets changed in a nanosecond."

I had no idea at the time how profoundly affected I was by that mid-morning conversation. The discussion turned out to be a career course correction I wouldn't fully recognize until years later.

I walked back to the AFS headquarters and Steve Rhinesmith beckoned me into his office.

"Two things," Steve said. Sandy Mistretta's latest financial spreadsheets covered Rhinesmith's desk. "First, South America."

"South America?"

"Look, the U.S. and Europe are coming around," Steve noted, sounding even more positive than usual. As well he should. AFS was still on shaky ground but things were looking up. "We need to make sure our reps in Central and South America are fully on board with the changes we're making."

"So, that means…?" I asked the needless question. The answer was obvious.

"That means touching base with our major offices in South America," Steve answered. "I'll get someone else to handle Central America."

Spend a couple of days in Brazil, Argentina, Chile, and Peru with national representatives in each location, Rhinesmith said. I would need to block out at least a week and a half on the road, at a time when I had a lot of other AFS projects already on the stove. Plus, I was among the senior management team members who had only recently returned from a meeting in Tunisia where Middle Eastern and African national reps had been brought together. What was supposed to have been a three-day workshop had turned into a marathon event because of a rare flash flood that hit the region trapping us in a resort outside Tunis for days.

My AFS job required a lot more time in the air and on the road than I had anticipated. So much so, I decided to give up pursuing a doctorate degree. I had accumulated most of the course credits for the NYU degree but to get across the finish line, I would need to invest at least another year or more to complete a research-based dissertation. Something had to give, and NYU was it. Even after putting an end to my graduate studies, business travel and a long daily commute still consumed many, many hours. I was missing too much time with my kids, who were now as rambunctious as they were endearing. And my work schedule was not helping an increasingly precarious marriage. Another long international business trip could have serious consequences.

"I realize this piles on the travel," Steve acknowledged. "It's asking a lot but you and I know this is really important."

I started to push back but Steve held up his hand.

"Let me get to the second issue. We're promoting you to vice president. Immediately."

Two weeks later, I was in the air flying from JFK Airport in New York to Rio de Janeiro and then on to Buenos Aires. The meetings in both countries were productive and enjoyable. Next stop was Santiago, Chile where things went in reverse in a hurry. Chile was still reeling from a military junta that had ousted a democratically elected, socialist-leaning government headed by Salvador Allende. The 1973 coup-d'état had been led by General Augusto Pinochet who wasted no time in converting the Chilean democracy into a de facto dictatorship. It was widely known the CIA had helped overthrow the Allende administration partly because his socialist administration was moving toward nationalizing the country's incredibly valuable copper industry. This was an odd turn of events since the U.S. continued to ballyhoo the importance of making the world safe for democracy. At the same time, Pinochet's Chilean take-over had been aided and abetted by Uncle Sam.

Salvador Allende   *General Augusto Pinochet*

Pinochet's regime was instantly repressive. Over time, 3,000 Chileans would be killed or go missing and an estimated 200,000 citizens would flee the country. If or how AFS could continue in a nation still in such turmoil was unclear. I met with a couple of AFS returnees to discuss options I would communicate back to Rhinesmith. The organization was determined to stay above whatever political fray was taking place in Chile – or any other country, for that matter. *"Helping the world learn to live together,"* was a primary AFS goal that transcended the political makeup of any nation. AFS was set up to be just as relevant in an open society as it was in a country ruled by an autocrat.

Following my quick visit with the Chilean AFS representatives, I took a cab to the city's busy international airport and boarded a plane scheduled to make a nonstop, four-hour flight to Lima, Peru. The aircraft was jammed, and I was stuck in a middle seat at the rear of the cabin. Minutes before we were to leave the gate, two uniformed men entered the plane carrying semi-automatic weapons in one hand and a glossy black-and-white photograph in the other. They slowly made their way along the aisle checking faces of passengers whose expressions ranged from uneasiness to sheer terror. When they reached my row, they motioned me to stand up. "*Recoge todas tus cosas!*" they ordered. A flight attendant gave me a worried look and translated the message. "They want you to collect whatever you have and leave the plane."

Sweat instantly dotted my forehead. I pulled a jacket and briefcase from the overhead storage bin and marched toward the front cabin door. Inside the terminal, I was taken to a windowless room and pushed into a folding chair next to a long table where piles of familiar-looking clothing, papers, and a camera were on display. My checked-in suitcase had been pulled from the plane and its contents were now spread out in front of me.

"Who did you talk to while you were in Santiago?" a man who looked to be about my age said. He spoke perfect English.

"What's going on here?" I replied with a question.

"Who did you meet with?" the man glared at me as he spoke.

I explained who I was and why I was in Chile.

"We need the names of the people you talked to," the man demanded.

The interrogation continued for several more minutes. I asked if I could make a phone call to my home office thinking Rhinesmith would circle back to an embassy official. I had no idea why I was being grilled but it was getting more and more apparent I needed outside help.

"Do you have anything on or in your body?" the interrogator asked.

"*What?* Is this about drugs?"

"Do you have or any encrypted information in or on your body?" the man continued the questioning.

"Encrypted ... Absolutely not."

The English-speaking interrogator studied my face. "Take off your clothes," he said.

"*What?*"

"Your clothes – take off everything."

I resisted but a burly man wearing a uniform yanked me to my feet. I was either going to strip on my own or things were going to turn *really* nasty. Once I was stark naked, someone tossed me a sheet I quickly pulled over my scrawny body. Two men were ordered to inspect my just-removed clothes which had been thrown on the long table. They had been huddled over a Canon F-1 camera that had been pulled from my checked bag. The camera had been taken apart and the film removed. The F-1 was a revolutionary new 35 mm camera purchased only a month earlier by AFS. I had snapped hundreds of photos during my previous stops in Brazil and Argentina which were to be included in upcoming editions of AFS publications. From all appearances, every roll of film had been confiscated.

"You see the man in the corner," the English-speaking interrogator said and nodded toward a sad-looking hombre holding a box of disposable latex gloves. "He's going to do the cavity search."

"What?" I croaked. "No, no, no ..."

"Frankly, the gentleman is not very good as his job. He has big fingers and is quite clumsy. The procedure can be painful and usually ends up bloody."

"Listen, this has gone far enough," I protested. "I want to speak to ..."

"We want the names of *all* the people you met over the past couple of days."

The door opened and a military officer walked directly to the interrogator. "*Lo dejó ir.*"

"*Señor?*"

"*La CIA lo quiere fuera de ella.*"

The interrogator looked dejected. "Saved in the nick of time," he said with disappointment. "You're fortunate to have friends at the CIA."

"I do?"

"Apparently so. You are free to go."

I quickly retrieved my clothes and dressed. Then I threw my belongings back into my suitcase.

"A suggestion," the interrogator said as he led me out of the room. "It would be wise if you did not return to Chile."

I managed to find a seat on another flight to Peru and landed in Lima still shaken but grateful my rectum was still intact. It would be a couple of years later when I would fully understand the reason for my being ousted from Chile. In 1976, an AFS returnee named Gabriela Salazar was arrested by Chilean authorities. Along with tens of thousands of others, she was jailed for her opposition to the Pinochet regime. Even though the U.S. had played a role in bringing General Pinochet to power, certain North American nonprofit organizations were viewed as prodemocracy threats to the dictatorship. AFS was on that list. A few European AFS country leaders would petition Chile to release Salazar citing no valid reason for her confinement. That action would prompt the AFS board of directors to reaffirm the importance of AFS *not* getting involved with politically-related actions taken by any country where the organization was carrying out student exchanges.

When I landed in Lima, I called AFS headquarters trying to reach Steve Rhinesmith. He was unavailable but Reed Whittle was in the office.

"I got harassed because I work for a U.S. organization," I exploded. "Oh, and by the way, that's the same U.S. that helped a *thug* overthrow a democracy!"

"No, you work for an international organization that's supposed to fly above country politics," Reed replied calmly.

"That's tough to do when AFSers spend nearly a year in the U.S. soaking up all the advantages of a free democracy and end up going home to a country that's been turned into a fascist hell hole. And they're not supposed to do anything?"

"*They* can do whatever they want – or whatever they think they can get away with," Reed answered. "But AFS *can't*. That's not this organization's mission."

"I'm not sure an organization like ours should sidestep situations like this."

"Keep in mind, the *situation* has CIA written all over it," noted Reed. "If you think the Chilean military gave you a hard time, try going up against the Agency."

"I thought AFS is about creating a more just and peaceful world."

Reed laughed. "Okay, now I get it. We're back to saving the world from itself, are we?"

"Look, I know AFS has value," I said. "But changing hearts and minds one kid and family at a time is fine until you run into a meat grinder like Chile. Then it's like throwing cups of water at an inferno."

"Could be the exchange business isn't your kind of gig," Reed concluded. "Maybe you should try snagging a job at the UN Foundation. Or figure out how to get the corporate world to stop kicking politicians into starting wars that are more about money than anything else."

"You think businesses are behind what's happening in Chile?"

Reed snorted. "You think the Pope's Catholic?"

Following a relatively uneventful couple of days in Lima, I headed back to New York City. In a money-saving move, the AFS travel department scheduled me for a one-night layover in Panama. I arrived at Tocumen Airport, about 20 minutes outside Balboa, a city district not far from the Panama Canal. It was Sunday and I took a cab to a Hilton hotel. It was mid-morning and much too early to be checked in. To kill time until 3 p.m. when a room would be ready, I dug through my luggage and found the Canon F1 camera. The Chileans had removed all the film cartridges but fortunately had not damaged the camera. I had purchased a few rolls of film in Peru which I used to take numerous photos in and around Lima. Taking a few more shots of Panama City would keep me busy for two or three hours.

After checking my bags along with my passport and a packet of traveler's checks, I left the hotel and walked to the grassy median that divided a picturesque roadway called Avenida Balboa. It was noon and I was shooting the Panama City sky-line when I noticed four men approaching from the rear. I was instantly apprehensive but because it was the middle of the day and there was traffic on either side of the median, I didn't panic. A major error in judgment. One of the men grabbed me from behind and put me in a chokehold. A second hit me hard in the chest. The two others rifled my pockets and yanked the Canon out of my hand. This all happened in seconds but long enough for me to momentarily lose consciousness. I was punched again and thrown to the ground. I didn't see the men leave but assumed they ran across the highway into a patchwork of buildings and alleyways.

Avenida Balboa   *Panama Canal*

I was bleeding from the nose and mouth which was messy but not as painful as the contusions to my neck and chest. I had trouble breathing and couldn't pull myself to a standing position. Cars and trucks whizzed by, not one slowing down. Ten minutes passed and finally a Panamanian Public Forces transport truck pulled to a stop. Two uniformed soldiers jumped to my side and piled me into the back of the vehicle. There was a lot of talk, all in Spanish which I didn't understand. We traveled a few miles until the truck stopped in front of a small, seedy police station tucked into a Panama City alley. The two soldiers dragged me inside and propped me against a waist-high counter. Iron bars ran vertically from the countertop to the ceiling.

"*Cuál es tu problema?*" asked a uniformed man seated in the small, cluttered room behind the row of metal bars. He was watching a live television broadcast of a bull fight and made no effort to get up from his chair.

"I don't speak Spanish," I gurgled through blood that still oozed from a deep cut that ran the width of the inside of my lower lip. "Do you speak English?"

"Some," the man said with a shrug.

"I was mugged. Four men stole an expensive camera and some cash."

"Here," the man said and pushed a one-page form and a pencil through the bars. "*Siéntate allí.*" He waved me toward a wooden bench and quickly turned his attention back to the bull fight.

I pushed myself away from the counter and then my legs gave out. I fell to a kneeling position on the grimy floor and threw up.

The man behind the bars leaped out of his seat. "*Tonto estúpida!*" he screamed. Jerking open a closet, he fished out a plastic bucket and a stained rag. Unlocking a narrow door at the rear of the small room, the man threw the pail and foul-looking cloth at me. "*Limpiarlo!*" he yelled "Clean it up, you fool!"

I was aware many Panamanians resented North Americans because of the lingering dispute over what country should control the Panama Canal. Negotiations were underway aimed at transferring ownership of the canal from the U.S. to Panama – but it would be a couple of years before President Jimmy Carter would sign a treaty making that change a reality. For now, I speculated Panamanians like the unpleasant police official who was back in his seat watching TV had little use for anyone from the U.S. A few minutes later while I was wiping my own vomit from the floor, I found out it wasn't just me the man treated with disdain.

A woman walked into the police station holding the hand of a small boy who looked to be five or six years old. She called out to the man watching TV and then pushed a photograph through the bars. I could only make out a few of her words but I knew *hombre muerto* meant "dead man." The police official never got out of his seat. He glanced at the photo and shoved it back through the bars.

"*No recogemos cuerpos el domingo,*" the man said.

The woman began protesting loudly, waving her arms, and pointing at the boy I assumed had to be her son. The photograph flew to the floor and landed at my side. It was a picture of the boy using a long stick to prod what looked to be a lifeless man sprawled on a patch of weeds.

"Don't pick up the dead on Sunday!" the woman said in broken English as she leaned over to retrieve the photo. I don't know what gave me away as being a non-Spanish speaking foreigner, but the woman clearly knew I wasn't Panamanian. "Been three days," she said. "Stinking mess in my yard. This *cerdo* doesn't care."

The woman and child left. I finished a poor job of cleaning the floor, put the puke-soaked rag in the pail and stood up. I was still having trouble staying on my feet and nausea came at me in waves.

"I need a ride to my hotel," I told the man who was far more interested in what was happening on television than anything to do with me.

"No ride," the man said. "Find your own."

"I don't have any *cash!*" I shot back, too loudly.

The man reluctantly swiveled in his seat and pointed a stubby finger toward the door that led to the alley. "*Afuera!*" he snarled.

Any hope I had about getting help from the police evaporated. I staggered outside, headed toward a more congested road and flagged a taxi. The driver stared at my bloody clothes and swollen face. Before he could keep me from climbing into the cab, I jumped in the back. "Hilton Hotel on Balboa Avenida," I said. It was not a long ride and when we arrived at the hotel, I told the wary driver to wait and ran inside. A desk clerk couldn't hide his shock when I lumbered through the lobby. I explained what happened, asked that someone pay the cab driver and promised to reimburse the hotel with a traveler's check once a porter retrieved my bag.

"Have you seen a doctor?" a well-dressed man asked. He was standing beside me, having just registered as a hotel guest.

"No."

"I'm a physician," he explained. "I would be happy to help you." The doctor was from Costa Rica. He escorted me to his room and examined my head and upper body. "You have a concussion and some slight damage to your neck," he said in perfect English. "There are no broken ribs but one or two are bruised and might be cracked."

"My mouth?"

"Lacerations that could use a few stitches," he said. "Unfortunately, I can't do that here. The hotel can probably arrange to get you to an emergency clinic. If you want, I have gauze you can use as a compress which should stop the bleeding. If it does and if you don't have any problems with headaches, loss of vision or nausea, you should be able to make it back to the U.S. Then be sure to see your own doctor. In the meantime, I can give you a mild painkiller."

I had a morning flight the next day and had no intention of getting trapped in a Panamanian medical maze. I would take what the Costa Rican doctor was offering and hope for the best.

"Thank you," I said with genuine sincerity. "How much do I owe you?"

"Oh, no," the doctor smiled. "Thank you for your offer. I'm just someone who happened to be able to help and am glad to have done so."

The next day, I flew to New York City. While I was still not feeling great, my head was clear and the nausea gone. As we landed at JFK Airport, I realized what happened in Panama was another **life lesson: value those the most who are the least indifferent.** The hundreds of cars that sped by as I lay on the side of Balboa Avenida and the totally disinterested policeman in Panama City were prime examples of how indifferent humans can be. The Costa Rican physician, on the other hand, exemplified an extraordinary level of caring and concern. We all default to being indifferent at times. But I learned those who regularly or more frequently rise above that less-than-admirable characteristic are people worth keeping close.

Months passed and AFS continued to make impressive strides under Steve Rhinesmith's leadership. As the organization grew stronger, I grew more restless. Reed Whittle and I were now very close friends and we talked freely about our aspirations. Reed helped me understand that while I lauded AFS and the people who ran the organization, I needed to get connected to an institution focused on more short-term social and economic challenges.

Those discussions were the perfect stage-setter for a headhunter who called me about two job openings. The woman said both non-profit organizations were looking for a communications/ development officer. I met all the qualifications for either position, she added. "We'd like you to schedule an in-person interview with both," she said. "We'll pay your travel and lodging."

"Where are these organizations?" I asked.

"The East-West Center in Oahu, Hawaii and the Asia Foundation in San Francisco."

I had no intention of checking out either or both options without telling Rhinesmith I wanted to start exploring an exit strategy from AFS. As expected, Steve was fully supportive and added that if I decided to remain at AFS, that would be his preferred outcome.

A few weeks later, I flew to the East-West Center situated on 21 spectacular acres in Honolulu. Established by the U.S. Congress in the 1960s, the Center billed itself as an independent nonprofit working on ways to strengthen relations between the U.S. and Asian nations. I was as impressed with the organization but very concerned about a comment made by one of the Center's program officers. "This is paradise but if you're the type who doesn't want to live in the middle of nowhere surrounded by a million tourists, you might not be a happy camper."

I flew back to the mainland and interviewed with the management team at The Asia Foundation, another nonprofit that got its start with the help of the U.S. government. The organization was based in San Francisco but had offices in more than a dozen Pacific Rim countries. The foundation's stated mission was to "improve lives across a dynamic and developing Asia" – no easy task given the spillover impact the war in Vietnam and Cambodia was having on the region.

I returned to AFS and met with Steve Rhinesmith and told him my decision had been made. Then I walked to Reed Whittle's office and let him know I would be leaving AFS in two months.

"So, which organization did you pick?" Reed asked.

I answered.

Reed laughed. "You're going to love working for the CIA!"

**

Much happened after my departure from AFS. General Augusto Pinochet would continue to rule Chile for 17 years until stepping down in 1990. When on a visit to London in 1998, he would be arrested and charged with numerous human rights violations. In failing health, he would be released and returned to Santiago. He would die at the age of 91.

The U.S. Congress would approve a treaty shifting control of the Panama Canal to the Panamanians. The transfer agreement would be signed in 1978 but the canal would not officially change hands until 1999. The treaty's provisions would be in jeopardy when Manuel Noriega became Panama's leader, a development that would prompt George H.W. Bush to authorize an invasion of the country. After a period of instability, the U.S. and Panama would resolve most differences and the 50-mile waterway would finally be turned over to the Panamanians.

Helen Hayes MacArthur would die in 1993. In recognition of her reputation as one of the greatest theatrical leading ladies of the 20th century, New York City would put her name on a Manhattan midtown theater.

My good friend, Reed Whittle, would leave AFS not long after I moved on. He would become a solo consultant working with investment and banking giants like Goldman Sachs. A master at orchestrating senior management transitions, Reed would be called upon by multinational businesses to convince executives it was time to change or leave their jobs. It would be a process called "Whittlization" and it was something no high-paid corporate leader ever wanted to experience.

Reed would make an astounding amount of money consulting with firms in the U.S. and Europe. But his work would eat away at his marriage. After his divorce from his very successful wife, Carolyn (a banking vice president and a prominent political figure in White Plains, New York), Reed would date a string of women ranging from legitimate princesses to lingerie models. Following my own remarriage, he would invite my wife and me to dinner at his East Side Manhattan apartment where we would meet and then days later evaluate his most recent dating interest. Dr. Whittle would eventually marry Sassona Norton, a wealthy Israeli-born sculptress and artist. The two would split their time between a stunning apartment on Manhattan's Upper East Side and an enormous mansion in Bedminster, New Jersey.

Reed was an avid sportsman and adventurer. On one occasion, he and a friend went on a survival trip in an unexplored part of the Amazon jungle. Whittle would contract a tropical disease which he confessed to me was possibly linked to his eating an uncooked monkey brain. The disease would later be associated with Sweet's Syndrome, an autoinflammatory ailment usually controlled by steroids. In Reed's case, the disease would lead to many other complications and he would die in 2008 at age 66.

Whittle and I were very much alike despite traveling on different tracks. Reed was driven by a determination to live as adventurously as possible, accumulate as much knowledge as was feasible and acquire money – a lot of it. I was driven by some unattainable pursuit of a better world order. But those drives were equally as ferocious; equally as uncontrollable. When I was with Reed, I would always see some of myself. And when Dr. Whittle died, so did a part of me.

Dr. Steve Rhinesmith would continue to lead AFS until 1982. He would take his management skills to the private sector when Holland American Cruise Lines would name him COO and president. Then, in 1986, President Ronald Reagan would give Dr. Rhinesmith the diplomatic rank of U.S. ambassador and charge him with overseeing exchanges between the U.S. and the Soviet Union. Steve would author several books and articles on international affairs, publications that would establish him as a much sought-after consultant among companies and nations looking to develop global leaders.

Dr. Rhinesmith would be summoned to all corners of the planet to assist businesses and countries. China's Tianjin University, Moscow State University, United Arab Republic, and Singapore Senior Executive program would call upon Steve as would a long list of corporations including Bank of America, Samsung, Ford, Burberry, and Merck.

Rhinesmith would excel as a diplomat, author, and lecturer. His most important contribution would be his tireless efforts to develop new leadership mindsets to move the world in a productive and peaceful direction – something I would never cease to admire.

AFS would continue to expand, bringing exchange students to the U.S. from more than 80 countries and sending Americans abroad to 50 nations. The organization would continue to hold true to its mission: "to prevent future conflict through educational and cross-cultural exchanges."

Chapter 8

The Asia Foundation (1976-79)

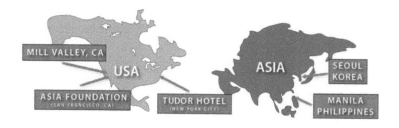

T he Tudor Hotel lobby was swarming with New York City cops. Flashing lights from two squad cars parked outside the hotel pulsated the foggy morning air that had settled over Tudor City, the three-block Manhattan district adjacent to the United Nations complex.

"What … what happened?" I stammered to a hotel receptionist who was staring wide-eyed at the mayhem playing out in front of her.

Tudor City – New York   *Ambassador Haydn Williams*

"There was a robbery," she said, her voice shaky.

"A robbery? Who?"

"An ambassador," she replied. "On the second floor."

"*What?*" I gasped. It couldn't be. "Not Ambassador Williams?"

"Yes," the woman said, looking surprised. "How did you know?"

I *knew* because I had booked Haydn Williams a room at the Tudor Hotel. My very first road trip with my new boss, a man who looked like he ate babies for lunch, and he ends up a robbery victim.

A couple of minutes passed, and the hotel elevator opened. Out stepped Ambassador Williams accompanied by two men dressed in poorly tailored suits, a New York police shield dangling from a lanyard roped over each of their thick necks.

"Haydn!" I called out. "I'm so sorry! What happened?"

"Call the damn Consulate General's office!" Williams snapped. "I need a new passport. And get somebody in the San Francisco office to wire me some damn cash!"

I pumped the desk clerk for details while Haydn grumbled at a plainclothes detective furiously scribbling on a pocket-sized pad. The clerk said one or more thieves broke into the ambassador's room sometime between midnight and 6 a.m. while Williams was sleeping. The door lock had been picked and the safety chain had been snapped probably by a bolt cutter, the desk clerk said, repeating what she had heard from one of the cops. The ambassador never woke as his wallet, passport, watch, and briefcase were removed from the room.

"Come with me," a short man ordered after flashing a badge and pointing to an alcove behind the registration desk. "You're with Ambassador Williams?"

"I work for him," I said. "For the past six months or so."

"Were you with him last night?" the man asked.

I explained that the two of us had arrived late on a flight from San Francisco. We had taken a cab to the hotel, checked in, and went directly to our rooms.

"Did you see the ambassador meet with anybody last night? A man? What about a woman?"

I had a déjà vu moment; a flashback to me sitting naked as a jay bird being grilled by a Chilean interrogator. "No," I replied.

"Was the ambassador at a bar on Lexington a few blocks from here?"

"What?" I blinked. "No. I mean, I don't think he was."

"There are 300 rooms in this hotel," the man informed me. "There are all kinds of United Nations' big hitters staying here. Why break into the ambassador's room?"

"I have no idea."

"Seems odd, doesn't it?" the man continued the questioning. "Why somebody wouldn't wake up during a robbery."

"I guess."

The man studied my face. "What was in his briefcase?"

"His briefcase?"

"Yes," the man repeated. "What ... was ... in ... his ... briefcase?"

I didn't know what Ambassador Williams had been carrying in his briefcase. For that matter, I didn't know all that much about the ambassador. What I did know was I was working for a man who headed an organization that claimed it was not a CIA cover but admitted it was once part of the U.S. intelligence network.

"Is this when you want me to say I told you so?" my friend Reed Whittle laughed when much later in the day I called the AFS office to tell him about the break-in. "Congratulations. You're now officially a spook."

"That's not true," I argued. "The Asia Foundation *used* to be CIA but not anymore."

Reed laughed harder. "Hey, my Brooks Brothers camel hair coat may make me look like an awesome dromedary, but underneath I'm a human and nothing's going to change what I am."

"Yeah, yeah, you made your point," I muttered. I wasn't sure Reed was right about the foundation being a CIA cover but then again, I wasn't 100 percent certain he was wrong. Before I took the job, I had done what I thought was proper due diligence. But looking back, I had to admit the organization had a history that needed a closer inspection. What became apparent was another **life lesson: if you only want to see what you only want to see – you will see what you want to see.** I took at face value what the organization told me before I accepted a position as vice president. Had I made a few inquiries to insiders at the U.S. State Department, who knows if I would have moved my family to the San Francisco Bay Area.

"Where we were years ago and where we are today are two completely different stories," was the foundation's standard line when pushed to discuss its past. With some reluctance, foundation staffers did confirm the organization was an outgrowth of a U.S. government group called the Committee for a Free Asia. In 1954, the Committee morphed into The Asia Foundation and quietly got funded by CIA under the mysterious code name "Project DTPILLAR."

The outside world was told the foundation was an independent nongovernmental organization (NGO) like hundreds of other international cultural, economic, and education nonprofits. Advocating for the building of democratic institutions in Asia, the foundation attracted a blue-ribbon board including the CEO of Standard Oil of California (Chevron), university presidents (Columbia, Stanford, UCLA, etc.) and even Pulitzer Prize-winning writer James Michener.

In 1966, the left-leaning *Ramparts* magazine (which sputtered to its demise in 1975) exposed several nonprofits being covertly funded by the CIA. High on the list was the Asia Foundation. Following the exposé, a special commission headed by then Secretary of State Dean Rusk determined the foundation's work should continue but its funding no longer kept behind a curtain. The Asia Foundation was declared a "quasi-nongovernmental organization" with the federal government using non-CIA channels to offset most of its expenses.

"Word is the foundation is still pretty cozy with the CIA," my old Ford Foundation friend said after the ambassador and I pitched a group of foundation program directors. We had met with the Ford Foundation only a couple of hours after police finished their work at the Tudor Hotel. Once the meeting was over, Haydn had returned to his room and I stayed behind in one of the Ford Foundation's stunning meeting rooms.

"Maybe I should have checked around before jumping on The Asia Foundation train," I said.

"Probably," the Ford staffer agreed. "Ambassador Williams is a pretty intense guy. What's he like as a boss?"

I could have explained away some of Haydn Williams *intenseness* by disclosing details about the early morning robbery. But Haydn had insisted nothing be said about the incident. So, instead, I served up a quick snapshot of the man.

Williams held a doctorate degree from the Fletcher School of Law and Diplomacy at Tufts University. He was a Navy air operations officer who was later named deputy assistant secretary of defense under both Dwight D. Eisenhower and John F. Kennedy. Then in 1971, he was appointed ambassador to the Micronesia and Mariana Islands which had been taken over by the U.S. following World War II. Dr. Williams was credited for helping to close out the U.S. trusteeship over the islands.

"Doesn't seem like the warm and fuzzy type," my Ford Foundation friend noted.

"Keeps a lot to himself." My reply was a huge understatement. Haydn was a walking secret. He rarely volunteered information and his gruff nature discouraged anyone from asking many questions. I guessed correctly the missing briefcase and other items stolen from the ambassador's room would not be part of any future conversation.

"Well, good luck," my Ford Foundation friend said in a tone that I translated to mean *glad I'm not in your shoes.*

That evening, Haydn and I met with a wealthy investment banker who was a major Asia Foundation donor. The next day, there were two more meetings with big dollar contributors, including lunch at the huge and ultimately ill-fated World Trade Center complex that had opened five years earlier. The quick East Coast fundraising trip ended with my taking an evening flight back to California and Haydn jumping on a shuttle to Washington, DC.

The night was unusually clear and calm on the approach to San Francisco Airport. The evening fog that so often rolled in from the Pacific remained offshore. From several thousand feet in the air, it was easy to make out a blanket of lights on the rolling hillsides just north of the Golden Gate Bridge. Amidst the glow would be the comfortable (although not particularly well constructed) house in Mill Valley where I had relocated my family. The community was still in its developmental stage and somewhat affordable. That would all change, as would most of the Bay Area once the tech industry took root and housing prices took off. Just 14 miles from the heart of San Francisco, Mill Valley was destined to become a choice location for the monied set, especially those with an eye toward the extraordinary natural beauty that bordered the town. Richardson Bay lapped at the community's shoreline while 82,000 acres of undeveloped, carefully protected land capped the town's hills and colored its canyons in green and brown. In the background loomed the half-mile high Mount Tamalpais, home to the famous Muir Woods.

In some respects, it was the perfect life. The kids literally could roll down a steep incline to an elementary school situated at the base of a hill. Our house was a few hundred feet above sea level and while nowhere near as impressive or expensive as the homes with a much higher elevation, it still had a decent view of the valley and part of the bay. My commute was the antithesis of a hardship. While there was bus service that brought riders into the center of the city, a far better option was to take a jitney to the ferry terminal in Sausalito and then sail across the bay. The half hour cruise gave passengers enough time for coffee in the morning and a cocktail on the late afternoon trip back to Marin County. "You live in nirvana," a tourist said to me one beautiful day as the ferry pulled away from Sausalito, the town looking as enchanting as any Mediterranean village. I smiled and held back elaborating on another **life lesson: reality is perfection's flaw.** As with anything thought to be ideal, nirvana had its blemishes and as I would come to discover, a dark underside.

Mount Tamalpais   *Ferry from Sausalito to San Francisco*

My next-door neighbor, Terry, had become my commuter partner and good friend. Terry was a banking executive who had a high-paying job, an attractive wife, and three adorable children. On our travels to and from the city, Terry and I mused about the pros and cons of California life. On the surface, Californians were more laissez-faire in their personal and business dealings. They seemed less driven, less pressured by daily challenges than those of us from the East Coast. But for some, this veneer cloaked deep, troubling feelings. At the extreme, there were a few who would climb to the mid-section of the Golden Gate Bridge and jump to their death. Each morning and night when our ferry glided by the iconic bridge, I recalled the terrified, distraught man hanging over the edge of the Mount Hope Bridge in Bristol, Rhode Island. The same scene was played out even more frequently on the Golden Gate. Over 20 people a year plunged 245 feet at a speed of 75 miles per hour, hitting the water with a force equivalent to a speeding truck striking a brick wall.

Tragedy didn't always end in suicide. Pain came in other unexpected ways. I found that out one morning when I walked unannounced into Terry's kitchen. This was my usual weekday routine, stopping by Terry's house on the way to the covered bus stop a few blocks down the hill where the ferry jitney would collect a few passengers. On this morning, Terry sat staring at the floor. I could hear his wife sobbing in another room at the rear of the house. Spread out on the kitchen counter were four proof sheets, each with several color shots of Terry's wife who was topless in many of the photos. Terry didn't go to work that day. Later, I reached him by phone. He told me his wife was being recruited as a TV news anchor and had been convinced the pictures needed to be part of her portfolio if she expected to land the job. It was the starting block for a rather quick divorce with Terry moving to an apartment in San Francisco and his wife moving to Los Angeles to become, ironically, … a television news personality.

With Terry no longer my commuter buddy, I developed more casual ties with others on my daily ferry ride. Over time, conversations grew more personal and we talked about families, kids, and marital strains. I talked about what happened to Terry. Others joined in with one story after another about separation and divorce. Then a woman, herself twice divorced, said:

"This is the place where marriages come to die."

Her words cut deep. I had removed myself and my family from the East Coast thinking a new venue might be what was needed for a restart. Instead, more than ever, my marriage was teetering on the brink. It would be here in Northern California that it would be permanently put to rest.

Weeks after the New York trip, Haydn asked that I pay a visit to a few Asia Foundation offices in a half dozen countries where we might find or meet business leaders and others who would be willing to co-fund key foundation projects. Soon thereafter, I was in the air heading to Tokyo, the first stop jammed into a nine-day trip.

"These people love proverbs ... you know, sayings," the foundation's head man in Japan said. We were eating steak in the swank American Club not far from Toyko's Grand Hyatt Hotel where I was staying for the night. Although I was in one of the most densely populated cities in Asia, I was in an American cocoon which gave added credence to what was said next.

"Let every fox take care of its own tail," the foundation representative said. "I think it's actually an Italian proverb. But whatever. It sums up how things ended this afternoon."

"I'm not sure I understand." Earlier, we had a polite albeit stilted meeting with two prominent business executives. Our goal had been to kick open the door to Keidanren, the giant organization known as the voice of big business in Japan. Apparently, we came up short.

"They basically told us to stay in our lane and they'll stay in theirs," the representative explained. He was fluent in Japanese and unlike me, had understood everything that had been said during the meeting. "We're seen as an extension of the U.S. government. So, we have deep pockets and should pick up the tab for whatever we do in Japan or anywhere else in Asia. They'll work through Keidanren and do their thing using their own yen."

The foundation representative gave me a quick Keidanren tutorial after finishing his Wagyu rib steak. Japan was leaning heavily on the private sector to drive the country's economic and social growth. Keidanren was one of three major business associations in Japan and was the most influential. It represented well over a thousand corporations. This news only added to my growing contention that the business community could be a powerful change agent – much more so than it usually was.

Keidanren Headquarters   *Carabao Water Buffalo*

The foundation representative predicted Keidanren would become even more of a force within Japan as well as other parts of the world. He was right. Keidanren would eventually link up with the Japan Federation of Employers' Associations. The official name of the combined organizations would be the Japan Business Federation but the Keidanren brand dominated. So much so, the new organization's 30-story building would be named Keidanren Kalkan.

The next morning, I flew from Tokyo to the Philippines ready to pitch the foundation to a pair of wealthy industrialists. A brief meeting was arranged at the Manila hotel where I was staying. Getting the men focused on the Asia Foundation proved impossible given their giddy anticipation of the upcoming "fight of the century" billed as *The Thrilla in Manila* at which two internationally famous boxers, Muhammad Ali and Joe Frazier, would pound each other for the final time. The only other topic to make its way into our conversation was how President Ferdinand Marcos was using martial law and other tough measurers to keep the Moro National Liberation Front (MNLF) in check. Not familiar with the Front, I asked questions that led to a vitriolic broadside about "the Muslim problem." The Philippines had been feuding for decades with millions of its own citizens living in Mindanao, an archipelago in the southern part of the country. The mostly Muslim population had been recently organized under the MNLF, an aggressive separatist organization. This was all interesting but not especially relevant to me until later that same day when I was seated in the large hotel dining room.

It was early evening and I had finished a light entrée when my waiter brought me a small complimentary dish of carabao ice cream. The dessert was a popular Filipino treat made from water buffalo milk which I was told I had to sample. Just as the dish arrived, a fiery blast lit up the far end of the room. The waiter yelled and flipped the table on its side, sending china and utensils flying. He threw himself behind the overturned table, pulling me beside him as he hit the floor. There were only a few other guests in the room but without hesitation, most reacted the same way. Tables became round protective barriers with diners and wait staff ducking behind them, anticipating the worst.

"*MNLF!*" someone screamed. "*MNLF!*"

From what I had been told earlier in the afternoon, Manila was an unlikely target for the Moro Liberation National Front. But a perceptible fear factor gripped the city and any act of violence triggered suspicion MNLF was responsible.

"*Paeng! Paeng!*" my waiter shouted at a boy running toward the dining room's main entrance. The boy's white serving coat and his long hair were in flames. "It's Paeng!" my waiter screamed and raced after the boy who dashed into the main hotel lobby. No one else moved, frozen in place by shock and fear. Much shouting and wailing could be heard from another section of the hotel. Then an eerie stillness took over the room, interrupted minutes later by a hotel executive who called out an apology for an "unfortunate accident." A hotel worker, he said, had tipped over a container of paraffin oil used to fuel decorative tabletop lanterns. The oil splashed onto the worker's clothing, which caught fire. Guests and waiters cautiously got to their feet. There would be no charge for food or drink, the executive added. He hoped we would return later in the evening once the dining room was put back in order. I didn't accept the offer choosing instead to return to my room. I walked out of the dining room, stepping over my now melted carabao ice cream.

When checking out the next morning, I asked about the employee who had been injured the night before. The victim was a boy named Paeng, an adolescent not yet in his teens. A porter said he heard the boy died shortly after being taken to an area hospital.

My next stop was Hong Kong and then on to Singapore. Both proved more promising for enlisting well-do-to businessmen as possible co-funders of certain programs and projects of interest to the Asia Foundation. As productive as the visits were, I was distracted by thoughts of what had happened in the Philippines. The glimpse of a young boy trying to outrun the flames that engulfed his small body turned into a recurring memory. But there was more to the incident than just that tragedy.

Everyone in the hotel dining room had assumed MNLF was responsible for what seemed to be a terrorist attack. Yet MNLF was not considered a serious threat to Manila. Still, its brand was so widely known and feared throughout the Philippines, by default the organization became the designated culprit. MNLF was to the Philippines what ISIS would be to the United States many years later.

MNLF's activism and to some, terrorism, created its national awareness. However, the organization's ability to equate its name with its cause distinguished MNLF from other separatist groups active in Mindanao. In an odd way, I was left with another **life lesson: build your brand when you can.** The MNLF acronym itself became as powerful as any demonstration or act of violence. The brand would give the organization enough standing to become the Mindanao representative selected to enter into peace negotiations with the Philippine government.

139

Decades after my tour of duty with the Asia Foundation, I would enlist the help of a national expert on cause marketing, social media usage, and branding to join me in helping non-profit leaders generate revenue. Joe Waters is a Massachusetts-based consultant who makes the point better than anyone that a major shortcoming for organizations is their inability to establish and communicate a viable brand. It's not just about designing a fancy logo or coming up with a memorable acronym, Joe points out. Organizations need to define their purpose and mission in a compelling, easy-to-understand sentence or two – What do they do that's important? How and why are they different from others? Then they should use an array of communication channels to promote the brand to create awareness and value to a clearly defined audience(s). Not the easiest undertaking but one that often leads to a major payoff.

The final leg of my Asia trip took me to South Korea. Without being asked in advance, I was the honored guest at a private dinner arranged by the foundation's country representative. In an upstairs room of a private Seoul club, I was introduced to seven Korean men most of whom worked in the financial field. We were seated at a long table, each of us paired with a young woman who sat behind us. The ladies were Korean *gisaeng* who were there to provide each man whatever services were required. Most of the women were not prostitutes, I was told. Modeled after the Japanese Geisha, they were skilled in conversation and many were trained dancers or singers. Their main role this evening was to provide comfort to whichever male was deemed their responsibility. Coming from America where women were well beyond acting as an attendant or minion, it was an awkward arrangement. As the night unfolded, though, my *gisaeng* proved to be my savior.

The night began with a small glass of soju, a potent rice-based liquor very popular in Korea. Reserved conversation gradually turned more open and one guest called out: *Titanic!* The rest of the room cheered and applauded. The *gisaeng* scrambled to an exterior room and returned with a tall glass and placed it front of me. The glass was half filled with Hite, a well-known Korean beer. Next, a shot glass was carefully floated on top of the beer.

"Don't sink the Titanic!" warned one of the men. He passed me a bottle of soju. I quickly learned Koreans loved drinking games and this one happened to be a favorite. The beer glass was passed from one person to the next. At each stop, soju was dripped into the buoyant shot glass until it took on such weight that it sank. The unlucky soul who sent the glass to the bottom was required to drink all the soju-laced beer. As the honored guest, I began the process by putting only a few drops of the rice liquor into the shot glass. Then the beer glass made its way around the table, soju added at each stop. When it returned to me, the shot glass was nearly full and barely able to stay afloat. I steadied my hand and sent a single drop into the beer tumbler. The shot glass sank like a rock.

"*Titanic!*" the group roared. After I guzzled the beer and soju, they all toasted me with a shot of soju.

On to round two. Because I had lost the first match, it was up to me to start the game again. I dribbled soju into the shot glass and it made its wobbly way around the room. When it circled back to me, the results were the same as round one. Not being a big drinker, I had to work at draining the mix of beer and liquor. My head was spinning, and I was panicky about sinking the Titanic a third time. If that happened, I was certain it would be lights out.

The tall glass was refilled halfway with Hite and a new shot glass bobbed on the beer's surface. I was about to pour the soju when my *gisaeng* nudged me. She spoke only a few words of English so she resorted to hand gestures to tell me I needed to put a lot more soju into the shot glass. That was the advantage player number one had – to start the round with the little glass so full it couldn't possibly make the return trip to its starting point. The strategy worked. I didn't lose again but was still very intoxicated.

Later I would read a report by the marketing and research firm, Euromonitor, that South Koreans hold the record for drinking the most hard liquor on the planet. They consume over 13 shots of liquor a week, mostly soju. They drink twice as much as Russians (number two in the ranking) and four times as much as Americans. From what I can recall about my private dinner in Seoul, those findings seem to be on target.

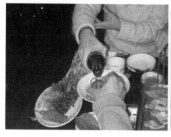 

Soju   *Gaegogi - Dog Meat*

The excessive drinking went on even after platters of food were brought into the room. Traditional kimchi, stir-fried noodles, rice, and meat called *Gaegogi* weighed down the center of the table. A rice wine infused more alcohol into the increasingly noisy group of men.

"So, what does the foundation do for the CIA?" the guest to my left asked loudly. The room went still waiting for my answer.

"We're not connected to the CIA," I replied.

A burst of loud laughter filled the room.

"No, really," I said emphatically. "We're not CIA."

The foundation rep sat silently and offered no backup.

"Please understand," one of the Koreans said. "We value the CIA and what you do."

"But ..." I tried interrupting but the Korean kept talking.

"We're sitting here just 35 miles from the DMZ. Knowing as much as we can about what's going on in the North keeps us one step ahead of being annihilated."

Most of the men nodded and grunted in agreement. They lifted their wine glasses and toasted the CIA.

I didn't want the evening to end without making it clear that as far as I knew, there was no direct connection between the foundation and the CIA. But before I could make a strong case, my *gisaeng* loaded my plate with food and used a pair of chopsticks to feed me. With my mouth full and my brain blurred, there was no way I could attempt to set the record straight. The night ended with my *gisaeng* helping me to a car called to drive me back to my hotel.

I woke the next morning with a horrific headache. After checking out, the foundation's Korean rep met me in the lobby and walked me to his car. As he drove to the airport, I asked him about the CIA discussion I barely could remember.

"Yes, the issue comes up now and again," the rep said. He was incredibly alert and looking not the least affected by the drinking fest that had gone on late into the night.

"So, what's the right explanation?" I asked.

"People need to understand how the CIA works. It grabs bits and pieces of information then puts them together. Like a jigsaw puzzle."

"And the foundation is one of those pieces?" I inquired.

"We support a lot of programs and organizations," the rep said, carefully avoiding a direct answer.

A few miles away from Gimpo International Airport on the western edge of Seoul, I asked the rep about the food choices for last night's dinner. "What was the meat dish?" I wanted to know.

"Ah, *Gaegogi*," the rep explained with a nod of approval.

"*Gaegogi?*"

"The meat of the dog."

I ordered the rep to pull over. I yanked open the passenger side door and threw up.

After the rep dropped me off at Gimpo, I made a long, uncomfortable flight back to San Francisco. Seated next to me was a Korean lawyer who told me more than I wanted to know about his country's penchant for dog eating. A special breed called *Nureongi* was the most common source of meat. But abandoned Labradors, cocker spaniels, and retrievers were sometimes sent to slaughterhouses. Most dog meat ended up in soups or stews.

However, good quality dog could be roasted and served as a meal's main dish.

For the next couple of years, I worked to expand the foundation's individual, foundation, and corporate donor base. The increase in private funding was slow but steady. Had the organization's CEO been more engaged in fundraising, the donor base would most likely have expanded. But the bulk of Ambassador Williams time was spent making sure the foundation's ties with Washington were strong. Given how much the organization depended on public dollars, it was the right decision.

The lack of senior executive involvement in soliciting private donations meant I was largely on my own in finding non-government funds with one important exception: Bill Bramstedt.

William Frederick Bramstedt was a retired oil executive who was a non-paid consultant to the Asia Foundation. He was given an office next to mine and spent four or five days a week offering advice and direction to anyone who cared to access his expertise. Few staff members ever knocked on Bill's door. I was the exception, grabbing as much of Bramstedt's time as possible.

Bill had been a longtime executive with Standard Oil of California (now Chevron) before being named president of Caltex Corporation, a joint venture between Chevron and Texaco. After his retirement in 1970, he split his time between a residence on San Francisco's prestigious Nob Hill and a home at the Silverado Country Club in Napa Valley. Wealthy but not at all pretentious, Bill was well connected to many of the West Coast's most prominent business leaders.

"I feel like a water boy for a big league sports team," I confessed one day while eating chilled Dungeness crab at the very exclusive Pacific-Union Club. Once the home of silver magnate James Flood, the club's member roster included San Francisco's top power brokers.

"What do you mean?" Bramstedt asked. He had been a longtime Pacific-Union member and frequently invited me to accompany him as a lunch guest.

Pacific-Union Club

"The Asia Foundation has been and probably always will be a quasi-government operation with a dab of private money here and there to make it look like an independent nonprofit," I groused. A proposal rejection from an East Coast bank had made it a tough morning.

Bill started with a counterargument but was interrupted by Bill Hewlett who stopped by the table to say hello. The co-founder of Hewlett-Packard was just one of the business celebrities in the room. I recognized Walter Hass, Levi-Strauss chairman, talking with Steve Bechtel who headed one of the nation's most important engineering firms.

"There has to be at least *some* private money coming in the door," Bill resumed our conversation. "The government won't pick up the whole tab."

"The feds are paying 85 to 90 percent of the foundation's costs," I said. "My job is to bring in a little loose change."

Bill paused while a waiter served a cup of vichyssoise resting on a bed of ice. It was another club specialty. "You sound frustrated."

"I am," I confessed. "At best, I can only make a marginal difference at the foundation. It isn't just that I'm a bit player when it comes to the revenue we get, it's also the fact that I have no say in how money is being spent. Haydn Williams, the field staff, and probably a dozen people at the State Department in Washington are making the important decisions."

"You're hardly 30 years old and the vice president of a major international nonprofit organization," Bill said with what I logged as another **life lesson: be wary of titles that sap ambition and foster grandiose delusions.** Many of my friends and associates had titles that denoted accomplishment and responsibility. For some, these badges came with enough social status to lull them into a kind of cruise control that overrode their drive to achieve more for themselves or others. Then there were those who assigned more importance to a title than was warranted. For me, my Asia Foundation title was appreciated but certainly not something that would keep me tethered to the organization.

"So, where is all this going?" Bill asked.

I hesitated with a response, knowing my next statement could be very consequential. "I'm seriously thinking about making a change."

Bramstedt rubbed his chin as he usually did when concerned or conflicted. "Making a change to do what?"

"Convince businesses to play a bigger role in dealing with social issues like education, poverty, the environment."

Bill glanced at the busy dining room crowded with captains of industry. "And just how will you do that?" he asked, skepticism weighing down each of his words.

"On my own," I replied and then added: "Hopefully with your help."

**

The 300-room Tudor Hotel would change hands and names over the years. Now the Westgate New York City, the hotel has preserved some of its 1930's features including trouser presses and unique lighting fixtures. Ambassador Williams' broken door locks were repaired.

The Moro National Liberation Front (MNLF) would sign a peace agreement with the Philippine government in 1996. Under terms of the agreement, an autonomous region would be established to include five provinces mainly inhabited and self-ruled by Muslim residents.

Bill Bramstedt would play an instrumental role in the next chapter of my life but would also remain associated with the Asia Foundation.

President Bill Clinton would name Ambassador Haydn Williams to serve on the American Battle Monuments Commission. Dr. Williams would be elevated to the Commission's chair and take the lead in raising money for the National WWII Memorial in Washington, DC (which would be formally dedicated in 2004). At the age of 96 and having served 25 years as president of the Asia Foundation, Dr. Williams would die of heart failure in 2016.

The Asia Foundation would spend over $100 million a year to continue its work "improving lives across a dynamic and developing Asia." The organization would remain reliant on U.S. government funding (80% or more per annum) to carry out programs in 18 Asian countries focusing on governance, empowerment of women, expanded economic opportunity, environmental resilience, and regional cooperation.

Chapter 9

Weeden Management Systems – Philanthropy (1980-90)

"Check this out!"

Don Kendall snapped a switch and, in the distance, a majestic water fountain erupted, its fine spray turning the afternoon's brilliant sunshine into a rainbow.

"Something, isn't it?" Kendall asked with a broad smile.

It was indeed *something*. Kendall was CEO of the soft drink behemoth PepsiCo and was rightfully proud of the 168-acre sculpture garden that turned the corporation's Purchase, New York headquarters into an art lover's paradise. Scattered among trees, water-lily ponds and fountains were works by renowned artists such as Auguste Rodin, Henry Moore, and Alexander Calder.

"Good to see you, Bill," Kendall said warmly to my new business partner, Bill Bramstedt. "What can I do for you?"

To call Bill connected would be a major understatement. Bramstedt was wired into dozens of CEOs who always made time for the affable one-time oil executive. Don Kendall was the first business chief we would ask to react to a new consulting venture – a service aimed at helping corporations design and carry out strategically focused social responsibility programs.

"Well, I think you may be on to something," Kendall said after listening to Bill and me outline our plans. "Think you could get more companies interested in the arts?"

Bill turned to me. "Yes, I think we can," I replied.

Kendall said he would consider how his company might use Weeden Management Systems, Inc. (WMS) to back up PepsiCo's company foundation. We were on the launch pad ready to land a deal with our first major client. But life and death would get in the way – and Kendall's kind offer to help WMS get off the ground was never accepted.

After leaving the picturesque PepsiCo campus, Bill and I headed south to Washington, DC for a meeting with the 43-year-old head of the U.S. Chamber of Commerce Foundation. "This guy's engine runs at full speed 24/7," Bill prepped me before we sat down with Tom Donohue. "What he's doing now is just a pit stop. It won't be long before he'll be top dog for a much bigger operation."

Bill had an uncanny way of sniffing out potential and as soon as I was introduced to Donohue, I knew Bramstedt was right. In addition to heading the Chamber's relatively new foundation, Donohue was charged with building the organization's grassroots political platform. That connected him with power brokers all over Washington. It would come as no surprise a few years later that the American Trucking Association would recruit him as its president and CEO.

Donald M. Kendall Sculpture Gardens   *Tom J. Donohue*

"I think Milton Friedman is right," Donohue said a few minutes into our meeting. "The only social responsibility businesses have is to make profit."

The reference was to an oft-quoted article that had appeared in the *New York Times* a decade earlier. Friedman was the American economist who won the Nobel Memorial Prize in Economic Sciences. He argued businesses shouldn't support charitable activities (especially higher education) because in a free-enterprise society, that kind of spending was an inappropriate use of business resources.

"But what if charitable support could legally and ethically help businesses make a *bigger* profit?" I asked.

Donohue hesitated and then said: "If that's do-able, I'm in."

Bill and I left with the U.S. Chamber Foundation agreeing to buy a couple of consulting days to review plans for ways the organization could secure tax-deductible charitable gifts to carry out programs and activities relevant to its member constituency. We had our first client.

The rest of the East Coast trip was a whirlwind with more top-tier meetings in New York. By the time we flew back to California, Bill had given WMS an incredibly valuable front-office buzz. Two days passed and while Bill was having lunch at the Pacific-Union Club with Tom Clausen, CEO of the Bank of America, I was on the phone with a Xerox vice president in Stamford, Connecticut. The word was out: I was available to help businesses either create or beef up their social responsibility portfolios.

The next week, I flew east to begin several days of work with a Xerox team. While at the company's headquarters, I was contacted by a high-level executive at Continental Group located only a town away. The corporation was a diversified holding business that had grown out of what was once the world's largest packaging firm, Continental Can Company.

"Confidentially, we're going to break up the company," the Continental executive said. "There will be repercussions in certain places."

"Places like where you'll be closing plants and offices?" I asked.

"Exactly," the executive confirmed. "We want to put together a plan that lessens the pain as much as possible. What kind of philanthropy can we use as part of an exit strategy? That's where we need your help and we need it fast."

Early the next week, I signed a non-disclosure agreement with Continental Group and learned how the business was going to be chopped apart both in the U.S. and Europe. While outlining recommendations for my newest client, I called Bill Bramstedt to check on developments back in San Francisco.

"Bank of America may want our help at some point in the future," Bill noted. "But for now, you need to touch base with

Merck in New Jersey. They just called and want to meet with you as soon as possible."

"Bill, all the action is happening on the East Coast," I pointed out the obvious.

"Seems to be," Bill agreed. "At least for now."

"But I'm living in California."

Bramstedt held off responding for a few seconds and then said: "Yes, well … that might have to change."

Bill was not only my business partner; he was my personal confidant. He knew all the details about my failing marriage, which had finally dissolved into a divorce. When not parked in a motel somewhere east of the Mississippi, my temporary home was now a two-bedroom rental in Tiburon, another upscale Marin County town just north of the Golden Gate Bridge. Under terms of the divorce, the Mill Valley house was sold and delivered a handsome profit. My now ex-wife moved 50 miles north to a ranch house in a rural town called Sebastopol close to her teaching job. While contentious at times, the divorce had ended with an acceptable division of property, a child support payment agreement but no alimony since my ex-wife was earning a reasonable salary. The one issue that cut deeply was child custody. The divorce proceeding included mandatory mediation that probed whether the kids would be better off with a mother whose work didn't take her far from home or a father who seemed to be increasingly nomadic. I tried to convince the mediator I could revamp my career path and find work that wouldn't require a lot of business travel – possibly even remaining with the Asia Foundation. The argument didn't resonate. "Given the ages of the dependents, affording the mother primary custody is determined to be in the best interest of the children," was the mediator's conclusion.

One of the darkest moments of my life was a bright California afternoon when my four children ended a visit to my small apartment. It was the day before they were to move to their new Sebastopol home. I watched from a front window as they walked from the front door to my ex-wife's car. Each step they took was a gut punch. For hours after they left, I sat weeping on the carpet of my sparsely furnished apartment trying to grasp the full enormity of what was happening. Divorce had exploded a family into pieces with the children likely to be scarred the most. And to a large degree, this was a calamity of my own making.

"Well, you can keep beating yourself up," Bill Bramstedt said later. "Or you can figure out how to make a bad situation a little less traumatic."

I confessed to Bill I didn't have a clue as to what to do. He parsed the issue in two and said first, I had a parenting obligation to my children even if that responsibility needed to be delivered long distance. "Second, you have a financial commitment," Bill added. "And a big one."

Bramstedt was right, as he usually was. My monthly child support requirements weren't overly burdensome but there were a lot of "add-ons." There would be travel costs needed to move the kids back and forth from Sebastopol to wherever I might be, supplemental expenses for clothing, entertainment, and more. But most of all, there were looming college costs. Although not spelled out in the divorce decree, I pledged to cover whatever college or comparable costs my kids would incur.

"You need to get the consulting business up to speed," Bill noted. "Build a client base on the East Coast and start making money. In the meantime, I'll keep on developing the West Coast client base. If things work out, hire somebody to take over the east and move back to California."

Thanks to Bill, at least I had a plan. He also pointed me in the direction of another **life lesson: some problems can never be fully resolved; but all problems can be mitigated.** Bill's observation was not only helpful to me personally, it proved important to many of my consulting clients. I was often hired to help a business facing a serious challenge. "I can't make the problem go away," I would sometime say at the start of my assignment, "but I can help lessen the consequences." For most corporations, that was good enough.

The consulting gigs kept coming one after the other. There was no need for advertising. With Bramstedt's connections and word-of-mouth recommendations, the business steadily grew. Over the years, Weeden Management Systems provided services to corporations in a panoply of industry sectors:

* Xerox	* Starbucks
* Continental Group	* Northwestern Mutual
(Continental Can)	* Hasbro
* Allied Signal	* Horizon Blue Cross Blue
(now Honeywell)	Shield of NJ
* Merck	* Wellpoint Health Networks
* General Motors	* Anthem
* Bank of America	* Shell Oil
* Amgen	* Newell Brands
* Chrysler (now Fiat Chrysler)	* Sony
* Novartis Pharmaceuticals	* Turner Broadcasting
* Becton Dickinson	* Noble Energy
* AstraZeneca	* Bausch & Lomb
* Cisco	* Johnson & Johnson

Most of my engagements would begin as rudimentary assignments with some turning far more interesting and challenging. Case in point: the pharmaceutical giant, Merck.

In the early 1980s, Merck's U.S. headquarters was connected to one of its manufacturing facilities in a gritty part of Rahway, New Jersey not far from the state's 27-acre maximum-security prison. Of all the pharmaceutical industry home offices around the nation, this was arguably the least impressive. This was a strictly no-frills operation overseen by a likeable CEO named John Lloyd Huck.

"Call me Lloyd," the top Merck executive said seconds after I was introduced to a man who looked like he had been chiseled out of a Brooks Brothers ad. Brooklyn born, Huck had worked his way up the Merck ladder via a sales and marketing route nabbing the CEO chair in 1978. "I want you to help Grace Winterling set up a first-rate corporate philanthropy program," he told me.

Grace was a kind, older woman who for years had worked alongside some of Merck's most senior executives. She had been moved out of her administrative assistant role to oversee the company's rather insignificant and disorganized charitable giving efforts. Grace was not that far from retirement, and for her this late-career assignment was a plum.

Like many other businesses, Merck spent little money or executive time managing its corporate philanthropy. But to Lloyd Huck's credit, he sensed there was potential in beefing up the company's social responsibility commitments. So, with his backing, Grace and I cobbled together a basic but functional corporate giving program including a "matching gifts" option that obligated Merck to match dollar-for-dollar those donations made by employees to certain nonprofit organizations. A few line and staff executives were pulled together as a corporate contributions committee that met periodically, mainly to take credit for whatever work Grace carried out.

As I was wrapping up my Merck assignment, Lloyd Huck called me into his office for two reasons: to thank me for helping Grace and to talk about Penn State. Lloyd and his wife were avid Penn Staters, so much so they would end up giving the university over $40 million.

"A friend of mine is a Johnson & Johnson vice president," Lloyd said. "I'd like you to meet him. He and I are both on the Penn State board. Sometime soon, we may need your help."

Little did I know the Johnson & Johnson introduction would have a profound impact on my career.

"Before I tie things up with Grace," I said, "there are a few products Merck might want to consider donating down the line." I handed him a short list of prescription drugs the company manufactured.

"Why?"

Like most other pharmaceutical and medical device manufacturers, Merck was already making occasional gifts of slow-moving and other less-valuable inventory to qualified nonprofit organizations. By doing so, the corporation took a modest charitable deduction for these donations.

"There's talk the 1962 tax law that set the rules for product giving is going to be changed," I explained. "The word is there may be a stepped-up tax write-off for certain kinds of product donations."

Lloyd took time to listen to my prediction and then told me to book a few more consulting days to make sure Merck would be ready to capitalize on the tax law change if it happened.

Lloyd Huck

Countries Affected by River Blindness

And it did happen. In 1984, the Treasury Department changed its regulations so businesses could give away product and be awarded with a "bonus" charitable deduction equal to the cost of the goods *plus* an "enhanced deduction" calculated as half the difference between cost and fair market value. The financially beneficial change prompted many corporations to get much more serious about "noncash giving." But it would be Merck that would be widely recognized as the king of product donations.

In 1987, Merck announced it would donate one of its drugs called Mectizan through a partnership with the Task Force for Global Health to treat a devastating disease known as onchocerciasis or river blindness. Restricted mostly to remote locations in very poor areas of the world (Africa, Latin America, parts of the Middle East), the disease gets transmitted by blackflies and left untreated usually puts victims on a path to a complete loss of vision. Labeled the Mectizan Donation Program, Merck would turn the initiative into the longest-running neglected tropical disease drug donation program in the world. Over 300 million people would gain access to Mectizan every year. It also became the gold standard for corporate noncash giving and inspired many other businesses to donate some of their inventory not just as a charitable commitment but as a wise tax strategy as well.

I was about to leave Merck's Rahway campus one late afternoon when I called my voice mail to check for messages.

"Curt, call me immediately!"

Before the woman left her name and phone number, I recognized her familiar voice. It was Geri Bell, one of my Asia Foundation colleagues. I returned the call bracing for what I knew had to be bad news. It was.

"Bill…" Geri hesitated and then stabbed me with her message. "Bill Bramstedt. He's dead."

The friend and counselor who was guiding me through the most traumatic transition of my life was gone. Bill Bramstedt was the gentlest, kindest, most non-judgmental man I had come to know over the years. His death left an immense void.

Months after Bill's funeral, consulting work became more and more concentrated on the East Coast. Without Bramstedt cultivating California clients, demand for WMS services west of the Mississippi was minimal. Any hope of my moving the business back to the Bay Area had faded so I traded my Tiberon apartment for an unremarkable second-floor walk-up in a New Jersey suburb. I did most of my work with businesses located along the Route 95 corridor from Delaware to Connecticut, and I was able to combine my few consulting days in California with visits with my children. Only rarely did I agree to short-term assignments with companies in the Midwest. One of those consulting jobs made a lasting impression. "Are those checks you're signing, sir?" I asked the man seated across from me. I had been invited to spend a few minutes with the CEO of General Motors, a business leader some considered the most powerful executive in America possibly even the world. I had just completed a cursory assessment of GM's philanthropy program.

"They are," Roger Smith replied, working his pen while he talked. "Checks and notes I send to charities."

"You … you hand sign contribution checks…?" I couldn't hold back my disbelief. This was the top dog of the then largest corporation on the planet taking time out of his day to put his name on a pile of checks. "It's the most satisfying part of my job," Smith said.

I don't know if Roger Smith was exaggerating or whether this display was mostly a show. He knew I was working with other high-level business executives designing social responsibility strategies. Maybe he thought I would spread the word to a slew of private sector movers and shakers that GM's CEO was personally invested in how and why his corporation connected to nonprofit organizations. If that were his goal, it worked. Because after Michael Moore released his searing but impressive film, *Roger & Me* in 1989, I was a counterweight.

"The man decimated Flint, Michigan," friends would tell me. "He closed plants all over the place and put thousands of people out of work!"

I didn't argue what was a well-publicized fact. Instead, I said: "But I saw another side of the man. He was one of the few CEOs who personally took time to connect his company with a lot of nonprofit organizations." Well, at least I thought he did.

Whether genuine or not, Smith had an awareness of how a corporation's perceived association with the nonprofit world could score points with different stakeholders – from investors to business analysts. These corporate-nonprofit connections would prove to be even more important to companies facing potentially catastrophic public relations challenges – companies such as Allied-Signal (now Honeywell).

In 1985, the New Jersey-based Allied Corporation – once known as the Allied Chemical Corporation – merged with Signal Companies, a huge West Coast oil and aerospace business. The newly combined business became increasingly dependent on government defense contracts. As part of its expanded operations, Allied-Signal operated the world's biggest chromium reduction plant near Baltimore Maryland's inner harbor. Chromium is not only used in making stainless steel and other metals, it is also important to certain ink and paint products. The 27-acre plant, formerly called Baltimore Works, had been in the chromium business for over 100 years, long before it was acquired by Allied. But in 1985, an investigation discovered that over 60 pounds of chromium tailings were being dumped daily into Baltimore Harbor. Contaminating a waterway so close to Washington, DC was not in the best interests of a corporation reliant on winning federal government contracts. Allied-Signal closed the plant in 1985 and a $110 million cleanup operation would soon follow. But even before the operation was shuttered, it was clear more needed to be done to redeem the corporation's sullied social responsibility reputation.

"There are a few members of Congress who are really important to us," Alan Painter said. "They can kill a defense contract opportunity in a nanosecond. What can we do to show them we're a decent corporate citizen?"

Alan was a retired Marine Corps lieutenant colonel and now Allied-Signal's director of community affairs. He reported to Ed Hennessey, a testy CEO who once studied to be a priest but had morphed into a business leader known more for his arrogance than his benevolence.

"These Congressional people who are so important to Allied-Signal – do they all come together on any other standing committee?" I asked.

Alan said he didn't know but would ask the company's Washington representatives to find out. Shortly after, we were told most of the key government players were on the U.S. House Permanent Select Committee on Aging, led by Florida's Claude Pepper who had a well-deserved reputation as a champion of the elderly.

"A branded program on aging," I suggested.

"What?"

"No corporation is known for taking the lead in dealing with problems facing older Americans," I noted. "Let's come up with an Allied-Signal initiative that will put the company in the spotlight as the frontrunner. It will get Pepper's attention, not to mention the other 65 members of Congress who sit on his committee."

"An interesting idea," Alan said. "But how do we even begin to make this happen?"

"With the right partner," I replied. Although not evident at the time, it was another **life lesson: a partner should bring as much or more to you as you bring to the partner.**

The Johns Hopkins Center on Aging was one of just a handful of academic centers around the country reputed to be on the leading edge of aging research. With some convincing and a sizeable corporate contribution, the university agreed to lock arms with Allied-Signal. It administered a program designed to "recognize and focus public attention to the works of individuals who make significant contributions through medical research, health care delivery or public policy in medicine and health care, all to enhance the quality of life for older persons." Each year, the corporation held an annual awards presentation at the Washington, DC Four Seasons Hotel where high achieving individuals were each presented with $30,000 in cash and a Steuben glass sculpture that quickly became heralded in the aging community. Present at the yearly awards event were older stage and screen celebrities as well as a long list of other notables ... including members of the Congressional Select Committee on Aging.

Eventually, Allied-Signal's chromium woes faded. The company enjoyed a much more positive recognition thanks in part to its private sector leadership in tackling an oft-overlooked social challenge.

Hardly by design, WMS had became a "go-to" resource for companies looking for ways to solve business problems, recruit or retain employees, and bolster their top or bottom line financial performance. Increasingly, WMS was straying from its main mission – to push corporations to allocate added funding for business-relevant nonprofit programs and activities. All this was happening at the same time corporate contributions as measured as a percent of pretax profits was on a decline. It was a development that triggered a decision to make still another career path adjustment.

**

Don Kendall would step down as PepsiCo's CEO in 1986. The company would honor the retired executive by naming the meticulously landscaped grounds surrounding its headquarters building the Donald M. Kendall Sculpture Gardens. The 168 acres with 45 pieces of outdoor sculpture would be open to the public.

Tom Donohue would return to the U.S. Chamber of Commerce as its president in 1997. He would lead the country's largest lobbying group, spending more money on lobbying than any other organization on a yearly basis. Donohue would earn a reputation as the "George Patton of the trade association world" with the *Washington Post* making this observation: "Nobody has mastered this new Washington game better than Thomas J. Donohue."

Lloyd Huck would retire from Merck in 1986. Six years later, the company would relocate its no-frills U.S. headquarters from Rahway to an opulent, hexagon-shaped building constructed on a former dairy farm in Whitehouse Station, New Jersey. A small forest of trees would be planted around the building, turning Merck's home into "the corporate cottage in the woods." Considered overly extravagant by some, the 1,000-acre campus would be sold to a California IT company, UNICOM Global. Merck would then move its headquarters to Kenilworth, another New Jersey location.

Called "one of the worst American CEOs of all time" by CNBC, Roger Smith would end his General Motors career in 1990 and die in 2007. He would be disparaged for poor acquisition, reorganization, and automation decisions. GM would be left with a mountain of debt before his departure from the corporation.

In 1999, AlliedSignal would spend $15 billion to purchase Honeywell. Although the enlarged company would keep its headquarters in Morris County, New Jersey, it would rebrand itself by taking on the more recognizable name, Honeywell. Edward Hennessy, the brusque CEO known for his hair-trigger temper, would leave his CEO post in 1991.

Chapter 10

Weeden Management Systems – Sidetracks (1980-90)

"From Tyson's down the road," the plump woman behind the cafeteria serving counter said proudly. She waved at trays of fried chicken, baked chicken, and a cauldron of chicken soup. For those who worked at the sprawling Walmart headquarters in Bentonville, Arkansas – a next-door neighbor to Tyson Foods - chicken was without question the main source of protein.

Arthur White, the well-known and much beloved marketing research guru, ordered a chicken salad sandwich. I picked the daily special: chicken a la king.

"You have any idea what Sam Walton is worth?" Arthur asked while carefully extricating two sliced pickles from his sandwich.

"Not a clue," I said.

"Two billion. And he still drives a pickup and eats chicken. A lot of chicken."

We were in Bentonville to work with a Walmart corporate team charged with putting together a "Buy America" campaign. The company's celebrated 66-year-old chairman was on a crusade to stop the flow of imports into the U.S. He had sent letters to 3,000 manufacturers and wholesalers telling them his 753 discount stores wanted to see more American goods. Arthur's company, Yankelovich, Skelly & White, was engaged as a partner to help monitor public (especially customer) attitudes about the campaign.

"American shoppers could be more price conscious than they are patriotic," I stated the obvious. "There's a chance they'll run to Kmart if imports are cheaper."

Arthur nodded. It wasn't his job to judge the logic of the new Walmart initiative, just to measure consumer reactions. Sam Walton had built his business and amassed his fortune on the buying practices of Americans who patronized his stores, most of which were in rural parts of the country. Walton didn't like seeing small-town workers losing jobs because imports led to plant closings.

"Arthur…" I began, not certain this was the right time to bring up a decision I had made days earlier. "I'm working with quite a few companies helping them with their cash and product giving strategies."

"Yeah, I know," Arthur smiled. "That's terrific."

Walmart Headquarters   *Spell Checker & Logo Trouble*

"I need to make it more terrific," I said. "It's supposed to be my core business, Arthur. The point is, I need to stop taking on side jobs."

"So, what are you saying?" asked Arthur. "What we're doing here in Bentonville isn't ... core?"

"For me, it's not," I said.

"More like a diversion?"

"Hmm ... More like a learning opportunity that's interesting but not what should be on my radar screen."

Arthur laughed. He got the point. We had known each other a long time and communication between the two of us had become honest and easy. Over the years, Arthur would call and ask if I could join him to handle certain special – and sometimes bizarre – projects. I rarely said "no" because spending a few days with one of the most engaging and genuinely caring individuals I knew was always a pleasure.

"If it weren't for me, you wouldn't be in Arkansas eating chicken at what is looking more and more like corporate America's king of the mountain," Arthur said, unaware of how accurate his prognostication would be.

"And a few months ago, you had me in Cincinnati saving Procter & Gamble from the devil."

"So I did," Arthur chuckled. "And wasn't that fascinating?"

Actually, it was. I had been added to the Yankelovich, Skelly and White team to survey customer attitudes about P&G after the company was accused of being in cahoots with the prince of darkness. A few evangelists had been spreading false claims about how the company's logo (since changed) was a disguised campaign to promote Beelzebub. The logo featured a line drawing of the man-in-the-moon with a stringy beard that to some looked far too much like three inverted sixes – which, according to the Book of Revelation, was Satan's favorite number combination. Calls to boycott Tide, Vicks cough drops, Mr. Clean, and a bundle of P&G's many other products were heard in a few parts of the country, mainly in the South.

"Our data helped convince the company to change the moon face to a friendlier, more modern look" Arthur reminded me.

"You're making my point," I said. "We spent time saving the company's top and bottom lines, not coming up with ways P&G could do more to save society."

Arthur knew I wasn't about to change my mind. I was at the front edge of another **life lesson: pursue purpose; deflect distraction.** On many occasions, Arthur and I had discussed my obsession with why and how businesses could and should do more to address social problems. That was my self-assigned course heading. To get where I wanted to go meant fending off other tempting but less relevant options. And when it came to Arthur White, there was never a shortage of project temptations.

Passing up future opportunities to work with Arthur was not an easy decision. He was an inspiring gnome, short and stocky with limitless ideas and boundless energy. He would forever be a friend, but I had to opt out of being his sidekick on time-consuming ventures that would take me off course.

"So, what about IBM?"

"I shut that one down," I answered. Arthur looked surprised and I could understand why. The IBM relationship had the potential to be both long-term and highly profitable. It was at a Mamaroneck, New York bar where a senior executive from Continental Group passed along my name to an IBM vice president looking for someone to teach effective writing skills to computer engineers. A couple of weeks later, I was in a room with a half dozen geeks outlining ways to convert a mishmash of technical information into simple, intelligible letters and business plans. The small-group seminars were helpful and I was asked to plug IBM into my consulting schedule on an ongoing basis.

"You dumped the spell check deal?" Arthur asked, looking more incredulous.

I explained how appreciative I was that IBM even considered me as a partner on an important project development team, but I had to decline because of time constraints. IBM was trying to stay ahead of the fast-developing spell checker field. The company had been first out of the gate with a spell-check system thanks to a group of six Georgetown University linguists retained to develop the software. That breakthrough led to a rush of competitors jumping into the spellcheck world including Macintosh, VAX, and Unix. By upgrading its word processing service to include more writing and grammar aids, IBM thought it could leapfrog back to the front of the pack. I would be part of the leapfrogging.

"So, you think you can do nothing but work on saving the world," Arthur chortled.

"I hope I can."

Arthur brushed a few crumbs from his pinstripe suit. "Impossible. I know you too well. You have intellectual attention deficit disorder."

"No, I don't."

Arthur gave me one of his *get real* looks. As it turned out, he knew me better than I knew myself. Many years later, he would point to three examples of just how right he was on that day in Bentonville, Arkansas.

Distraction #1: Merryman Engineering – blind luck?

I don't recall who introduced me to Wayne and Joan Merryman. What I do remember is being invited to their ranch-style home in Lafayette, a town on the eastern side of California's Berkeley Hills, connected to San Francisco by the Bay Area Rapid Transit system. The Merryman's cozy house was wrapped in vines, shrubs, and vegetation common in a town known for its Mediterranean climate.

"Do you know anything about steel mills?" Wayne asked me over a tall glass of lemonade. It was summer and hot. The temperatures in Lafayette would sometimes crack the100 mark.

"Not really," I admitted.

"When steel or just about any other material is manufactured in rolls, sheets have to fall within a certain tolerance range," he said. "In other words, when rolled out, a sheet can't be too thick or too thin."

"Okay."

"Making sure product isn't too thick is usually not a problem," Wayne went on. "But rolling steel that's too thin? Well, that's tricky. It's a bad day if a steel roll doesn't meet spec, meaning the roll gets rejected and sent back to the plant."

I had no idea where the conversation was going. But the lemonade was tasty, so I kept listening.

"What manufacturers do is add a little extra steel during the rolling process just to make sure they don't fall short on the thin side. In most cases, what's added is more than what's actually needed."

Wayne paused and fumbled to find a napkin to wipe the sweat from his lemonade glass. "Supposing steel mills had a measuring device so accurate they could reduce the amount of excess metal by just a fraction of a millimeter?"

I took a guess and replied that steel companies would save a lot of money.

"Millions and millions of dollars," Wayne confirmed. "Come with me."

We went inside to what looked to have once been a bedroom. Wayne lifted a plexiglass cover from a small but complicated-looking device hooked to a computer. He walked me through an explanation of how this contraption worked and ended with a compelling pitch about how his device was a manufacturing game changer. His problem? He needed to catch the attention of someone fairly high up in the steel industry who would be willing to give his invention a chance to prove itself.

"You can get me into Bethlehem Steel," Wayne said.

"I can?"

"That's what a friend of a friend told me," Wayne replied. "You know people all over the place."

It was an overblown compliment aimed at convincing me to kick open a door or two. Another hour and a lemonade refill later, I agreed to make a few phone calls.

"Why would you do that?" a friend asked days later after I reluctantly confessed how I gave in to Wayne Merryman's request. "You said you weren't going to let yourself get sidetracked from kicking businesses into being better corporate citizens."

"Not exactly my words," I said. "But you're right. This puts me on an off-ramp but it's something I think I have to do."

"But *why?*"

"Because ..." I paused. "Because Wayne Merryman is blind."

Well, not 100 percent blind. Wayne could make out objects one or two feet in front of him. Anything else was lost in a colorless fog or total darkness. He relied on his wife and his requisite white cane to navigate his home and too frequent trips to doctors who treated him for medical problems unrelated to his vision impairment. For years, Wayne had squinted to piece together his ingenious electrical measurement system, applying an old technology to a contemporary need.

"Know anything about the Doppler effect?" Wayne asked me while I was at his home.

"Not a clue."

"Doppler was an Austrian mathematician who played around with frequencies," Wayne said. "He figured out back in the 1800s that sound waves change when bounced off things that move."

I knew Wayne was dumbing down the explanation and I appreciated him doing so. He stopped talking and gave me a first-hand demonstration of his invention. He switched on a mini rolling device designed to replicate steel being processed through a huge roller. A metal arm stretched out over a loop of fabric moving at a dizzying speed. Small cylinders mounted on the arm shot ultrasound beams into the cloth.

"In a steel mill, this computer will collect ultrasound readings and then control the rollers that determine how thin or thick the metal should be," Wayne said proudly. "Using the Doppler method, steel can be rolled more accurately than ever before."

I had no idea if Wayne was on to something or just blowing smoke. But he was so passionate about his invention, I agreed to look for someone in the steel industry who might be willing to give it a fair evaluation. I had just finished a consulting assignment with the pharmaceutical company AstraZeneca in Delaware and recalled a vice president telling me he had a friend who was high up at Bethlehem Steel's massive plant at Sparrow's Point in Baltimore, Maryland.

"Ever see the inside of a steel mill?" the Bethlehem Steel executive asked me weeks later. Thanks to AstraZeneca, I had been extended an invitation to drive to the spit of land once used for growing peaches and now the site of an enormous industrial complex.

"Nope."

"I'll give you a quick tour." The manager tossed me a hard hat and led the way into a massive building stretching four miles from end to end. If there were any place on the planet that mimicked hell, this was it. Molten steel ran like a river as open hearths spewed fiery bits of glowing metal into the air.

"This plant made girders for the Golden Gate Bridge!" the manager shouted over a thunderous roar than shook the building. "Cables for the George Washington Bridge!"

We spent several minutes perched on a catwalk watching liquid metal turn into steel ingots. Then the manager motioned me back to his quiet office. He asked to see the pictures of Merryman's Doppler device I had brought with me.

Bethlehem Steel – Sparrow's Point, Maryland

"Well, we've never tried anything like this," the manager said. "Interesting idea. We could run a trial at our headquarters lab in Pennsylvania. Would Merryman be willing to send us his device so we could play around with the thing?"

Wayne was more than willing. His invention was shipped to a corporate address and over the next month, the Doppler system was tested in a secure laboratory by a covey of intrigued engineers. Merryman's equipment sparked a lot of interest and a long list of technical questions. The next step was to bring Merryman east to meet face-to-face with the company's research and development team.

Wayne and his wife, Joan, booked a flight to Philadelphia two weeks later. The plan was for Joan to rent a car and drive to the company's headquarters located in a small city aptly named Bethlehem. Wayne had talked me into showing up for the meeting to help map out next steps assuming the corporation wanted to move forward. I wasn't keen about giving up another consulting day but saying "no" to Merryman was difficult to do.

I made the drive to Lehigh Valley in Eastern Pennsylvania and had no trouble finding Bethlehem's 21-story headquarters building. It was the tallest structure in the city. Opened in 1972, the building was a showstopper constructed in the shape of a cross, giving most every office a window view. When it was first occupied, the mini-skyscraper was a towering testimonial to the steel industry's economic muscle. Things would radically change in the years ahead.

"We just got word from Mr. Merryman's wife," one of nine engineers seated in a handsome meeting room said. "Seems he became ill at the airport in California. He won't be with us. Perhaps you can stand in and answer some of our questions."

I gulped and braced myself for what would turn into one of the most uncomfortable 30 minutes of my life.

Will your readings be the same for 18-gauge mild sheet metal as well as stainless? What about grade 403 stainless – will the system be as accurate as with grade 316? Are you familiar with the Tresca yield criterion? Does the unit get repositioned depending on recrystallization?

I danced around as many questions as possible, constantly reminding the nine men (no women) I was technically challenged, especially when it came to steel production. It didn't take long for everyone to realize this meeting was a total waste of time, so one engineer pushed back his chair and headed for the door. "See if Mr. Merryman can send a back-up who knows what he's talking about if we ever do this again," he called out to me.

Since all was now lost, it didn't matter what I said in response. "Seeing isn't easy for a man who's blind."

The engineer who was about to exit turned to face me. "Mr. Merryman is *blind?*"

"Pretty much."

"A *blind* man made this system?"

"He did."

Murmurs filled the room.

"Tell Mr. Merryman we'll get back to him."

I drove back to New Jersey convinced Bethlehem would pass on Merryman's measurement device. Had I not been a technical moron, the meeting might have ended differently. I also felt guilty about playing the vision impairment card. Wayne was not the type who courted sympathy for his disability. He wanted his invention to win favor based on its own merits. Too late now – this deal was finished.

About a month later, a late evening phone call. "They want it!" Wayne Merryman yelled.

"What?"

"Sparrow's Point! It will be a trial. But it will go on a line at Sparrow's Point!"

I was too stunned to say anything. Bethlehem signed a contract with Wayne that included a small consulting fee and travel expenses for him to oversee the test at Sparrow's Point. I was astonished Bethlehem had agreed to go ahead with a trial given my calamitous performance weeks before. Merryman was thrilled and so was I. But the joy was short-lived.

The Sparrow's Point test was a complete disaster. As impressive as Wayne's device was in a controlled, contaminant-free laboratory, it was totally useless in an environment where bits of metal flew in all directions. Merryman's ultrasound readings were incessantly disrupted by fragments of hot steel burped out of a roll as it went through the processing cycle. On all accounts, Wayne's invention was a giant flop.

Shortly after his return to California, I called Merryman to tell him how sorry I was about the Sparrow's Point outcome. Wayne didn't seem overly upset and said he was working on a protective cage that would keep his ultrasound equipment from being distorted by a steel mill's flying debris. I wished him the best of luck. Many months would pass before I made a follow-up call to check on Wayne's progress.

"Well, he's had some medical setbacks," Joan Merryman told me. She apologized that Wayne was sleeping and couldn't come to the phone.

"I'm so sorry."

"Oh, it's not like he's stopped thinking about ways to come up with the next best thing," she said. "He's always been something of a visionary. Still is."

Wayne would continue to struggle with his health and eyesight until his death. While I wish he could have left behind a measurement instrument destined to become a manufacturing staple, he did leave something for me – a valuable **life lesson: visions that are possible are not always probable.** I learned how important due diligence is in weighing any opportunity whether professional or personal. Before going all in on a strong possibility, calculate the probability of success. Scout out potential negatives that could impinge on promised positives. The goal is not to pour cold water on a hot vision but rather to establish the odds for getting to the finish line. If the possible is only remotely probable, then time and resources might be better pointed toward a more achievable vision. Put another way, it's probability and not possibility that should be the main litmus test for any idea. It turns out Wayne Merryman's calibration system was not his only invention. Looking back, I think I could have served him better by advising him which of his many visions had the greatest probability of crossing the goal line.

**

In 2001, Bethlehem Steel – once the second largest steel producer and largest shipbuilder in America – declared bankruptcy. The headquarters building was vacated in 2007 and stood empty for years. A decision was made to demolish the building in 2019.

Joan Merryman died in 2008. She asked that donations made in the memory of her late husband be directed to the Books on Tape Merryman Endowment Fund at the Lafayette Library.

Distraction #2: Healthcheck Communications, Inc. – weighty opportunity?

Only 5% of dieters succeed.
Only 90+% of people who lose weight keep the pounds off.

So opened the business plan for Healthcheck Communications, one of a profusion of enterprises all aspiring to help people shed weight and make a lot of money at the same time. Healthcheck's point of difference?

"We bring people together to assist them in building new healthy behaviors via the privacy and convenience of the telephone."

Hatched in the 1980s, a decade before the internet became a viable commercial tool, Healthcheck jumped into what was at the time a $10 billion-a-year market. More importantly, it was a field wide open to new business ventures as an ever-growing number of overweight Americans cycled through one diet plan after another. Numerous players vied for customers ranging from weight loss clubs (Weight Watchers, Diet Center, Overeaters Anonymous), liquid fasting products (Optifast, Medifast), special foods (Nutri/System, LeanLine), and even video/audio services (Deal a Meal, Sybervision). Still, because plus-sized consumers were so ready to try "the next best thing" in the dieting world, Healthcheck was pitched as a sure-fire winner.

"I need you in the game," John Simon said after buying me a beer at a New Brunswick, New Jersey pub.

"Let me get this straight." I said. "You want *me* to help peddle a dieting scheme."

John shook his head. "It's not a scheme. It's about getting people to adopt healthy eating and exercise habits. And yes, I want you to be part of this deal."

I stood up. "Look at me. I'm super *skinny*! Practically the invisible man. Heavy people resent beanpoles like me."

"Heavy people aren't going to see you," said John. "I'm the one who needs to see you. And so does Johnson & Johnson."

John Simon was in his early 40s and admired for both his intelligence and his ability to sniff out money-making business opportunities mainly in the health field. John was a fellow in preventative medicine at Harvard Medical School and an instructor at the Georgetown University School of Medicine. He was also my good friend.

"John, this whole thing is so out of my orbit it's ridiculous to even ..." I was cut off before debunking what was an insane idea.

"$150,000."

"What?"

"Johnson & Johnson will put $150,000 on the table as start-up funding with more to come if we hit a few milestones," John explained. "But J&J wants you working with me or the deal's going to be a whole lot more difficult to sell."

I had established a growing relationship with J&J including working on a few big-dollar acquisitions. I assumed J&J wanted me in the mix just to minimize the risk of having its investment go up in smoke.

"I just don't have the time," I protested.

"Mostly after-hour stuff," John explained. "Beef up the business plan. Work over multi-year revenue and margin forecasts. You can do this in your sleep. And this doesn't have to be long-term. A couple of years and I can buy back your share of the business."

After another two beers, I reluctantly agreed to take 49% ownership in Healthcheck Communications, Inc. John was the majority shareholder. Since my life's plan was not to run a weight-loss enterprise, I would exit Healthcheck within three years and leave behind any management responsibilities that might have come my way. John would have the option of buying me out based on an agreed-upon valuation of Healthcheck's stock.

A week later, we put together a more robust business plan. J&J wasted no time in coming through with its $150,000 in exchange for a small equity position in Healthcheck, which immediately diluted my stake in the company. I should have considered this an omen, but at the time, I was dazzled by John's insistence that this was going to revolutionize the diet world.

Healthcheck Communications offered four different products all dependent on the telephone:

First, a library of three-minute taped messages about all aspects of dieting and exercising accessible to callers on a pay-by-the-minute call-in 900 number available any time day or night. Dial up information such as … *How to beat impulse eating. Ways to stay under 1,500 calories a day. Calorie information about fast foods.*

Second, another 900 call-in chat line open to those who wanted or needed to connect with other weight-challenged callers anywhere in the USA.

Third, special "Weight Support Groups" scheduled to convene (by phone) 30 minutes every week. Four paying participants linked up with a trained weight-management counselor to discuss diet goals and challenges.

And fourth, the ultimate and most costly option – a personalized 24-page weight analysis and diet plan tailored to a participant's age, sex, lifestyle, occupation, and other factors. A weight loss counselor would set up a series of 15 minute consultations to make sure participants didn't stray from their weight loss goals.

From day one, I was under-whelmed by what Healthcheck had to offer. It was far from the snazzy dieting breakthrough John made it out to be. But my new business partner cautioned me not to judge – after all, I never had to walk in the shoes of a heavy person.

"We have J&J's money," I said, putting aside my skepticism. "Now what?"

"Mall intercepts, a national phone survey, and a couple of focus groups," John replied. "Then at least two TV ad spots – 30 and 60 seconds."

And that's what happened. Healthcheck hired a firm to corner hefty-looking shoppers at a mammoth mall in Livingston, New Jersey. Reactions to the four program options were used to construct a survey instrument that was then given to a telemarketing firm. Over 800 random household calls were placed and the results were less than encouraging. The call-in group counseling idea was a bust. The personal weight counseling concept came across as "probably too expensive." The three-minute taped messages and chat line were of some interest largely among younger people (women) who were looking to lose ten pounds or less.

"I think we have something here," John said after pouring over the phone survey results.

"We do?" I scratched my bald head. Was I looking at the same spread sheet as John Simon?

"Enough to go to a couple of focus groups with sample TV spots pushing the tape library and 24-hour-a-day talk line."

John was well connected to the ad world and in short order, we had a 30- and 60-second demo featuring a couple in their mid-30s who were almost as lean as I was.

"The woman – she looks like a Barbie doll," I commented.

"Exactly," John smiled. "She looks the way women *want* to look." He reminded me that our research confirmed Healthcheck's target audience was the 56 percent of American women ages 25 to 64 who wanted to lose weight.

Focus Group Observation Room   *Focus Group "Incentives"*

We took the TV spots and sample print ads to a "qualitative research" company in Princeton, New Jersey. The firm organized small focus groups that mimicked whatever audiences a company most wanted to reach. At 7 p.m. on a spring evening, John and I stood in an observation room watching eight chubby women and a portly man introduce one another. They were on the opposite side of a one-way glass panel; we could see the focus group, but they could not see us. The nine were seated around a large conference table eyeing two trays of doughnuts. A facilitator walked into the room, explained why the group had been brought together and then added, "Oh, please help yourselves to the doughnuts."

Within ten minutes, three dozen glazed, jelly, cream-filled, and plain doughnuts were gone.

"Jeez, John," I shook my head. "That was unreal!"

"Nope," John said. "What you just saw is *very* real. These people never met a pastry they didn't want to pounce on. Healthcheck is going to change all that."

It was a noble objective, but I was growing more and more uncertain about Healthcheck's product line. After the focus group watched and reacted to the two TV spots, I was even more dubious. The nine responded to the ads with comments such as "might follow up…" and "possibly would be interested…" but no "absolutely want to try this…" or "wow! This is definitely worth doing …"

The focus group research firm reviewed participant reactions and sent John and me a short report recommending changes to the television ads and suggested we adjust the price-per-minute charge for the tape library and chat line. The firm concluded Healthcheck might be profitable if the company was willing to make a *big* investment in front-end electronic and print advertising.

John interpreted the findings as a "go" and produced a 12 month spreadsheet forecasting over 250,000 calls a month to Healthcheck's tape library at $2.68 a call. His projections for the chat line were 150,000 calls each month at an average of $3.86 per call. Company revenues would top $14 million a year but the expenses were high driven by TV, newspaper, and magazine ad spending.

To me, John's numbers simply did not add up. I had doubts Healthcheck could ever turn a profit and even if it did the margins were thin. A lot of risk for a small return. More of a concern was the likelihood this would end up as just another weight management come-on pumped up by questionable claims. It had taken a while, but I had reached the end of the line: I wanted out.

Divorcing oneself from a business relationship while trying to maintain a close friendship turned out to be a challenge. John was not happy with my decision and asked that I stay in the game for at least another year. By doing so, it would make it easier to win the next round of funding. But I made the hard decision to cut the cord and, in the process, learned another **life lesson: if the train is moving in the wrong direction, get off.** And get off as soon as possible. It would have been much easier to stay on board for the next several months. Instead, I turned over my Healthcheck Communications shares to John without stipulations or conditions. That helped make my exit from Healthcheck less distressing but the separation still left a scar on a long-term friendship. John and I were never as close as we were before Healthcheck Communications bonded us as business partners.

**

John Simon did receive another round of funding for his weight-loss company. But not long after, Healthcheck Communications closed its doors, never rolling out a media campaign for its tape library and chat line. Three factors led to the company's demise ...

First, in 1988, the government allowed several commercial email providers to build and operate links to the Internet. It was the start of a communication revolution that would make accessing weight loss or any other kind of information more accessible on a PC or laptop than a telephone.

Second, John found himself pulled in two directions. Growing Healthcheck became more and more challenging as time demands mounted within his new venture, the Keren Group, a health communication and medical marketing firm he would lead for years. One of his notable accomplishments was his design of a marketing plan for Healthcare Satellite Broadcasting that delivered continuing education to nurse executives via television throughout the country. Developing two businesses at once proved to be too much. Healthcheck was put to rest.

And, third, John's health would slowly and painfully deteriorate. An incurable disease would send my brilliant friend into a long, debilitating decline. John Simon died in 2006 at the age of 59.

Distraction #3: Yankee Doodle Noodle – pasta possibility?

The low-slung building tucked into a mini-industrial park was among the least notable structures in the tightly packed town of

East Brunswick, New Jersey. The community was largely a residential haven for 47,000 people and had little room for any major manufacturing facilities. Still, there were small pockets of land tucked away on less-traveled side roads where small businesses had won permission to set up shop to produce everything from specialty plastic materials to packaging supplies. But what was going on inside that obscure one-story building I passed so frequently when driving from my East Brunswick home to the New Jersey Turnpike was a complete mystery. Until a chance encounter with my across-the-street neighbor.

"Noodles."

I gave Stan Smulewitz a quizzical stare. "What?"

"Noodles," Stan said again. "Ramen noodles. You know, the instant noodles you put in boiling water. Comes with a flavor packet."

Of course I knew ramen noodles. They were a primary food staple while I was in college. "Let me get this straight," I said. "You make ramen noodles in that office park building at the other end of town."

Stan explained he manufactured and sold a ramen product called Yankee Doodle Noodles. Then he tacked on a question: "You do marketing for companies, right?"

"On occasion," I confirmed. "That's not my strong suit but every once and a while I get attached to a marketing team."

We were sitting in Stan's living room which faced a narrow street lined with similar-looking homes all beginning to show their age. Diagonal to the Smulewitz residence was my two-story house which was in plain view from Stan's picture window.

"So, I could use a little advice," Stan said.

"I don't know anything about noodles." I felt another distraction heading my way.

"Making noodles is not my problem," Stan noted. "It's getting the grocery trade to put what I'm making on the shelf."

Stan invited me to tour his operation, which I did a few days later. It was a relatively simple manufacturing process that started with wheat flour, water, salt, and an alkaline additive dumped into a large blender. The mixture was then extruded onto a conveyor that pulled the dough through a series of processing steps. The end product was a neatly packaged, cellophane-wrapped "noodle block" labeled *Yankee Doodle Noodle*. The blocks were hand-packed into cartons ready for transport to different food stores.

Ramen Noodle Production   *Ramen Noodle Block*

We moved into Stan's small office where he went into detail about his business operations. The cost of producing ramen noodles was low – ingredients were cheap, and he didn't need skilled labor. What he *did* need was a production supervisor to monitor the few workers on his payroll. Quality control became a concern after an "incident" where a now ex-employee was seen tossing the remnants of a marijuana joint into the noodle blender.

"The unit costs are certainly reasonable," I said after scanning the numbers. "But the selling price – it doesn't look like you can make much money on each package sold."

"Exactly," said Stan. "This is a really low-margin product. Which means I have to sell a *lot* of noodles."

"Who does the selling?" I asked.

"Mostly me," Stan replied. "That's where I could use some advice. Know anything about product placement on a grocery store shelf?"

Having done work with a couple of businesses that dominated the over-the-counter drug world, I was familiar with the basics of retail sales. "Ideally, you get your item displayed at eye level at the end of an aisle," I said.

"The big boys pay to reserve that space," Stan said. "Small guys like me? My stuff gets jammed into a bottom shelf in the least trafficked part of a store. Unless I play the game."

"What game?"

"If you get to the right store manager, your product will show up in a primo location for a few days. But you need to slip him a gratuity."

"What kind of gratuity?"

Stan shrugged. "Like a color television you leave on the loading dock."

Stan and his wife, Grace Mary, were wonderful people and great neighbors. I wanted to do what I could to make Yankee Doodle Noodles a colossal success. But my expertise and time were in short supply. I did talk through a few marketing and promotion ideas with Stan only to become more convinced this enterprise would soon be on life support. Stan talked about widening his sales territory to build demand for his noodles. He even proposed marketing his product south of the Mason Dixon line.

"Somehow I don't see Southerners giving up grits for Yankee Doodle Noodles," I said.

Stan sighed. He was grasping for ways to make his business sustainable and I wasn't handing him a rescue plan. Cutting the price for each noodle block in an attempt to drive up sales wasn't an option Stan could afford. We even discussed reaching out to large food producers or distributors who might be interested in acquiring Yankee Doodle Noodles. That, too, was a stretch since there was nothing unique about Stan's manufacturing line or his ramen except its brand.

With little else I could do to help Stan, my time with him diminished. In an ironic twist, I was on a walk past a neighborhood elementary school when I heard a familiar song drifting through the open windows of a first-grade classroom:

Yankee Doodle went to town
A-riding on a pony
Stuck a feather in his cap
And called it macaroni

That same week, I learned Stan had closed the door on his ramen noodle business. A Korean company purchased his manufacturing equipment. Stan, Grace Mary, and their kids would eventually leave East Brunswick and move to Highland Park, a town only a few miles away. Stan did not ride off on a pony, but he left with a valuable feather called experience tucked in his cap. He had launched and run a small company in a very tough industry. He would leverage that experience to go on to become a successful businessman.

***

Arthur White turned ninety in 2014. There were so many well-wishers who wanted to celebrate his birthday, two large parties were held. One in New York and another in Washington, DC. I was invited to the Washington event.

"How's the 'no distractions' plan working out for you?" Arthur asked during a brief lull in the festivities. He turned to Vivien, his wife of 65 years, and winked.

I laughed. "You were right. I can't seem to fend off side jobs."

Arthur smiled, leaned forward and gave me an important **life lesson: the two most consequential words in any language: yes and no.** "You're good at saying yes," Arthur observed. "You need to work on saying no." He was right, of course. Being unable to say *No* would be a constant nemesis throughout my career.

In August, only a few months after his birthday, Arthur White suffered a stroke. He died shortly after.

Chapter 11

Weeden Management Systems – the Johnson Effect (1980-90)

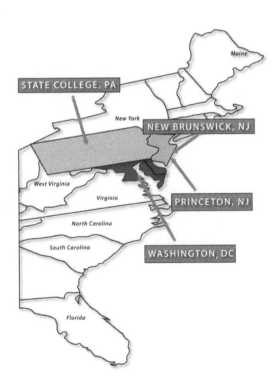

A tall fence walled off John Seward Johnson Jr.'s compound making it impossible for Princetonians to catch a glimpse of the eccentric sculptor or the wolf-dog hybrids allowed to roam his grounds. I had only met Seward a few times before but each trip to his guarded estate made me uneasy. This visit was no exception. I swallowed hard and pushed the *speak* button on the intercom at the side of the compound's main gate.

"I have an appointment with Mr. Johnson."

A minute later, a middle-aged woman appeared and led me to Seward's office.

"Sit down," Johnson ordered.

On command, I sat waiting patiently for Seward to handwrite a message on what looked to be an order for one of his increasingly expensive works of art. In his mid-50s, Seward didn't have the appearance of a man rumored to be a millionaire many times over. He was rather nondescript except for a telltale tan that told me he had been spending more time than usual at his Nantucket home – or maybe his property in Bermuda.

"You have the recommendations?" Seward asked when he finally raised his head. I handed him two sheets of paper and he fell silent again. While he studied a list of small grants proposed for Princeton-area charitable organizations, one of Seward's hybrids marched into the room and slumped to the floor only a few feet from me. The animal pointed its laser-like eyes at my face. I took the glare to be a warning that it would be unwise to upset the wolf-dog's master. After all, Seward was already upset enough these days.

Seward had been born into extraordinary wealth and might have been even more affluent if it hadn't been for a Polish chambermaid who years earlier caught his father's eye along with his $400 million estate. Seward Johnson Sr. died in 1983 but not before he changed his will and left most of his fortune to Barbara Piasecka, a Polish immigrant most knew as "Basia." According to Seward Jr. and his five siblings, Basia was a clever manipulator who convinced old man Johnson to trade in his wife of 32 years for a woman who spoke little English but who had mastered the language of seduction. Basia, 42 years younger than her new husband, served up a different story claiming she was a devoted and loving wife. As such, she insisted she was deserving of her departed husband's millions as well as the couple's Princeton mansion called Jasna Polana (Polish for "bright meadows"). At 54,000-square-feet, the residence with its 39 bathrooms along with its air-conditioned dog kennel was surrounded by 226 acres of prime Princeton acreage.

"You and Bob going to Harbor Branch?" Seward Junior asked while still studying the papers I had given him.

"We are," I confirmed. "Next month." Bob was Robert Campbell, a trustee of the Seward Johnson Sr. Charitable Trust. He was also Johnson & Johnson's chief financial officer. And he was the reason why I was sitting across from one of the country's most intriguing, controversial, and wealthiest artists.

Seward was by every measure an unusual man. He was hampered by dyslexia, a condition he had never tried to hide. His only higher education was at the University of Maine where he studied poultry husbandry for a couple of years before dropping out to enlist in the Navy. After a few years on the high seas, Seward was roped into a management position at Johnson & Johnson which was a move doomed from the start. He left the company at about the same time he married a thrice-divorced woman whose alleged infidelities led to a scandalous incident in the early 1960s. With divorce on his mind, Seward hired a pair of detectives to spy on his wife. He arranged to have the two private eyes enter his house one night hoping they would catch his wife *en flagrante delicto.* Instead, Mrs. Johnson, who at the time was alone in her bedroom, heard the men and shot one of the detectives thinking he was a late-night intruder. Predictably, the marriage officially ended in 1964.

Seward wed again and his second wife, the novelist Joyce Horton, encouraged her husband to pursue his art interests. With little training, Seward established himself as a widely recognized (although not always highly regarded) sculptor. His life-sized bronze figures, each meticulously detailed, became more and more popular – and more and more pricey.

Jasna Polana – Main Gate   *Harbor Branch – Fort Pierce, FL*

"Harbor Branch," Seward said. The familiar words caused the wolf-dog to stir. "Find out their top two or three funding priorities. Get back to me on that."

Seward glanced again at the list of proposed contributions to Princeton nonprofits. He returned the two pages to me and nodded his approval. The small donations would be paid out of a pair of trusts set up by his father. The same trusts provided ongoing support to the Florida-based Harbor Branch Oceanographic Institution, a nonprofit research organization founded by Seward Sr. and Edwin Link, an aeronautic and oceanographic expert best known for his invention of the flight simulator. Seward Jr. would carry on the Johnson family interest in Harbor Branch, even taking the lead as the nonprofit's president for a time.

After leaving Seward's compound, I stopped to call Bob Campbell. "It's all good," I said. "He was pretty mellow."

"Great," Bob replied and meant what he said. Meetings with Seward could be uneventful or could easily blow up with the sculptor firing not-so-veiled charges that the two Seward Sr. trusts were being mismanaged. Most of Seward's displeasure, when it surfaced, was pointed at a Princeton attorney, Jim Hill who was another trustee. Hill and Bob Campbell had totally different personalities. Often found at the town's somewhat stuffy Nassau Club, Hill's appearance and behavior reeked upper crust. He frequently referenced his Deerfield Academy, Williams College, and Columbia Law School education. Bob, on the other hand, was more unassuming and enjoyed a reputation as being among the most likeable people in New Jersey. His college days were vastly different from Hill's. Bob commuted from Passaic, New Jersey to Fordham University in the Bronx. While Bob didn't drop the Fordham name that often, it was clear he valued his experience at the university. He and his wife, Joan, would later make a $10 million gift to Fordham, one of the largest in the school's history.

"Seward wants a few funding options for Harbor Branch," I reported.

"We'll be there in a few weeks," Bob noted. "There's no shortage of things there that could use money."

I had visited Harbor Branch once before. Spread over 146 acres along the Indian River Lagoon north of Fort Pierce, HBOI (as it was called by locals and those in the oceanographic world) was launched in 1971. Comparable to the more well-known Woods Hole in Massachusetts, HBOI was established as a marine research and education facility. It was also home port for an ocean submersible large enough for four crew members and sturdy enough to probe some of the world's deepest seas.

"Thanks for your help with this deal," Bob added before we disconnected. "Glad you've been 'Johnsonized.'"

Johnsonized? How did that happen? A look at my consulting log for the past couple of years proved Bob was correct. Johnson & Johnson and its connected parts such as the Seward Johnson Sr. Trusts had become a magnet, pulling me slowly but steadily into J&J's incredibly expansive orbit. This had all come about since my first date with the corporation which had followed a phone call from Merck CEO Lloyd Huck to J&J's public relations vice president, a sometimes-fiery but highly competent professional named Lawrence (Larry) Foster.

"Lloyd tells me you did some work for Merck," Larry said. "Huck and I are on the Penn State board of directors. We're looking for a new university president. I could use some help."

Not long after, Larry and I were on one of three J&J company planes en route to State College, Pennsylvania for a series of interviews with Penn State faculty and administrators. My job was to log expectations and frustrations that would serve as a roadmap the trustee search committee could use in its hunt for the university's next chief executive. Many of the meetings were brief and unmemorable. The one exception was a lengthy conversation with the legendary Joe Paterno whose regal status on campus stemmed not just from his football coaching prowess but also from his genuine decency. Shockingly, "JoPa's" reputation would tank many years later following the arrest and trial of Jerry Sandusky, the defensive coordinator for Penn State's wildly successful football team. Sandusky would be found guilty on 45 counts of sexual abuse and, in turn, Paterno would be haunted until his death by allegations he tried to cover up the scandal.

"The top-rated presidents of other state universities – find out who they are," Larry ordered on our flight back from State College. Later in the week, I handed Larry a short list. Stanley Ikenberry, CEO of the University of Illinois was among the college executives with very high marks. "Set up a meeting – I want to talk to him," Larry said and not long after, he commandeered the J&J plane for a trip to Urbana, Illinois. More interviews were scheduled over the next several weeks and the feedback was used to fashion a job description for Penn State's next top administrator. Ultimately, the university picked Bryce Jordan from Texas as its fourteenth president.

"Good job," Larry complimented me. "Ready for another assignment?"

I shrugged. It wasn't easy to say "no" to Larry Foster.

"Herb Kaiser is a retired diplomat," Larry said. "He was posted in South Africa. While he was there, he was diagnosed with advanced melanoma. That got him knee-deep in South Africa's medical system. What he saw, he didn't like. He and his wife, Joy, are setting up a nonprofit to raise money to make health care more accessible to the country's people of color."

"And you want me to …?"

"The Kaisers are good people, but they don't know squat about setting up a nonprofit. Go help them get the thing off the ground."

Penn State's Nittany Lion   *Herb & Joy Kaiser with Nelson Mandela*

My first of many meetings with the Kaisers was in their small kitchen. Along with the couple's son, Paul, we sat for hours honing an organization mission statement and going over the basics for incorporating a 501c3 charity.

"South Africa has a black population of over 20 million people and most go without good health care," Herb told me. "A hospital for South African blacks usually has a 300 percent occupancy rate. Know what that means? Two patients in the same bed and one on the floor."

I quickly discovered both Kaisers had gentle, compassionate personalities that masked a fierce determination. Their new organization, named Medical Education for South African Blacks or MESAB, would raise money for training students of color seeking health careers.

"Fundraising in the U.S. for a project in Africa won't be a walk in the park," I warned Joy and Herb.

"We're not about walking," Herb said. "To make a difference in South Africa, we need to be running and running fast."

And run they did. For 22 years until MESAB's sunset in 2007, this remarkable couple would collect $27 million from individuals, corporations, and foundations. The money would be used to educate 10,000 black doctors, dentists and nurses – a feat so astounding the Kaisers would win acclaim from notables such as South African President Nelson Mandela and Archbishop Desmond Tutu. Even more impressive than the Kaiser's resolve to get MESAB off the ground was their tireless effort to keep the organization going. They left me with another **life lesson: creating can be hard; sustaining**

can be harder. Most new initiatives, although difficult and even painful to start, are born with a luster. But that sheen often fades over time. Keeping an organization alive and healthy long after its launch can be the ultimate test. Through grit and persistence, the Kaisers passed that test with high honors.

After MESAB came a flurry of other Johnson & Johnson jobs. I was billing so much of my consulting time to the health care giant, the corporation offered me free office space at its NJ headquarters building. Moving some of my files into the old but impressive brick building overlooking the shallow Raritan River, it was now obvious the gravitational pull of this huge company was altering my career path. At the same time, an even more profound change was propelling my personal life into a new trajectory.

Marriage.

This has about as much chance of lasting as a scoop of rocky road on a hot summer day. It was understandable why popular opinion would bet my second marriage would go south in no time. My bride was a strikingly attractive blonde who dressed impeccably, loved classical music, and worshiped ballet. I, on the other hand, was a bald string bean, professionally hyperactive, and the father of four kids living on the West Coast. How could this relationship possibly work? While we were officially wed at a private, low-key ceremony in the spring, we delayed celebrating the marriage until the summer when we could more easily bring family and friends together. The reception was held at the Hill-Physick House in Philadelphia, the 18th-century mansion once home to Philip Syng Physick, the father of American surgery. Seeing this new blended family in one place at one time was eye opening. My wife brought a tiny toddler from an earlier marriage into the fold. Along with the four West Coast children, we were a curious collection, to say the least. Tall and short, black and white, boys and girls – this was an amalgamation so out of the ordinary that we drew stares wherever we went.

"Why would a woman so amazingly beautiful marry a guy like you – with four kids, no less?" was a question asked of me many times by close male friends. I didn't have an answer and still don't. I am only grateful she took the plunge and was willing to endure the hard work and sacrifice essential to holding together such a diverse family. There would be many hurdles including serious medical challenges offset by exhilarating highs such as the birth of nine grandchildren. The marriage that couldn't last has gone on for nearly four decades thanks largely to the love and support of a woman who somehow has managed to make it all work.

With J&J asking for an ever-increasing amount of consulting time, my wife and I decided to move closer to the corporation's home office. We purchased a modest, two-story home on a quarter acre in East Brunswick, less than a half-hour commute from downtown New Brunswick. The neighborhood was a typical middle class, suburban mix of families, most with children. The house wasn't huge but big enough to accommodate the west coast kids when they were with us for the summers or for other special occasions. Friendships came easily and have endured over the years.

Most of my J&J consulting time was spent helping the company construct an ambitious and ultimately highly regarded philanthropy program. But two assignments took me in vastly different directions.

"A thousand times sweeter than sugar," Ray Regimbal said, and handed me a vial the size of a small test tube. The white powder inside could have been easily mistaken for a few grams of cocaine. While not a narcotic, I would soon find out the substance was a kind of Wall Street drug billed as a product that would give shareholders a rush.

"What's it called?"

Ray retrieved the vial. "Sucralose. You're looking at millions of dollars *if* we can get the stuff approved for use here in the U.S."

Ray, the Canadian-born J&J executive known for his deep religious roots, tapped the vial. "We need a marketing and branding strategy ready to go once the FDA give us a thumbs up."

So began a multi-year relationship with Ray. My job was to evaluate and challenge market entry ideas that would give G.D. Searle a run for its money. Searle made aspartame, commonly known as NutraSweet or Equal. The Skokie, Illinois company was headed by Donald Rumsfeld who joined Searle after serving in the Gerald Ford administration as Chief of Staff and Secretary of Defense. Rumsfeld had a "take no prisoners" reputation and Searle was already well aware that a J&J affiliate called McNeil Nutritionals was planning an assault on the sweetener world. Grabbing a portion of Searle's stronghold on the market wouldn't be easy. But as we would soon learn, marketing challenges were minor compared to getting a stamp of approval from the Food & Drug Administration.

Sucralose didn't belong to J&J. It was discovered by UK-based sugar giant Tate & Lyle in the mid-1970s. The company, along with a partner university, found that by chlorinating sucrose, a unique artificial sweetener could be produced. But the use of chlorine as part of the process prompted safety concerns from day one. "People shouldn't be ingesting anything made with bleach," one dubious scientist commented. Although test after test showed the chlorination method had no adverse effect on animals, sucralose would have an ongoing PR problem because of its links to chlorine. But because sucralose was found to be three times as sweet as aspartame and twice as sweet as saccharin, its market potential was so great that both Tate & Lyle and J&J pledged to find a way to counter public suspicions.

"Here's the kicker," said Ray. "Unlike other sweeteners, sucralose is stable when heated. That means it can be used in baking and as an ingredient in products that need to have a long shelf life."

The artificial sweetener market was growing fast – on track to reach $1.5 billion with much of the growth driven by the soft drink industry. The commercial appetite for sucralose became even more extreme when companies such as Coca-Cola and PepsiCo experimented with sucralose as a fountain drink option. Since carbonated beverages containing sucralose didn't generate much fizz, less liquid was lost as overflow when poured from a commercial fountain dispenser. As more and more potential customers lined up salivating for the new sweetener, the FDA moved at an agonizingly slow pace in reviewing an application for approval. Anticipating sucralose would find its way into an array of consumer goods, the FDA expressed concerns about the product's long-term effects. So, more and more animal tests were required with J&J obligated to eat most of the costs. Patience was wearing thin and Ray was under increasing pressure to come up with a plan to push regulators to decree sucralose was safe for human consumption.

One afternoon, Ray called me to his office following a particularly contentious meeting he had with a few other J&J executives. "Time is running out," he announced.

"You mean the company is going to cancel the Tate & Lyle deal?" I asked.

"No," Ray said, his voice unusually soft. "Time is running out for me. This project is stuck in neutral and we all know it isn't going to move for quite some time. So, in the meantime, the corporation is considering a management shakeup. My guess is they'll be bringing in a new quarterback."

I was stunned. "That won't speed up the FDA review."

"True," Ray agreed. "But a leadership change will make the analysts happy."

Ray was on target. It was the beginning of the end of his J&J career. This devout man who frequently met with a small group of other corporate executives to start the day with a prayer breakfast would soon be pushed into early retirement by circumstances that were never in his control.

The day it was confirmed Ray would be stepping down from his role as captain of the sucralose team, I drove home listening to an FM station play the Supremes' *You Can't Hurry Love*. There was an irony to the lyrics:

You just have to wait
You gotta trust; give it time
No matter how long it takes

If Ray Regimbal had a failure it was his inability to make J&J and Tate & Lyle understand that approving a new noncaloric ingested substance would take time. A lot of time. For Ray, it was a career killer. For me it was another **life lesson: caution is a speedbump to progress and a magnifying glass to outcomes.** I should have advised Ray to make the case that any short-term benefit stemming from excessive pressure on the government to approve sucralose might be dwarfed by serious long-term consequences. Better to have the project fail in its pre-release stage than to have a hastily reviewed product become a health hazard and a financial disaster. Had Ray been able to buy more time, he would have been drinking champagne in 1998 when the U.S. *finally* gave a thumbs up to sucralose. It wouldn't be long before the sweetener, branded with the name Splenda®, would go on to capture 62% of the market overtaking Equal, the once dominant-brand in the field.

While sucralose soaked up a hefty amount of my J&J consulting time, so did another project that had its origins in the mid-1970s. That is when I caught my first glimpse of a sandy-haired man walking across a bridge connecting New Brunswick to a neighboring New Jersey suburb, Highland Park. It was winter, a nasty wind whipping over the ice-covered Raritan River. The man leaned into the gusts of frigid air.

"Who is that?" I asked a J&J manager sitting in the front passenger seat of my car. We were on our way to Newark Airport.

"John Heldrich," was the answer. "He's a big hitter. One of the executive committee members. Lives just across the river."

"The executive committee?" I asked, thinking I had misunderstood the response. The executive committee was the small collection of men (no women) who were at the helm of the world's largest diversified health care corporation. "But he's *walking* to work – in the middle of winter!"

"He does that a lot. He's a tough bird who heads up corporate administration. In charge of everything from employee benefits to paper towels. Loves J&J and loves New Brunswick even more."

Weeks later, I was introduced to John. It was the start of a long and fascinating relationship. The son of German immigrants, John lived in a modest two-story home that belied his financial worth. A prominent daily newspaper would claim John's J&J stock holdings made him one of the richest men in New Jersey. But like other wealthy J&J executives, personal extravagance was not on display. He would occasionally travel to Yankee Stadium to watch his favorite team. His wife, Regina, would drive herself to New York's Lincoln Center. There would be infrequent vacations usually to the Caribbean. The couple had a large family, but their children had long since grown and moved to other parts of the country. The Heldrich's charity was generous but not hyped. The Catholic Church, Rutgers University, and various nonprofit organizations committed to resuscitating New Brunswick were the usual beneficiaries.

"Gary Gorran works the numbers," John said to me months after we got to know one another. "I need somebody else to work the words – to take my ideas and put them in writing."

That "somebody" would be me and the "ideas" would be copious. Fortunately, Gary Gorran was as friendly and willing to help as he was financially astute. John was heavily dependent on Gary for dollar projections tied to several projects both inside and outside J&J. Gary was not only competent with numbers, he knew the innerworkings and politics of J&J's complicated organizational structure. The corporation billed itself as a "family of companies" made up of many affiliates all of which were given some degree of autonomy. Converting any of John's ideas usually meant running to Gary's office to get clarification on how and what I needed to do.

"This might not be pretty," John warned one morning as we walked to J&J's front office. It was the mid-70s, years before Bob Campbell told me I had been *Johnsonized.* There would be many, many other meetings I would be asked to attend going forward. None would compare to this one. None would tell me more about the people and principles of the Johnson & Johnson corporation.

"This is where the company got its start and this is where we're staying," John stated emphatically a few minutes after the meeting got started.

"Just because the office is close enough for you to walk home for lunch doesn't mean it's the right place for our headquarters," Dave Clare shot back. A MIT graduate, Clare had only recently been named president and chairman of J&J's executive committee. He had a reputation for being as hardnosed as he was wise when it came to making business decisions. "By the way, this isn't your call, John."

"We have roots here," John said, turning to another man in the room. "We owe it to this city to stay put."

Jim Burke was half paying attention to the Heldrich-Clare debate that was escalating to an argument. Burke was J&J's CEO, technically one notch above Clare. But it was common knowledge the corporation had two men in charge. Burke was wading through his inbox while jumping into the conversation at the same time. He was famous for doing at least two things at once.

"We need a new home office," Jim looked at John. "To keep a New Brunswick address, it will cost us. Cost us a lot. And it isn't just about constructing a new building, John. This city is a mess. We would have to pour even more money into making it a place where we can recruit and retain the right kind of people."

John took a breath and studied Burke who had returned to flipping through a pile of paper on his desk. Before the meeting, John had predicted it would be a struggle convincing the company to remain in New Brunswick given the options the corporation had for moving elsewhere. J&J owned an expansive tract of land in Skillman, a bucolic town in adjacent Somerset County that could easily accommodate a much larger corporate campus.

A second alternative was a multi-acre land parcel J&J owned adjacent to Ethicon, an important corporate affiliate. Not openly discussed were the personal circumstances of the company's top two leaders. Burke lived in Princeton, a 43-minute drive to the south. Claire's home was in Westfield 40-minutes to the north. Neither had any vested interest in New Brunswick. They were also correct about the city's worn-out and in some cases dilapidated condition.

"Either of you going to tell Dick Sellers we're even *thinking* about relocating?" John asked. It was one of his trump cards and he was playing it early. Although I was seated in the corner of the room taking notes and out of the line of fire, I sensed the meeting had just taken a turn. Sellers was J&J's former CEO and chairman and known to be tight with several corporate board members. He was also as much of a cheerleader for New Brunswick as John Heldrich.

"When we lay out how much we'll save by getting out of here, he'll come around," Clare said.

"Really?" John gave Clare a hard stare. "Did you ever listen to Dick? *The survival of our country depends on the survival of its cities –* that's one of his favorite talking points. If you think he'll agree to let this town go to hell in a handbasket without a fight, you don't know Dick Sellers."

Burke pulled off his reading glasses. "I don't know, John. No question Dick's got a dog in this hunt, but we have an obligation to thousands of shareholders who ..."

New Brunswick, NJ Viewed from   J&J Worldwide Headquarters
the Raritan River

"The Credo," John said, cutting off his boss. The second trump card was now out in the open. John walked to the far wall of the office and pointed to a framed document, his finger tapping one of the four paragraphs printed below the heading *Our Credo*.

We are responsible to the communities in which we live and work and to the world community as well.

We must be good citizens – support good works and charities and bear our fair share of taxes.

"Everywhere you go Jim, you tell people it's the Credo that makes J&J different," John reminded Burke. "We need to do more than talk. We need to do the right thing."

"The *right* thing is to maximize a shareholder's return on investment," Clare bristled.

Burke raised a hand and the room went still. John's Credo reference had scored a direct hit. The short statement had been crafted in 1943 by General Robert Wood Johnson. Since then, the simple yet profound document had been used as the bedrock for building the corporation into an international powerhouse. For Burke, it was his manifesto that had helped carry him into J&J's driver's seat.

"Bring me some options," Burke said. "With numbers. I want to see how much it will cost to stay put."

Clare shook his head as John and I walked out the door. Later, I would learn this kind of no-holds-barred exchange was a common occurrence inside J&J's C-suite. But on this occasion, I was so stressed that my lightly starched white shirt (part of the standard suit and tie uniform at J&J's headquarters) was soaked with sweat. Once John was back in his office, he asked Gary Gorran to start crunching numbers. It was the beginning of New Brunswick's revitalization.

Not only did J&J's corporate headquarters remain one of the most important anchors in New Brunswick, the company played a lead role in turning around a deteriorated urban community that had been on the decline since the 1960s. Through a new organization called the New Brunswick Development Corporation (DevCo), J&J helped upgrade the city's center and several blighted and neglected neighborhoods. The corporation provided the financial backing for a new Hyatt hotel and conference center as a way to attract conferences and special events to the city. Commuters would later be lured to an upscale housing development within walking distance of a much-improved train station that offered rail transportation to New York City or Philadelphia.

J&J's most important contribution to the city was its new corporate headquarters designed by the I.M. Pei architectural firm (known for the John F. Kennedy Library in Massachusetts and the controversial glass-and-steel pyramid that sits atop the Musée du Louvre in Paris). Called a "park in a city and a company in a park," the complex included indoor atriums and exterior grounds that sloped into surrounding sidewalks and streets with few barriers and walls. When J&J moved into the new offices in 1983, the price tag for the new building was thought to be north of $120 million. Over the years, J&J would continue to open its checkbook pouring millions more into the city.

Dave Clare was right about the high cost of staying in a location badly in need of revitalization. Jim Burke was right to show employees, customers, and shareholders that remaining in New Brunswick was consistent with the company's credo mandate. And John Heldrich would be right for joining with Dick Sellers in fighting hard for keeping Johnson & Johnson in the city where it was born.

The showdown in Jim Burke's office revealed the power of J&J's deceptively simple corporate credo. The company used just four paragraphs as an organizational GPS system to make key decisions – not the least of which was deciding to stay put in New Brunswick. The credo became another important **life lesson: principles are more meaningful and actionable when translated into responsibilities.** Most organizations have mission statements that bundle aspirations with principles as a way of defining their *raison d'etre*. Robert Wood Johnson singled out his own set of principles which he used as the underpinning for his business (hold to the highest possible standards when making products or delivering services; respect the dignity and merit of employees; be decent citizens especially in locations where the company has a presence; and make a sound profit for stockholders). General Johnson could have melded those principles into the kind of mission statement most corporations promote as their lodestar. But those mission statements can frequently be fuzzy and largely disregarded. So instead, the general turned the company's most important principles into responsibilities. And along with each responsibility came *accountability.* The Credo was used to evaluate all J&J employees - including those at the very top of the organization. The result? A highly *principled* corporation.

Over time, I would be confronted with another J&J-related **life lesson: a statement of purpose or expected behavior should not be static.** While J&J termed its credo its "moral compass," it was also the company's way of assessing standards of behavior for the thousands of people who worked for the corporation. J&J worked hard to avoid having employees conclude this was essentially a top-down performance mandate by giving everyone in the company a chance to periodically "challenge" the credo. The corporation solicited input from its worldwide workforce asking questions such as: Was J&J living up to credo provisions? Should the credo be modified to reflect changes outside the company? The process gave employees a sense of credo ownership that, in turn, made the document's four paragraphs even more relevant. These "Credo Challenges" would also do something else: lead to changes in credo content. In 1979, J&J would add "protecting the environment and natural resources" to its roster of responsibilities. Then in 1987, the credo's first paragraph would be modified to recognize the importance of a healthy work/life balance. There were other minor changes – not Titanic adjustments but alterations that proved the credo could be adjusted to keep it as timely and pertinent as possible. How J&J works hard to keep its credo contemporary by building in an allowance for carefully-deliberated change serves as a case study for other organizations to consider – including government.

Much of my Johnsonization period was spent in and out of Heldrich's spacious corner office. Although guarded fiercely by his administrative assistant, Jean Szymborski, I had easy access to John's inner sanctum as did Gary Gorran. When John retired in 1991, both Gary and I worried about the transition. Who could replace a man so influential in the internal as well as external activities of one of the nation's largest corporations? That worry disappeared when J&J's chief counsel, Roger Fine, took over John's position.

Shortly after taking on his new role, Roger walked into my office unannounced and closed the door behind him. "I want you to come inside," he said.

"Inside?" I reacted with surprise. I had become so Johnsonized I thought I was *already* inside.

"I want you on the J&J payroll," Roger explained. "Vice president."

I blinked. The idea of becoming a J&J employee had crossed my mind but I had dismissed that possibility mainly because I wanted the freedom to work with more than just one corporation as a way to kickstart the private sector into becoming more socially responsible.

"Here's something to think about," Roger said after it was clear I wasn't jumping at his offer. "You can be a whole lot more effective in convincing companies to focus on the business advantages of corporate philanthropy, employee volunteerism, and a lot more if you actually had experience in *running* a company's social responsibility office."

Roger was right, as he usually was. There was a weakness in my consulting portfolio. I didn't have any executive-level management experience inside a class-A company. J&J was already recognized as one of the most thoughtful and progressive leaders in the social responsibility field. Joining the team at a vice president level was an offer Roger thought I shouldn't refuse.

"Consider it a buy-out of your consulting business," Roger noted. "We'll make it worth your while. Oh, and if you accept, plan on continuing your work with the Seward Johnson Sr. Trust."

"I don't know if I can promise to make this a long-term commitment," I said.

"Try it for a few years," Roger replied. "Turn our corporate philanthropy program into one of the best in the country. Then if you want to go back outside, dust off your consulting shingle and hit the road again."

Roger left. I called my wife and discussed the offer. Then I called Roger.

I was now 100 percent Johnsonized.

***

Seward Johnson Jr. would continue to gain recognition and occasional disparagement for his *trompe l'oeil* painted bronze statues. The life-size castings would become familiar art works from New York City to Australia. The court battle that pitted Seward and his siblings against their stepmother Basia dragged on. The case would be settled out of court with the Johnson children awarded 12 percent of Seward Sr.'s fortune. In 1992, Seward would launch "Grounds for Sculpture," a 42-acre sculpture park situated on what was once the New Jersey State Fairgrounds. Seward's legal entanglements would continue when the Johnson family argued Seward's daughter, Jenia Anne Johnson (known as "Cookie"), should not be eligible for a share of Seward Sr.'s trust money. The court disagreed. Cookie would be added to the list of beneficiaries.

The Harbor Branch Oceanographic Institute would continue receiving added support from the Seward Johnson Sr. Charitable Trusts. In 2007, the Institute would partner with Florida Atlantic University in Fort Pierce. The deal would bring $45 million in construction funds and provide the Institute with nearly $9 million a year in operating support.

Johnson & Johnson would exit the sweetener field in 2015, turning over its Splenda brand to Heartland Food Products Group (based in Indianapolis). The decision to give up the popular sugar substitute would follow a barrage of legal and Better Business Bureau complaints from competitors contending J&J was carrying out a misleading marketing campaign by citing Splenda as "made from sugar, so it tastes like sugar." The Sugar Association, an influential trade group, would loudly protest to the Federal Trade Commission that "Splenda is not a natural product ... it is not cultivated or grown and it does not occur in nature..." Looking back, J&J's long and bumpy history with Splenda was, at best, bittersweet.

In 1982, seven people in the Chicago metro area would die after ingesting Extra Strength Tylenol laced with potassium cyanide. No one would ever be charged with the drug tampering crime, but the incident would lead to a decision by Jim Burke destined to make him a private sector folk hero. Burke would order 31 million bottles of Tylenol, the best-selling over-the-counter pain reliever in the country, to be removed from store shelves. It would be one of the largest product recalls in U.S. history. The gutsy – and, at the time, contentious – move would become a gold-standard business school case study on crisis management. Burke would step down from his J&J post in 1989 and spend much of his retirement advocating for the nonprofit organization, Partnership for a Drug-Free America. He would be named by *Fortune* magazine as one of the 10 greatest CEOs of all time.

Dave Clare would retire from J&J but stay active in the health care field working with the Pew Health Professions Commission and the President's Drug Advisory Council. He would split his time between New Jersey and his home in North Palm Beach, Florida where he would die in 2014.

"Let's meet at Panico's," John Heldrich suggested a week before I was to be in New Brunswick. The Italian restaurant was tucked into a side street not far from J&J headquarters and was one of John's favorites even after he retired from the corporation.

"How's the Old Sage feeling?" I asked before disconnecting. John had earned the title because he was constantly being asked for advice by a cadre of government, business, and civic leaders all involved in New Brunswick's revitalization.

"The Old Sage never misses a meal," John laughed. "So, don't be late."

I worked my schedule to be in New Brunswick once each year or two so I could spend time with John mostly to reminisce about the "old days." This visit would be especially important because John's wife, Regina, had died only a few months earlier. The Old Sage lived in his modest Highland Park home, his only companion a beloved pet dog.

The Old Shepherd's Chief Mourner   *New Brunswick's The Heldrich*

On a gloomy October day in 2014, I was waiting for an Amtrak train to take me from New York City to my lunch with John when my cell phone buzzed. "John died this morning." I was told. My one-time boss, mentor, and friend was gone.

His dog was by his side when they found him, I learned later. The news triggered a memory of John talking about a painting he admired – *The Old Shepherd's Chief Mourner* by the English artist Edwin Landseer. The famous oil happened to also be one of my wife's favorites, which helped explain why I recalled John's reference to the sad portrayal of a dog lamenting the loss of his master. John's dog had become the Old Sage's chief mourner but it was the entire city of New Brunswick that also grieved the loss.

John's profound impact on New Brunswick would not be forgotten. The Heldrich name continues to resonate in many parts of the city and nowhere is it more prominent than above the front entrance to a downtown hotel called The Heldrich. With 248 guest rooms, the hotel stands tall as a monument to a man who refused to turn his back on a city he loved.

Chapter 12

Johnson & Johnson (1990 – 1999)

An air horn blast sent 36 golf carts scattering across the close-cropped lawn of a popular Central Jersey golf course. It was the start of the first annual golf outing organized by a nonprofit organization called the First Baptist Community Development Corporation (later renamed the Central Jersey Community Development Corporation). I was Johnson & Johnson's chief representative for the sold-out event.

"Let me get this straight," I said to the short but trim African-American man parked next to me in the passenger seat of my cart tagged with a huge sign that read: *11ᵗʰ HOLE.* "You've never played golf before."

"Putt-putt golf," the Reverend DeForest Soaries chuckled. "Fact is, I don't know much about the game. What does *shotgun format* mean, anyway?"

I laughed. "You're in charge of this tournament and you don't have a clue what's going on, Buster!"

My playing partner gave me an uncharacteristic shrug. The young Reverend Soaries was known to most as just plain Buster, a name many considered ill-suited to a man widely regarded as an up-and-coming religious and community development powerhouse.

"Groups of four golfers are sent to each of the course's 18 holes," I explained, as our cart bumped its way toward the eleventh tee box. "When the air horn goes off again, each foursome begins playing at the same time. Called a shotgun start."

"Okay," Buster grinned. "So, now I won't come across as a complete idiot."

Buster Soaries had been called many things – charismatic, egocentric, dynamic, inspirational, even politically motivated. But an "idiot" he was not. Far from it. Buster was the head pastor at a mega-church in Central Jersey called First Baptist of Lincoln Gardens. His sermons were electrifying, and his oratory talent was getting attention far beyond New Jersey. One out-of-state reporter even suggested Buster was an up-and-coming Martin Luther King.

"Listen, when it's your turn to tee off…" I babbled while jerking the cart hard to the left. The abrupt turn sent Reverend Soaries flying out of the cart and down a steep embankment.

I screeched to a stop and slapped the side of my head. "Oh, my god!" I wailed. "I just killed the next MLK!"

Buster lay still for a few seconds, then slowly got to his hands and knees. He brushed clumps of grass and dirt from his hair and clothes. When he was fully upright, he shook his head and scampered up the mogul. "That was one wild ride!" he said with a wide smile.

It was just one of many wild rides Buster would take over the years. He would become the driving force behind an ambitious campaign to develop low-and moderate-income housing in New Jersey's crowded midsection. Buster would author books (e.g. *My Family Is Driving Me Crazy*, a survival guide for adolescents), spearhead the start of a Christian recording studio, and produce videos aimed at encouraging teenagers to practice sexual abstinence. Later in his career, he would be recruited as New Jersey's secretary of state and go on to chair the Congressionally-authorized U.S. Election Assistance Commission.

Buster, a one-time wannabe professional baseball player, turned out to be a pretty good golfer. But his game would never match his ability to preach. His words could move multitudes. Behind the pulpit, Buster was a master orator who became so popular crowds would jam his 2,000-seat church on a Sunday. Latecomers were left to watch the action on a big-screen television in an overflow room. As inspirational Buster was to a crowd, his one-on-one interactions with adults, adolescents, and children were frequently life-altering. During the years I worked with him, Buster taught me another **life lesson: for rousing the masses, use a homily; for achieving transformational change, get personal.** To a crowd, Buster was as much a messenger as he was an entertainer. His popularity left no doubt he had a remarkable ability to engage large audiences. But where Buster made the most difference was behind closed doors when he turned counselor, confidant, and mentor. A kid skipping school. An ex-offender in deep depression. A young adult struggling with addiction. Buster's fame was forged behind the pulpit, but his influence was never more significant than in the privacy of his office. As someone who would do his share of public speaking (albeit with far less flair than Buster), I would welcome audience applause but ever mindful this was mostly surface noise. Modifying behavior or opinion usually required the kind of personal Buster-like engagement that too often didn't come easily to me.

Buster began his ministry with First Baptist of Lincoln Gardens in 1990, about the same time I was officially named a Johnson &

Johnson vice president. He was one of many extraordinary people outside J&J's inner circle who were part of the nation's extensive and quietly influential network of religious, education, cultural, health care, and civic nonprofit organizations. Dozens of unsung and under-compensated leaders working in the nonprofit field would prove tremendously helpful to me over the years ahead. But I would also be guided by another remarkable team who surrounded me *inside* J&J.

Before he stepped down as CEO, Jim Burke had issued a directive that became one of his most important legacies. He ordered the formation of a J&J contributions committee, calling it the engine needed to carry out key provisions in the company's credo: ...*we must be good citizens – support good works and charities* ...

Burke enlisted several of the company's highest-ranking executives to serve on the committee. He made it clear this was not to be a side duty. It was serious business and there would be little tolerance for anyone missing a meeting or dodging an assignment dealing with the corporation's social responsibility. New Brunswick-advocate John Heldrich was named chair of the committee and upon his retirement, the responsibility was handed to Roger Fine, a lawyer who had been moved from the corporate law department to head J&J's international administration division. The committee met regularly, usually every couple of months with an 85 percent attendance record. And annually, committee members all showed up for a one-or two-day retreat to draft a detailed strategic plan that linked J&J's philanthropy priorities with current and near-term business interests. In a fascinating twist, these off-site social responsibility sessions would sometimes impact manufacturing and marketing plans.

As a consultant, I had been invited by companies other than J&J to help organize or revitalize "corporate contributions committees." Most were pick-up groups with three or four senior executives brought together (some reluctantly) to discuss philanthropy issues too often extraneous to P&L priorities. The J&J process was completely different and was one of the compelling reasons I made the decision to become an "insider." Aside from Heldrich and Fine, the J&J committee included an array of other socially conscious executives who had responsibilities as different as their personalities:

- Bob Gussin headed J&J's Corporate Office of Science & Technology. Like his predecessor, Bob Fuller, Gussin oversaw a proposal process that led to the annual awarding of millions of dollars in grants mainly to universities for carrying out nonproprietary "basic research." While these grants were of no direct commercial benefit to the company, they did allow J&J to peek into top-notch laboratories where the corporation found other discoveries judged to be viable (and profitable) products.

- Bill Nielsen who would move into Larry Foster's seat as head of J&J's communications and public relations operations. Bill underscored another important **life lesson: what you say can be as important as what you do.** J&J rarely used a bull horn to promote its good works. But the company grasped the importance of sending the right (often tempered) messages to the right audiences at the right time.

- Ed Harnett had management responsibility for J&J's challenging hospital service business. American acute care hospitals were shifting to a "just-in-time" supply system which put great strain on medical supply companies. Despite the pressure, Ed was never frazzled and was always good for a joke or upbeat story that made committee meetings as enjoyable as they were productive. Ed would become the company's leading advocate for using a portion of J&J's philanthropy to address the needs and interests of the nursing profession. Nurses, Ed accurately noted, were instrumental in making hospital purchasing decisions ranging from sutures to pain relievers. These under-appreciated and under-valued health care workers should be a priority for J&J, Ed said.

- Andy Markey was the corporation's treasurer who calculated contribution funding levels needed to carry out major contribution projects. Andy was also an avid Villanova University supporter and a prime example of a high-earning executive who took full advantage of J&J's generous matching gift policy. For every $1 an employee contributed to a qualified nonprofit, the company donated another $2. Andy's generous annual support of Villanova turned into a super-generous commitment thanks to one of the most magnanimous matching gift programs in the nation.

- The only African American on the committee was Al Cooper, the former mayor of New Brunswick. A one-time star basketball player for the University of Connecticut, Al was a warm, gracious J&J representative who directed cash contributions to several leading minority-focused nonprofits. Al constantly reminded both the committee and other J&J decision-makers that people of color represented a major customer base for J&J. "They will become increasingly important to us," he predicted, perhaps not fully understanding how right he would be.

- The committee also included a few line management executives who were the most essential pistons in J&J's massive economic engine. These were the individuals whose careers hinged on "making the sales and revenue numbers" on a regular basis. No one in this category was a better contributions committee member than a company group chairman named Bill Dearstyne.

"I'm at Carter Hall," Bill Dearstyne informed me after I answered the phone one afternoon.

"Carter Hall?" I asked, showing my confusion. "You mean Project HOPE's Carter Hall?"

"Right," Bill confirmed. "I'm in Millwood, Virginia?"

"Bill, I thought you were taking a day off. What are you doing at Project HOPE?"

"Unannounced inspection."

It was vintage Dearstyne. He would use his own time to run a quality control check on one of J&J's most important nonprofit partners. Project HOPE was a well-regarded international health and humanitarian relief organization based in Virginia and active in over 20 nations worldwide. It was one of only a handful of nonprofits qualified to distribute narcotic-based medications which J&J donated on a regular basis.

Bill Dearstyne's roadmap for professionalism was J&J's Credo. He measured every business decision against the company's deceptively simple four-paragraph doctrine. It wasn't unusual for him to carve out hours or even days either in the U.S. or abroad to personally visit a nonprofit organization funded by the corporation. His commitment to prudent philanthropy and all other aspects of the corporate Credo ran deep. Even after his retirement from J&J, Bill never lost his determination to continue his responsibility to "support good works and charity." He and his wife, Maude, moved to Austria where they launched a program called START aimed at finding ways to integrate immigrants into Austrian society.

Project HOPE   Bill and Maude Dearstyne's START Program in Austria

When I accepted the offer to sign on as a J&J employee, I planned to stay with the company for about five years – enough time to earn my stripes as a corporate contributions manager and reap most of the financial benefits of my front-end employment deal. Five years stretched into nine, a far longer tour of duty than anticipated. Certainly, the added financial incentives factored into the decision to remain on the job. But it was mostly people like Bill Dearstyne and so many others like him who were determined to make a difference that made it difficult for me to leave the corporation.

Top-tier executives were not the only J&J employees who practiced admirable professional and personal responsibility. Gary Gorran, whose financial efforts were so important to the rejuvenation of New Brunswick, continued to be a crucial part of the corporation's philanthropy efforts. Jim Burke's one-time administrative secretary, Helen Hughes, was moved to the contributions team and proved to be among the most revered emissaries for the business. Not only did Helen's multi-tasking competency win wide admiration, her friendly demeanor was enough to placate the harshest J&J critics.

But the corporate insider who was most instrumental in luring me to my J&J role and keeping me on board was Roger Fine. Intelligent and modest, Roger was a devout Jew. He would eventually serve as a trustee of a modern Orthodox movement called the Ohr Torah Stone Institutions of Israel. As someone long fascinated by the allure of – and allegiance to – organized religion, I would engage Roger in many conversations about Judaism and its sometimes-bumpy interaction with other faiths. Those discussions would occasionally become lengthy and engrossing talks usually carried out behind Roger's closed office door. As a corporate vice president and a member of the J&J executive committee, Roger was afforded a spacious office that included a handsomely decorated seating area. Framed photographs, mostly of family members, were strategically positioned on credenza cabinets and display shelves. Most prominent was a picture of a Puerto Rican nun named Sister Isolina Ferré, known affectionately to many as *Mother Teresa of Puerto Rico.*

"You're Jewish through and through," I said to Roger. "Yet a picture that stands out in your office is a snapshot of a Catholic nun. Why am I confused?"

Roger laughed. "Remember when we met Sra. Isolina?"

How could I forget. Months earlier, Roger and I had made a trip to Ponce, the most populated Puerto Rican city outside of San Juan. The municipality had taken a beating on many fronts in recent years. Thousands were left without jobs when a huge iron works factory closed. Then an even larger oil refinery shut down, adding to the unemployment misery. Prostitution was rampant and the overall crime rate was staggering. Against this backdrop of despair, a tiny woman literally plucked the poor off the streets and provided them with health care and education along with a strong dose of hope.

"*Tikkun olam,*" Roger said in Hebrew. I needed no translation. It was one of Roger's favorite expressions.

"Yes, I know," I nodded. "Repair the world."

"And that's exactly what she's doing," Roger noted. "Better than anyone I've met. I might not practice her religion, but I want to at least try practicing what she does."

So, Sra. Isolina looked over Roger's shoulder, constantly reminding him he was in a position few others could ever hope to find themselves. While not solely in command of J&J's multi-million-dollar charitable giving budget, Roger and those who worked with him had tremendous influence over how those funds were dispensed. "How many people get to use somebody else's money to make a difference?" Roger would periodically ask. The privilege Roger was afforded was never taken lightly. He was guided then and still is by an overriding mandate: *tikkun olam.*

"Word is Sra. Isolina may get the Presidential Medal of Freedom," I repeated a rumor circulating in a few Washington, DC circles.

"Can you think of anyone better qualified?"

Ponce, Puerto Rico   *Medal of Freedom*

I couldn't. I had met scores of women and men who devoted their lives to helping others. But Sra. Isolina was a cut above. Born into one of Puerto Rico's wealthiest and most influential families, she exchanged what could have been a life of luxury for a Catholic

Church vow to help Puerto Rico's poorest citizens. She founded a small hospital and a resource center (including a school) in La Playa, arguably the most poverty-hardened district in Ponce.

While deeply religious, Sra. Isolina was also a consummate activist who rarely bumped into a social problem she didn't try to fix. She was the inspiration for another **life lesson: faith fosters hope; confrontation fosters change.** Like many in the clergy, Sra. Isolina knew how and when to use faith to mitigate hopelessness. But she also had a strong secular bent that turned her into a confrontationist when faced with social inequality and injustice. It will never be known how many souls Sra. Isolina saved. But the impact of her earthlier confrontations *is* known. In those sections of Ponce where this extraordinary woman was a force, change happened. She used more than prayer to create opportunities and conditions that led to a 20 percent reduction in crime. Thanks to Sra. Isolina, I learned that although confrontation gets a rap for being a negative force that can push people in the wrong direction, it can also be a necessary intervention that produces positive results.

It was understandable why Roger wanted the tiny nun looking over his shoulder.

Roger changed subjects as he picked up a folder marked *Johnson & Johnson Community Health Program*. We walked to the headquarters executive garage, boarded a car waiting to drive us to Trenton-Mercer Airport where the corporation housed its three fixed-wing aircraft and a helicopter.

"Just a quick trip to DC and back, Mr, Fine?" one of the J&J pilots asked, glancing at a manifest.

Roger confirmed the flight plan.

"We've got the Gulfstream today," the pilot said and escorted us to the largest and most luxurious plane in J&J's aviation fleet. Usually it was reserved for much longer trips including trans-Atlantic travel. Maintenance crews were working on the other aircraft, the pilot explained. Of all the many perks J&J offered its senior staff, having access to company planes was close to the top of the list.

Gulfstream Corporate Jet   *J&J Nonprofit Partner: "NACHC"*

Once we were in the air, Roger scanned an updated report detailing one of J&J's most successful philanthropy programs. J&J had forged a relationship with an office inside the federal government's Department of Health & Human Services responsible for funding a wide network of community health centers. The partnership also included a third participant, NACHC - the National Association of Community Health Centers.

"Some of these health centers are doing amazing things," Roger correctly observed. He flipped through pages of examples underscoring the way health care providers were stretching dollars to meet the medical needs of millions of underserved Americans.

"Federally-funded community health centers get high marks from the government," I pointed out. "The Office of Management & Budget gives them an A-plus."

"And what we're doing adds value?" asked Roger.

"According to people like Tom Van Coverden, it adds a *lot* of value. J&J Community Health grants give centers the horsepower they need to try new ways of delivering medical services especially to women and kids."

Van Coverden was NACHC's president and CEO. He was also the most vocal and respected voice in support of the country's community health care movement. I was scheduled to meet Tom later in the morning to review plans for administering the next round of J&J community health program grants.

Roger looked up from the folder. "Let me ask you something. Of all the major philanthropy programs we're funding in the U.S., which gives us the biggest bang for the buck?"

I needed clarification. "Meaning what? Which program does the most to help people in need?

"That and which delivers the most return benefit to J&J?"

It was a difficult question to answer. Under the leadership of John Heldrich and Roger Fine, the company had a few highly regarded "signature" initiatives – charitable-giving programs branded with the Johnson & Johnson name. I asked Roger to give me a few minutes to think about his question. I mentally tried prioritizing a lot of good options including:

- Johnson & Johnson Focused Giving Grants. Cash awards to scientific investigators working in the basic research world were winning stellar reviews. Thanks to contributions committee member Bob Gussin, the program was garnering nothing but praise for J&J.

- The Johnson & Johnson Community Health Program. Roger was looking at indisputable evidence that grants to community health centers singled out by an independent selection panel meant a lot of dirt-poor adults and especially kids were getting health care services they otherwise might not have received. Funneling company pretax profits into a contributions pool used, in part, to address unmet health needs in the U.S. did not go unnoticed by government regulators and elected officials. Score more points for J&J.

- Johnson & Johnson's Pediatric Institute. Funding a program aimed at saving and improving the lives of mothers and babies added to the public perception that J&J was the country's number one "baby company." By partnering with the American Academy of Pediatrics, the Institute kept the corporation close to an important group of customers.

- Johnson & Johnson Bridge to Employment. Aimed at young people 14 to 18 years old mainly from economically disadvantaged locations, "Bridge" grants were used to keep kids in school and expose them to career options including the health care field. The longer-term hiring benefits to medical, pharmaceutical, and related businesses (J&J included) along with health care providers were obvious.

- Johnson & Johnson School Nurse Program (later changed to J&J School Health Leadership Program). In partnership with J&J's next-door neighbor, Rutgers University, the corporation approved grants to empower school nurses to do more to improve student health practices. By urging young people to make prudent lifestyle choices including those involving drugs and alcohol, the program impacted health outcomes. More praise for J&J.

The Gulfstream was on its descent when I finally answered Roger choosing two other J&J signature programs as my top selections. "Forced to pick, I would say our Head Start and Wharton programs are our two front runners."

Roger thought about the response and then nodded. "No question – they're both winners. What do you think about giving each an extra push?"

"What kind of push?"

"Start with Head Start," Roger leaned forward. "It's still *really* popular in the U.S., right?"

"Definitely."

"The feds pick up most of the cost for Head Start but is it fair to say J&J is the program's biggest corporate funder?"

"It is." My department had just done a thorough review of Head Start's private funding.

"A lot of people including investors might be wondering why we're at the front of the pack when it comes to Head Start."

I jumped in with an answer already well-known to Roger. "Because part of Head Start's mission is to deliver health and nutrition services to underserved kids. It's not just a preschool program."

"Exactly! The program is a reminder that J&J's interest in Head Start is to get decent health care services to kids living at or below the poverty line."

I nodded, wondering if the government's Bureau of Head Start could do more to broadcast that message. Although housed in the

Health & Human Services' bureaucratic labyrinth, the Bureau had been a remarkably cooperative partner in carrying out J&J's program. Even more helpful was the UCLA Anderson School of Management which was at the heart of J&J's effort to help the Head Start movement. I made a mental note to contact UCLA as soon as possible.

The Gulfstream thumped onto the tarmac as Roger reached into his briefcase and pulled out a second folder.

"Head Start gives us a lot of domestic exposure," Roger said. "But we're a global corporation and we need to start thinking more creatively about social responsibility ideas for countries outside the U.S."

Roger handed me a sheet of paper. It was the just-released consolidated financials for the corporation. "Notice how U.S. sales barely account for half the corporation's revenues?" he asked.

The numbers were obvious and not surprising. J&J had grown into a worldwide behemoth with the U.S. representing a smaller and smaller percentage of the annual financial pie. Roger didn't have to say much more. J&J had over 200 subsidiaries in 60 countries. Revenues were aggregated into a corporate pot with some of that pooled money used to finance the company's contributions budget – most all of which was earmarked for just the U.S.

"We should pump up our international philanthropy activities," Roger stated.

"What about all the products we donate that go overseas?" I asked. "We give away products worth hundreds of millions of dollars each year to dozens of countries around the world."

"Not many of those end up in the countries where our affiliates are sending us a ton of money."

Roger was right, as was usually the case. J&J's product giving was pointed mainly at developing nations where contributed pharmaceuticals as well as other consumer and medical goods weren't being marketed by J&J. Developed nations where company operations were registering impressive sales and profits rarely received a product contribution.

"We're putting together regional contribution groups in the U.K., Brussels, and Singapore," I noted. "They're already working on coming up with cash giving strategies for Europe and Asia."

"That's moving us in the right direction," Roger said. "But while that's happening, what about taking a program we've branded in the U.S. and seeing if we can internationalize the thing?"

"Like Wharton?"

Roger shrugged. "Why not? Think it can it be done?"

"Worth a shot," I replied. Another mental note: contact University of Pennsylvania's Wharton School.

We exited the Gulfstream and headed in different directions. Roger was en route to J&J's Washington office and I was driven to NACHC's headquarters where Tom Van Coverden and his team were waiting. It was 2004 and J&J's Community Health Program selection panel had already singled out several health centers that would be awarded sizeable J&J grants later in the year. NACHC recommended scheduling an award ceremony at each selected site. J&J should be represented at all presentation events, NACHC said. One grant was to be given to a neighborhood health center in New Orleans' Lower Ninth Ward. The funds would be used to launch a disease prevention project to be managed by a neighborhood health center. I agreed to be on hand for the award presentation along with a J&J community affairs specialist, Nancy Lane. No one was aware at the time that our community health center visit would precede a disaster so devastating that much of the Lower Ninth would be obliterated. Less than a year after the J&J grant was presented, Hurricane Katrina would hammer the Louisiana coast. The storm would spare no Ninth Ward home, business, or health care facility. Weeks after Katrina's ruinous landfall, the district would be hit again, this time by Hurricane Rita. The damage would be so severe, the area would remain under curfew for months. It would take years for volunteers and residents to begin the rebuilding process.

Following the NACHC meeting, the Gulfstream flew me back to New Brunswick where I checked my calendar. Roger Fine's suggestions about Head Start and Wharton became high priorities for me. Fortuitously, I was scheduled to be in Los Angeles the next week to take part in a Head Start dinner at UCLA. I called the program director, Al Osborne, and asked if we could get together a day early to map out a plan to put more emphasis on Head Start's efforts to keep low-income kids healthy.

"You play golf, right?" Al asked.

"I could be the world's worst golfer," I confessed.

"Good," Al said. "I'm just picking up the game and I need to play with someone who's as bad as I am. By the way, I joined the Bel-Air Country Club. You and I will shoot a round next week."

Bel-Air, I thought. This was totally out of my league. One of the best courses in the country, Bel-Air was famous for its Hollywood connections. The 14th fairway was where Howard Hughes landed a plane to impress Katharine Hepburn who lived adjacent to the course. I gulped and reluctantly accepted Al's invitation.

Next, I dialed Shel Rovin at Wharton's Leonard Davis Institute to schedule a meeting to explore ways to bring the Johnson & Johnson-Wharton Fellows Program in Management for Nurses to a location outside the U.S.

"Nanyang," Shel interrupted me before I could finish explaining what J&J had in mind.

"Nanyang?"

"Research University in Singapore," Shel explained. "Just so happens, they contacted me a few days ago. If we can put together a two or three-day seminar, the J&J-Wharton program goes on the road."

The Johnson & Johnson – Wharton Fellows Program in Nursing was a corporate philanthropy success story. Years before I was added to the J&J payroll, contributions committee member Ed Hartnett enlisted a seasoned marketing vice president to find a prominent university business school willing to launch a short-term management education for high-level nurse managers. Phil Doyle was a vice president attached to J&J's hospital services business. Phil, who was Boston Irish from top to bottom, was as knowledgeable about the U.S. acute care hospital world as he was about the Boston Red Sox. Like Hartnett, Phil was keenly aware that nurses (especially nurse managers) were key players when it came to making purchasing decisions. Phil also knew nurses too often were victims of what he called "the Rodney Dangerfield effect." When it came to strategic, non-purchasing decision-making, nurse executives were frequently not brought to the table. "They don't get no respect," Phil quipped, his deep Boston accent ruining his attempt at a Dangerfield-like imitation.

Phil had recruited me to work with him to develop a plan for equipping nurse executives with a mini-MBA degree from a university that had both a credible business school *and* a highly-regarded nursing school. There were not a lot of candidates. Our first stop was Harvard, where we were rebuffed in short order. But we hit pay dirt when we visited Wharton and met Professor Sheldon Rovin. Shel was a one-time forensic dentist who for a never-understood reason, u-turned his career to become a Wharton professor. Under Shel's direction (with Phil keeping a watchful eye), a three-week, intensive management program for nurses was designed. It would become the gold standard for short-term management education.

"Nanyang's open to running a kind of two- or three-day J&J-Wharton program for health professionals from different parts of Asia," Shel said. "Malaysia, Thailand, as well as Singapore. Maybe other countries as well. The program needs funding and J&J country managers will need to figure out who gets to attend."

Shel added that Nanyang wanted to fast-track the project, which meant getting contributions committee approval in the U.S. and finding the right J&J executive-level personnel in Asia to assist with the project. I made a quick trip to Bill Dearstyne's office and asked for his help. Bill had business responsibilities for parts of Asia and could pull all the right levers. As always, Bill agreed to get the project off the ground. The "internationalization" of the J&J-Wharton program was on the launchpad.

Now, on to Head Start.

Dean Al Osborne   *Nanyang Technological University (Singapore)*

A week after my NACHC meeting, I walked into the majestic Bel-Air clubhouse at mid-morning on a warm, cloudless Los Angeles day. Al Osborne was waiting at the front entrance and gave me a quick tour of the facility. In short order, we were on the first tee box. As Al's guest, I had honors and turned the day's opening drive into an out-of-control calamity. My ball flew to the left, sailing into a thicket of trees. I overheard my caddy whisper *This is going to be a long day.*

"Jeez," Al laughed. "You really are bad."

Al, tall and muscular, teed up his ball and fired. His shot flew high in the air and disappeared to the right of the fairway. Al's caddy shook his head and began what would be a pointless search for the missing ball.

And so it went for most of the morning. Al and I made up for the lack of golfing skills with conversation about the Head Start – Johnson & Johnson Management Fellows Program.

"Head Start directors are some of the most incredible people I've met," Al noted. This was a true testimonial to Head Start executives because Professor Osborne knew a *lot* of incredible people. Al directed the Price Center for Entrepreneurship & Innovation at the UCLA Anderson School of Management. As professor of global economics, management and entrepreneurship, he had educated and mentored a small army of MBA students who had moved into leadership roles around the country. What made Al a standout in the higher education field was his commitment to moral, value-based leadership, which won my admiration – and a lasting friendship.

"You've been on the board of directors of companies like Nordstrom, Times Mirror, USFilter (now Evoqua), Kaiser Aluminum, and Greyhound just to mention a few," I said as we walked to the tee box on hole number seven. A foursome ahead of us was nearly 300 yards down range standing just a chip shot away from the green. "And you're handing out compliments to Head Start directors most of whom haven't taken a business course in their lives. How come?"

Al waited to respond while I fired a ball into a sand trap to the left of the fairway.

Al teed up his ball. "The fact they *haven't* had any management training but are expected to run multi-million-dollar programs is pretty amazing, don't you think?"

Al took a vicious swipe at his ball, his driver striking its target so hard the thunderous crack rattled Bel-Air like a small earthquake. For the first time since we began play, a golf ball flew straight down the center of a fairway. Our caddies watched wide-eyed as the ball stayed airborne for over 250 yards and then rolled forward until finally striking the shoe of a chunky man just as he swung his lob wedge. When the man's ball plopped into a sand trap at the right of the green, he slammed his club to the ground. Then he turned and screamed at Al. Fortunately, we were too far away to hear most of the profanity.

"Wow," I said, astounded by what I had just seen. "I never thought you could hit a ball that far. And straight, no less!"

Instead of reveling in what he had just managed to do, Al seemed more concerned about being tossed out of Bel-Air. "How do we fix this?" he asked his caddy. That's when we learned in the world of pricey golf clubs, diplomacy is sometimes best left to the caddies. After the turn at the ninth hole, we were informed the foursome in front of us – a group including a toy company executive, movie producer, and two other moguls – were playing for several hundred dollars a hole. Al's ball assaulted the golfer whose game was deep in the loss column.

"So, is there room in the UCLA program to help Head Start directors find a way to put more emphasis on health and nutrition services?" I asked over a cold beer following what might have been the most outrageous game of golf ever played at Bel-Air.

"We'll make it happen," Al promised.

It was a promise kept.

Professor Osborne was the most talented management educator I had ever met. He earned a PhD from Stanford and had worked to resolve complex challenges including helping the Securities and Exchange Commission deal with liquidity and capital market access issues. But what Al loved most was entrepreneurship. He found that once he peeled off the social service skin from most Head Start directors, they had innate business capabilities. It was Al and his instructors who unleashed the leadership and management skills of scores of Head Start leaders. This was all accomplished through the Head Start J&J Fellows Program when directors were brought to UCLA where they lived for two weeks on campus immersed in an intense learning environment. Did it work?

- "… our agency has doubled our staffing, increased funding by 250% and reengineered our purpose to meet the changing needs of low-income children and families…" Triumph Head Start (Taunton, Massachusetts)
- "… the best experience I have had in 27 years with Head Start…" (Missouri Valley Human Resource Head Start)
- "… the most comprehensive, challenging, inspiring, life-changing and rewarding experience of my life …" (Stanislaus County Child & Infant Care Association – Ceres, California)

Yes, it worked. Hundreds of times over and with a lasting impact on the health as well as early childhood education of economically disadvantaged kids throughout the nation. After Bel-Air, I flew back to New Jersey not at all surprised to find Bill Dearstyne already putting together a framework for a Wharton mini-program to be rolled out in Singapore. Bill had recruited a small group of his direct reports who had responsibility for J&J businesses in a cluster of Asian countries. Their assignment? Come up with strategies for selecting hospital nurse managers and others who would most benefit from a modified Wharton experience.

It took a few months to nail down the necessary logistics. But thanks to Dearstyne setting the stage, Nanyang Technological University welcomed Shel in late spring of the following year. His Wharton affiliation made him an instant authority as was obvious by how he was greeted. One of Shel's requirements for taking on the overseas' assignment was that I tag along, ostensibly to help with instruction, but largely to be on the scene in case the program blew up. For the next two days, dozens of Asian health care executives – all with varying degrees of English language proficiency – listened to organization design concepts and theory. Shel did most of the lecturing and his audience seemed locked in on his every word. Participants scribbled notes after each of Shel's statements which were mainly extracted from his book, *Redesigning Society*, co-authored with noted systems theorist Russell Ackoff.

Having known each other for over a decade, Shel and I had become the kind of good friends who could banter about anything. After a long day at Nanyang, he and I were invited for drinks and dinner at Raffles, the century-old and iconic luxury hotel located a half hour away from the university.

"I watched everyone in the classroom when you were speaking," I told Shel while we were alone in a seating area near the hotel's famous Long Bar. "Whatever you said, they bought it. No matter what – they bought *everything*!"

"If you're an authority or a hero, most people will buy whatever you're selling," Shel shrugged. "I have a shingle hanging from my neck. Know what it says? *Wharton*. That's all it takes."

"There are limits," I argued. "Your credentials will only take you so far."

"Think so? How about a little wager?" Shel cocked his head toward a group of five health care graduate students who had crept into the back of a Nanyang classroom to monitor one of Rovin's lectures earlier in the day. These academic groupies had apparently tracked Shel to Raffles. "I'll bet you a Singapore Sling I can get those students to believe something totally ridiculous about hospitals. *And* I can do that in less than ten minutes."

This was a set-up, I thought to myself. Still, since Singapore's national drink was on the line, it was worth a gamble. "Just how far are you willing to go with this?" I asked.

Shell looked around the room, its tropical-like interior decorated with deep red furnishings and lush greenery. "Pick something," he waved at his surroundings. "I'll work with whatever you give me."

I ran through a few possibilities and then said, "socks."

"Socks?" Shel jerked back, not expecting my choice.

"Yeah, compression socks." I didn't even try to figure out why *socks* came to mind.

Shel rubbed his chin and then motioned me over to the five young Asians encircling a small table. The group gave Shel a look of awe.

"Tomorrow, you're welcome to sit in on a discussion we're going to have about one of the most serious problems facing hospitals in the United States and possibly the world as well," Shel began. "Know what it is?"

No one replied.

"Compression socks."

The five looked at one another, obviously confused by the Wharton professor's pronouncement.

"Totally off the radar, right?" Shel said. "Tomorrow, we'll talk about why we all have an obligation to deal with a medical menace that gets just about no attention."

One woman, who looked to be in her early twenties, asked: "Socks are that much of a problem, sir?"

"Surprising, isn't it?" Shel kept the fraudulent ball rolling. And then, glancing at me just to be sure I was paying attention to what was going on, Shel turned back to the woman. "So, tomorrow when I ask the question, *What's one of the most serious issues facing hospital patients that few people talk about?* you will answer...?"

"Compression socks!" two students replied gleefully. "The answer is compression socks, professor."

With that, Shel hooked my elbow and dragged me back to the Long Bar.

"Jeez, Shel," I muttered after we were alone. "You're just going to let that nonsense sit there?"

Three of the Asians were writing furiously in the notebooks they carried with them.

"Hey, post-surgical socks are important," Shel said and then ordered a pair of Singapore Slings. The Raffles' bartender nodded with a smile and poured jiggers of gin into a mix of pineapple and lime juice, Bénédictine, and curacao. "They prevent venous disorders."

"Yeah, yeah, I know. But making compression socks sound like they're in the same league as a staph infection or…"

"Don't worry, before they leave, I'll correct the record."

"By telling them what?"

"That I use socks as a way of making a larger point," Shel shot back without hesitation. "Great hospital care is a sum of the parts. All parts. Even small parts. Like socks."

Before we headed to dinner, Shel revisited the five students. He explained his sock logic and there were nods and smiles all around. Had there been no clarification, I was convinced dozens of Asian hospitals would have soon implemented mandatory sock alerts. Shel's spontaneous and largely bogus performance left me with an unsettling **life lesson: Accepted authoritarianism puts truth in jeopardy.** I had just witnessed five smart young people seemingly absorb a fabrication without so much as one serious challenge.

Over the next few years, J&J steadily internationalized its philanthropy and related social responsibility programs. The growth occurred without diverting any funds from those highly successful signature initiatives that continued to be fully supported inside the U.S. Taking into account the fair market value of donated products along with hundreds of millions of dollars in cash donations, the corporation now ranked as one of the world's most generous businesses. On the anniversary of my fifth year with the corporation – the deadline I had given myself for staying with J&J – I took stock of my situation. I had a dream job supported by a team of competent professionals at all levels of the company. Maybe a couple more years before leaving J&J's comfort zone; a couple more years before renewing the fight to push the private sector to mirror what J&J was doing. A couple more years ...

Then in 1996, the corporation made several high-level executive moves. The most consequential change affecting me was a decision to name Roger Fine general counsel. Unexpectedly, I had a new boss, a lawyer picked to be J&J's vice president of administration and a corporate executive committee member. Russell Deyo had been recruited by J&J years earlier after serving as head of the public corruption unit inside the New Jersey U.S. Attorney's Office. Anyone who had responsibility for prosecuting big-name, notorious crooks had to be a hardnosed, take-no-prisoners type. Wrong. As I quickly learned, Russ was as easy-going as he was pleasant.

"Favorite part of my job," Russ said a few months into his new role. It had taken him no time to pick up J&J's corporate philanthropy reins. Like Roger, he became an ardent advocate for the company's contributions program. Russ and I forged close professional and personal ties that would continue long after both of us were no longer on J&J's payroll. Russ would later play an important part in another forthcoming venture of mine and in turn, he would call on me as a *pro bono* aide after Congress appointed him to a top executive position at one of the federal government's largest and most complex departments.

"Russ, it's time." My announcement was delivered one spring morning in 1999.

"Time for what?" Russ looked puzzled.

"I promised myself I would stay at J&J five years," I said. "I've been here nearly twice as long as I had planned."

"And that's a problem because...?"

I explained how I had only a few professional years left and needed to pick up a crusade I had left at J&J's door when joining the corporation. America's private sector needed a better understanding of how and why it should be partnering more extensively with nonprofit organizations, I said. Russ countered with several compelling reasons why exiting J&J made absolutely no sense. But I was steadfast and when our long conversation ended, Russ knew there was no reversing my decision. We agreed I would make a slow withdrawal, giving the corporation as much time as needed to find the right replacement.

"You're *what?*" one of my J&J colleagues exclaimed. It had taken only hours for the news of my planned departure to trickle through the company's rumor mill.

"The golden handcuffs are getting a little too tight," I explained. More accurately, they had become *very* tight. Although my job was to leverage a portion of J&J's profits to ease global pain and suffering, I did so while living like a prince. Each day, my car was valeted, gassed, and cleaned. I lunched in the executive dining room enjoying daily fare that would rival the best restaurants in the world. My wife and I had been invited by TV networks to three Olympic games (Japan, Norway, and Atlanta). I traveled mainly in private jets and I was compensated handsomely.

"But you'll be leaving *millions* on the table," was the expected reaction. "You're not even 60! You're going to walk away from years' worth of stock options, certificates of extra compensation, cash, and stock bonuses…"

"The money's tempting," I admitted. "But fortunately, my wife is on my side when it comes to piling up more cash. We don't have any debt. We own a modest house and a couple of older cars. We've paid for the kids' higher education and we've set aside a small fund for grandchildren if they need help with college."

The look of dismay wouldn't go away. "What are you going to do?"

I hesitated with an answer. "A good question," I finally responded. Then I followed up with an unsettling postscript: "I'm not sure."

***

Buster Soaries continues to be the inspirational senior pastor for the First Baptist Church of Lincoln Gardens. His career path took a sharp turn when he was recruited as New Jersey's first male African American secretary of state (1999-2002). Since then, Buster has been multi-tasking on many fronts: community development, finding solutions for foster care kids, and launching the Financial Freedom Movement (teaching people to break free from debt).

After a long, debilitating illness, the powerful Jim Burke died in 2012. His business leadership and post-J&J activities won him the nation's highest civilian honor, the Presidential Medal of Freedom. At age 64, he retired from the private sector and became chair of the Partnership for a Drug-Free America (now called The Partnership at Drugfree.org). His creativity helped the Partnership become a force in combating substance abuse. Jim taught me another important **life lesson: Gray power is America's most unexploited energy source.** There are nearly 50 million retired workers in the U.S. Most are in reasonably good health. Linking an older person's time and talent to a social need or opportunity taps a potential that remains far too untapped.

Once retired, Bill Dearstyne and his wife relocated to Austria. He took much of J&J's credo philosophy with him. Bill has been instrumental in expanding the START Project, a unique scholarship initiative set up to help migrant students or financially strapped young people who have a migration background.

After logging 30 years at J&J, Roger Fine retired but was soon named chairman of the world's largest public health nonprofit – the Robert Wood Johnson Foundation (RWJ), which *Fast Company* singled out as "one of the 10 most innovative not-for-profits globally." Roger divides his time between his foundation responsibilities and the venture capital firm, Windham Venture Partners.

Cancer claimed Shel Rovin in 2009. He was 76. As professor emeritus at both the Wharton School and the University of Pennsylvania School of Dental Medicine, Shel was a nonstop advocate for more creative thinking especially among health care organizations. He was unrivaled in his belief that nursing was at the core of a successful medical system.

Predictably, Al Osborne's golf game excelled as did his status at UCLA. He was appointed interim dean of the Anderson School while continuing to promote his belief that entrepreneurship and innovation are essential nutrients for communities, states, and nations. "Societies that don't innovate are destined to die," Al would write.

Russ Deyo would replace Roger Fine as J&J's general counsel and executive committee member, a position he would hold until 2012. Three years later, he would head to Washington as undersecretary for management at the Department of Homeland Security. Russ would be promoted to deputy secretary before leaving his government post in early 2017.

Chapter 13

ACCP (1999- 2009)

CHARLESTON

SAVANNAH

PALM COAST

The first call came at 11 p.m. Had it not been for an enormous Maersk container ship gliding by the window of my Hyatt Regency hotel room, I would have been asleep a half hour earlier. But the Hyatt had cleverly installed tiny lights in each of its guest rooms facing the Savannah River that went live when a mammoth vessel approached. The waterway to Savannah's commercial port was busy day and night. On this fateful evening, there was more boat traffic than usual and I was captivated by the passing parade of ships.

I lifted the house phone after the second ring. "I'm *really* sick," the woman said, her voice shaky. "I just wanted you to know in case I'm not able to make the class tomorrow."

The container ship cruised away, its wake turning the river turbulent. The choppy waters turned out to be an omen.

The second call came a few minutes later. Six of the 20 participants attending what was presumptuously called the Contributions Academy were men. The call was from one of the six. The Wells Fargo manager informed me that he was on his way to the emergency room. Nonstop vomiting and debilitating cramps.

Two more calls followed, both detailing their gastrointestinal issues. I phoned the front desk, explained what was happening, and made sure the local EMS was put on alert if the medical calamity worsened.

The next morning, I walked into a Hyatt meeting room adjacent to the main lobby on the first floor. The conference space had been reserved for a three-day workshop designed to provide "management fundamentals" to 20 corporate contributions managers who had traveled to Savannah from around the country. I counted only eight participants in the room along with my instructor partner, Don Greene.

"Should we call it off?" Don whispered as I walked through the door. "We don't even have a quorum."

A recently retired Coca-Cola executive, Don had seen his share of meetings including a few that went sour. In his 30 years with Coke, Don had spent nearly half that time as president of the company's foundation. On top of that responsibility, he served as Coca-Cola's corporate secretary.

I quickly scanned the room. The seven women and one man all appeared healthy. Don, on the other hand, looked pale.

"Some of these people traveled thousands of miles to be here," I pointed out the obvious to Don. "They're all paying customers, Don. Sending them back to California, New York, Michigan means refunding ..."

"I know, I know," Don interjected. "But there are a dozen participants too sick to climb out of bed. What about them?"

Maybe this was a 24-hour virus, I thought. "Let's do this morning's session as planned," I said. "Hopefully we'll have a full classroom later in the day."

Don wasn't buying my decision and his next comment explained why. "I'm not feeling that great myself. Not sure I can make it through the morning,"

"It's all in your head, Don," I said, uncertain I was right. Don was not the psychosomatic type. "Once we get started, you'll be fine. How about we open with a couple of jokes? It will lighten things up and get your mind off your stomach."

The eight healthy participants pulled their chairs into a semi-circle around a flipchart resting on a portable easel. Don and I stood on opposite sides of the large pad, the words *Corporate Contributions Academy* printed in Magic Marker on the cover sheet.

"So, Don, did you hear the one about the nun, the rabbi, and the philanthropist?"

Don's face flushed and his cheeks puffed out. He mumbled a few words and raced out of the room heading for the hotel's main foyer. That's where he threw up.

"May I have a word?" the hotel's general manager beckoned to me after Don was escorted to a restroom. I was led to a private room where two men wearing dark suits and the hotel's head chef were seated. The chef was in tears.

"Homeland Security is making it impossible for us to continue service," the manager announced while shooting the two suits a venomous stare.

"*What?*" I was dismayed.

"Apparently when a large number of guests become ill at the same time, there's a government policy that requires a hotel to cease all restaurant and catering operations," the manager went on. "Under the circumstances, we can't accommodate your group. For the record, several members of a church organization staying here also became ill last night. They'll be leaving as well."

All eyes pointed at the chef who was trying unsuccessfully to control his weeping. Food poisoning apparently was not a step in the right direction for a cook anxious to move up the culinary profession ladder.

"We have to check to make sure this was a food contamination issue," one of the men explained. "If it's something else ..."

"I have 20 people here for three nights and four days," I moaned. "What am I supposed to do?"

"Terribly sorry," the manager responded. "I'm sure the Hyatt home office will make things right. In the meantime, there are a couple of loose ends we need to address."

"Excuse me?"

"One of your participants has been hospitalized and is quite sick," the manager said, his face showing more concern than the tone of his voice. "And another woman enrolled in your program was seen leaving the hotel very early this morning. She seemed quite disoriented. Is anyone missing from your group?"

I was beyond words. I stared open-mouthed at the manager.

"We'll process a missing person alert in a day or so if the lady isn't located," one of the seated men said calmly.

Fortunately, the hospitalized participant recovered and flew home to Southern California about the same time the Hyatt re-opened in Savannah. Without informing anyone, the missing woman (an oil executive based in the San Francisco Bay Area) had booked a last-minute plane ticket to her mother's home – in Hawaii. The lady later said she had only a vague recollection of the trip and was still experiencing the aftereffects of the Savannah event.

The resilient Don Greene rebounded quickly and we began discussing when and where to reschedule the Academy management forum. None of the 20 executives seemed overly enthused about a re-do. Even so, in our claim to the Hyatt, we included a line item for travel and housing of 20 corporate managers to make their way to another hotel *not* in Savannah. Hyatt's home office did eventually settle, offsetting all participant expenses. The hotel also compensated the Academy for loss of business and other damages.

Savannah Hyatt Regency with view   *Book Release: 1998*
of the Savannah River

The Savannah incident was just one of several memorable chapters in the evolution of an organization that would quickly grow into the nation's largest professional association for corporate responsibility professionals. The venture began before my "out-the-door" party at J&J. In 1998, I convinced Steve Piersanti, president and CEO of Berrett-Koehler Publishers, to produce a book titled *Corporate Social Investing.* Subtitled *The Breakthrough Strategy for Giving and Getting Corporate Contributions,* the book never made the *New York Times* best seller list. But thanks to forewords by actor and philanthropist Paul Newman, and the investment genius Peter Lynch, the publication did catch the attention of a lot of corporations across the country.

Corporate Social Investing gave me a platform to develop a concept that clicked into place immediately after my last day at J&J. My wife and I decided to trade New Jersey's cold, wet winters for Florida's warmer weather. We settled in an out-of-way community called Palm Coast located halfway between St. Augustine and Daytona Beach. The town was in its early stages of development and didn't have a lot to offer – except for a small conference center and motel overlooking the Intercoastal Waterway. It was the perfect location for the launch of the Contributions Academy. Business representatives who showed up in Palm Coast would have no distractions and could focus intently on designing strategies to make corporate philanthropy far more effective.

The first Academy class was as much a social gathering as it was a mini-thinktank. Among those who trekked to Palm Coast were Karen Davis (Hasbro) and Ed Wallace (Sony). Both were on track to become vice presidents within their respective companies. Patrick Dexter, the community relations advisor to ExxonMobil, and Conrad Person, a forward-thinking J&J director, expanded the industry mix at the inaugural forum. But it was one of the few women employed by the Michigan-based Visteon Corporation who would become vitally important to the Academy. Melinda Bostwick managed a 20-country philanthropy program funded by Visteon, the automotive electronics supplier spun off by Ford Motor Company in 1999. Melinda would be named to the Academy's board of directors and years later, recruited as a staff member.

From a management training vantage point, Palm Coast was an ideal location for a professional development program. There was simply not much to do other than conceptualize ways to build stronger corporate social responsibility initiatives. It was this same isolation that drove my wife stir crazy. I had married a woman who relished being only an hour from an American Ballet Theatre performance at Lincoln Center prefaced by dinner at the Metropolitan Opera House's Grand Tier restaurant. It became increasingly clear that we needed to relocate to a more cosmopolitan part of the country before she became stark raving mad.

One of our children was completing her advanced nursing degree at the Medical University of South Carolina in Charleston. The city was yet to be ranked one of the top tourist destinations in the country. Even without that distinction, it was a southern cultural center, crammed with excellent restaurants and an easy 80-minute flight to New York's LaGuardia Airport. Leaving Palm Coast was not complicated since we were renters who wisely had delayed buying a house. We did, however, own two vacant lots that were possible home sites. Both were easily sold.

Charleston offered enough potential for us to gamble on staying put long enough to warrant building a house. We settled into a modest one-story home on the edge of a marshy creek that ran through a section of Mount Pleasant, a Charleston suburb about to experience a population explosion that would make it the fourth largest municipality in the state.

The Academy shut down operations in Florida and moved to rented space in Mount Pleasant. Academy management forums were conducted at a hotel in downtown Charleston with special events plugged into the experience that gave attendees a snapshot of the city's history and culture.

It was then the Academy ran into an unexpected bump in the road.

"We can't go to Charleston anymore," one of the Academy's directors said bluntly. He was calling from his office just outside Washington, DC.

"I don't understand," I replied. "What's wrong with Charleston?"

"Nothing South Carolina couldn't fix."

Next came the distressing explanation. "No going to meetings in South Carolina until the Confederate flag comes off the top of the statehouse."

There had been rumors some corporations might boycott South Carolina because of the Confederate battle flag that crowned the state's capitol building in Columbia. Trying to stay one step ahead of this potential problem, I had been in touch with the state NAACP leadership arguing the Contributions Academy should be exempt from any boycott or campaign aimed at keeping tourists and business events out of South Carolina.

"Look, the NAACP gave us a pass," I explained. "We're in the clear." The NAACP decision was based on the Academy's ability to bring dozens of corporate philanthropy decision-makers to Charleston. Most, if not all, attendees would help build the case against continuing to fly the controversial flag atop the copper dome that capped the blue granite state house.

"Doesn't matter," the caller batted down the NAACP news. "Until the flag is off the dome, we're out."

A few days later, I fielded two more calls from businesses expressing "deep concern" about holding meetings anywhere within the South Carolina borders. The Academy's new venue was in trouble. Not only was I facing a loss of revenue because the business community was making a wide circle around the state, so was Charleston and probably other South Carolina cities as well. I wrote an op-ed for the local daily newspaper underscoring the economic downside of not removing the flag.

The same day the piece appeared in print (reworked as a letter to the editor with my name and town prominently noted), that's when the phone rang.

"You should move your Yankee ass back north where you belong," the caller said. He made no effort to conceal his identity. He was a limo driver and a proud member of the Sons of Confederate Veterans. I let him ramble on for a few minutes listening to how the flag is a symbol of Southern ancestry and heritage. I did learn a few things. The battle flag was designed for the Army of Northern Virginia under the command of Robert E. Lee. South Carolina's own Strom Thurmond brought considerable attention to the flag in the 1940s when his Dixiecrat political party became nationally prominent.

"Look, I don't want to waste your time or mine arguing the legitimacy of the flag," I finally cut into the caller's diatribe. "Put it on display somewhere other than where it is now and South Carolina lands a lot more business."

"It's not going anywhere," the man snarled. "If anything goes, it's you."

I didn't bother debating the caller by referencing facts I had researched while digging into the flag's past. A vast majority of Southern blacks regarded the flag as a symbol of racism. As for Americans in general, a small percentage had a positive attitude about the flag; about 90 percent of the population had either a negative impression or were neutral.

The limo driver left me with another **life lesson: the past can be a guidepost for the future or a headwind to progress.** Even before I threw myself into the South Carolina flag debate, I was aware history cut two ways. The past can help us understand how earlier decisions can lead to either positive or not-so-great consequences (e.g. "never forget…," etc.). But the past can also be a super-magnet so strong it impedes efforts to move forward. The highly charged flag debate had locked people in place, at least in the short term. This was not an issue that would be resolved anytime soon. Academy workshops and events had to be moved.

"What about Georgia?" asked Bill McCargo, the long-time executive at Scientific-Atlanta (acquired by Cisco Corporation). Bill had deep Georgia roots, so the suggestion did not come as a surprise.

"Georgia has its own problem with the Confederate flag," I contended.

"Not anymore," Bill replied and then brought me up to speed on a decision the state assembly had recently made. From 1956 until 2003, Georgia flew a flag that featured a prominent representation of the Confederate battle flag. Growing vocal opposition to the flag nudged Governor Sonny Perdue into authorizing a new design. The proposed flag (with no obvious Confederate symbolism) was turned into a statewide referendum. When the votes were counted, 73 percent of Georgia voters gave a thumbs up to the replacement flag.

Confederate Battle Flag *Georgia State Flag (as of 2003)*

Bill suggested Atlanta as a decent alternative to Charleston. I recommended Savannah because of its historic and cultural similarity to Charleston. Plus, there was my drive time consideration – three hours to Savannah and at least five to Atlanta. Bill convinced me to poll a few Academy alumni and there was unanimous agreement that Savannah was the right venue for future Academy workshops. Business executives soon were flocking to the "Hostess City of the South" giving Savannah high marks until several were knocked off their feet by what was rumored to be contaminated shellfish. Neither Homeland Security nor Hyatt would confirm or deny what caused the hotel shut-down on that fateful day.

Miraculously, the Academy navigated around the roadblocks encountered during its early years. The program experienced slow but steady growth.

"You know, those of us who have been through the Academy would like to stay connected," Brian Glowiak said. He was vice president of the Chrysler Corporation's company foundation. "What about an annual reunion?"

Glowiak's idea sparked a spirited discussion among a half dozen contributions executives who were listening in on the conversation. "This organization has turned into something more than just the Academy," said Jennifer Steiner, then the executive director of the Toledo-based HCR Manor Care Foundation.

"Where are you going with this, Jennifer?" I asked.

"Make the Academy part of a larger operation. Get companies to sign up as members. In addition to running the Contributions Academy, schedule an advanced management conference at least once a year. Start an internet newsletter to keep us up to speed on who's doing what in the field."

A lot of heads nodded in agreement.

The four-day Academy workshops were already keeping me working full-time. Adding a large annual conference in addition to other services might prove too much. "This would mean setting up a new nonprofit organization," I said. "What would we call the thing?"

"An association," Jennifer answered quickly. "Call it the Association of Corporate Contributions Professionals. ACCP."

"It's a mouthful," Brian and I said at the same time. "Still, the name says it all."

And so, on March 5, 2005, ACCP was officially born. Articles of incorporation were filed in South Carolina and the IRS granted the new organization a 501c6 status – a nonprofit category covering chambers of commerce, business leagues, and professional associations. ACCP named its first board of directors – 15 contributions executives selected from a cross-section of industries:

* Becton Dickinson (or BD)
* Boeing
* Chrysler (now Fiat Chrysler Automobiles or FCA US)
* ExxonMobil
* Hasbro
* Johnson & Johnson
* Lockheed Martin
* Northwestern Mutual
* Sony
* Starbucks
* Tupperware
* Turner Broadcasting
* Verizon
* Visteon
* WellPoint (merged with Indianapolis-based Anthem in 2004)

ACCP was an immediate success. Annual "reunions" turned into large events held in different cities around the country such as San Antonio, San Diego, and St. Petersburg. Attendance was sufficiently large enough to attract businesses selling services to corporate philanthropy departments as paying exhibitors. A new revenue line was created.

"We need to talk," said Donna Kraemer. Donna was ACCP's most important employee. Although her title wasn't chief operating officer, that is exactly the role she played. I had hired her years earlier when she answered an ad for a part-time assistant. She, her husband, and two kids had just moved to the Charleston area from Pennsylvania where she had been (among many other things) an information technology specialist. Her part-time work quickly exploded into a fulltime position and then some.

She handled ACCP's finances, meeting planning, IT issues, and a dozen other tasks.

"Is there a problem?" I asked, knowing there had to be. Donna rarely needed me to deal with an issue. This couldn't be good, I thought.

"The hotel manager has asked us to come to his office," Donna explained. "One of the maids has registered a complaint against a guest."

"Who?

"A vendor."

Donna and I walked to the hotel's administration offices. This was one of our largest annual conferences that had attracted over 100 member companies and nearly a dozen vendors. We didn't need this kind of disruption.

"What happened?" I asked.

"The maid opened the door to the vendor's room and he was wearing a tie," she said.

"A tie? A lot of vendors dress in a suit and tie."

Donna shook her head. "No suit. No shirt. Nothing on but a tie."

"You mean...?"

"He asked her to come into the room, wagged his tie a couple of times, and sent the maid screaming to her supervisor."

The hotel manager greeted us without an attempt at a smile. "The guy has to leave. Now."

We discretely confronted the vendor who denied some but not all of the maid's story. He was asked to close his exhibit display and check out of the hotel. He did so without further incident.

The tie fiasco was the latest in a string of events that made running training forums and larger meetings a challenge. I reflected on other indelible memories:

* A suicidal woman whose professional life was marred by a chauvinist boss and a marriage that was falling apart.

* A heavy-set lady who sat on a hotel toilet only to have it shatter into a pile of ceramic shards some of which penetrated her back end.

* A drunk participant who fell down a flight of stairs.

"Maybe it's time I take a break from doing these meetings," I said to Donna.

"You can't just bow out without putting together a management team to keep ACCP alive," Donna replied.

"Well, the organization has you," I reminded her. "And we hired Melinda Bostwick." The one-time Visteon employee was now on the ACCP payroll and a membership coordinator. She had made close connections with most of the corporate member representatives, a move that greatly stabilized the organization.

"That's not enough," Donna stated strongly. "You need to find someone who can replace you and who can take ACCP to the next level."

Donna was right, as was always the case. It really was time to pass the baton to a new leader who had the vision and capacity to grow ACCP. The organization began a national search for someone with the knowhow to oversee a small team of talented, specialized personnel; someone willing to take a gamble that a relatively new enterprise could continue to be professionally relevant and financially stable.

Our first serious candidate was an experienced communications executive from California. We were close to negotiating an employment agreement, when he was involved in a traffic accident and lost the use of his hands. The development put us back to square one. That's when I boarded a plane for Orlando.

"You're asking me to take on a lot of risk," Mark Shamley said, as he whacked a golf ball straight down a par five fairway.

"Well, we have a steady financial revenue flow and a pretty strong asset base," I answered as I used a three wood to trickle a ball 10 yards from my tee.

"Let me get this straight," Mark looked me in the eye. "You want me to run a small nonprofit organization after being the point man for sealing the deal on a $480 million events center in Orlando."

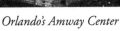
Orlando's Amway Center   *Mark Shamley*

I nodded sheepishly. Mark oversaw community relations and government affairs for the NBA basketball team, the Orlando Magic. He had won high marks for helping to convince public and private sector officials to invest in the new sports and entertainment venue in downtown Orlando. For the city, it was a herculean project called the "Centroplex" that was to include the new arena, a $375 million performing arts center and a major expansion of the existing Citrus Bowl.

"I know you had a big win in Orlando," I conceded. "You could probably name your ticket to whatever next job is out there."

This was not an exaggeration. Before joining the Magic, Mark had headed the global citizenship department at Tupperware and was executive director of the company's Children's Foundation. He had an MBA (Rollins College) and was well known to senior managers all over the country.

"So why would I even consider making a move to ACCP?" Mark pressed.

I had nothing left except: "Because you could make a real difference in the corporate social responsibility field. Do the right thing and put in a few years, Mark."

It wasn't much but it resonated. Several conversations later, Mark agreed to take over as the association's CEO and president. Minus the usual for-profit compensation add-ons (options, stock), he accepted a pay cut. But in exchange, ACCP agreed Mark and any new hires would be housed in an office to be rented in Orlando. Donna Kraemer would remain in South Carolina and Melinda Bostwick in Michigan – both would work remotely. In 2007, it was official. Mark Shamley was ACCP's new leader.

"So, now what happens with you?" Donna asked midway through the leadership transition.

"I've been pushing corporations to pump up their contribution budgets," I said. "Been at it for decades and there's not a lot to show for all the effort." That was an understatement. Recent data showed a *decline* in charitable giving on the part of corporations when measured as a percentage of pretax net income. "Maybe I've been poking the wrong bear."

"Meaning what" Donna asked.

"Meaning maybe I should help nonprofit organizations get more savvy about how to tap into a company's cash register and its workforce."

"Oh, no," Donna winced. "Not another organization."

I shrugged my shoulders. At my age, I wasn't certain I was ready to give birth to another startup. However, if nonprofits could be given the tools to raise more money ...

***

In June 2015, a 22-year-old white supremacist named Dylann Storm Roof walked into the Emanuel African Methodist Episcopal Church in downtown Charleston. Asked to sit and take part in the Wednesday night prayer service along with 10 black worshipers, Roof accepted the invitation. Then he stood and fired a Glock 41.45-caliber handgun. Nine parishioners were murdered, another seriously injured. Roof was captured and he and his neo-Nazi views soon became international news.

A week after the Emanuel Church massacre, then-Governor Nikki Haley called for the removal of the Confederate battle flag from atop the state house in Columbia. Following a contentious, 13-hour debate, the state legislature agreed to the governor's request. After flying over the capitol for more than a half century, the flag was taken down and moved to the Confederate Relic Room and Military Museum. South Carolina had at last cast off a symbolic shackle of the past but not before paying a hellish price.

Following ACCP's change of leadership, the cast of characters who had been instrumental in bringing the organization to life traveled in many directions:

Don Greene moved from the Academy to serve as the program director for the Conference Board Contributions Council. In 2009, he made a major career shift and joined his son and wife in raising alpacas. The Greene family own and operate Snow Diamond Alpacas in Bend, Oregon.

Melinda Bostwick remains a key player at ACCP in an elevated role as vice president of member services. She is a strong nonprofit advocate and even launched her own "Picture Me Project," a venture providing pro bono photographs to nonprofit organizations.

After Scientific Atlanta was acquired, Bill McCargo served as community relations vice president for Cisco Systems. He left to become president of the Atlanta Education Fund before opening his own consulting firm, B Mac & Associates.

Brian Glowiak followed up his long stint with the Chrysler Group by accepting a vice president position for the SME Education Foundation in Dearborn, Michigan. In 2019, he accepted the CEO position at Metro Community Development, a finance-focused organization based in Flint, Michigan.

Jennifer Steiner was recruited from HCA ManorCare to take on increasingly more expansive management responsibilities at three other organizations before being named CEO of Alsana, a national nonprofit initiative with locations across the country all aimed at helping people recover from eating and related disorders.

Donna Kraemer continues as the cornerstone for ACCP. The Penn State grad has been named the organization's chief financial officer and continues to be credited for much of ACCP's growth and success.

Mark Shamley remained in ACCP's wheelhouse for nearly 11 years before electing to return to the private sector. After a lengthy national search, he was replaced by Carolyn Berkowitz, former head of corporate social responsibility programming at Capital One Financial Corporation.

ACCP has continued to grow and remains the largest professional organization of its kind in the country (see appendix for list of corporate members). While the ACCP acronym has not changed, its official name has: the organization is now called the Association of Corporate *Citizenship* Professionals. The wording modification reflects the widening scope of responsibility shouldered by business executives charged with planning and executing a broad range of programs and activities that define a company's overall responsibility to society.

Chapter 14

New Strategies (2010 – 2020)

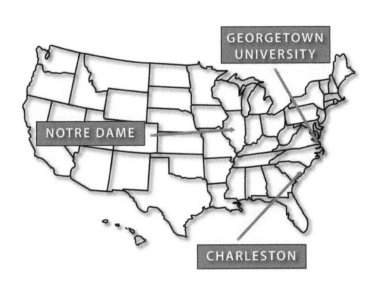

GEORGETOWN UNIVERSITY

NOTRE DAME

CHARLESTON

With an hour to kill before my meeting at Notre Dame's Mendoza School of Business, I used the time to tour a small part of the university's rambling, 1,250-acre campus. The grounds were meticulously maintained and the buildings – most no more than a few stories high – framed many of the quads scattered about the property. According to *Travel & Leisure,* Notre Dame has one of the most beautiful college campuses in the U.S. *No understatement,* I thought as I admired the surroundings.

My walk ended at the entrance to the famous Notre Dame football stadium, the 80,000-seat home field for the Fighting Irish.

"Hey, mister!" a sandy-haired man with two kids and a wife in tow called out. "You're a coach, right?"

I was confused. "A coach?"

"Listen, coach, could you do us a favor and take a picture" the man said, pushing a pocket-sized camera into my hand. "In front of Lou Holtz."

"But I …"

"Won't take a minute, coach," the man babbled while herding his family in front of a statue of the celebrated coach and two of his Notre Dame football players. "I gotta take this picture back home with me. Make sure you get me and the wife in the photo, ok? She graduated a year after I got out. We love Coach Holtz. Both of us *love* the man. You know him, right? I bet he's something."

I tried again to set the record straight but there was no interest in an explanation, only a snapshot. I clicked a few frames and returned the camera to the man, who quickly dragged his family toward Legends, the on-campus ale house strategically situated not far from the stadium.

Lou Holtz Statue

Notre Dame Football Stadium

"Well, you're wearing a sport coat and tie," Tom Harvey said a few minutes later. "Not many people dress like that especially around the stadium unless they're on the coaching staff."

"Nobody's ever mistaken me for a jock," I said. "I'm skinny as a nail and have no hair."

"You can be bald and still be a coach," Tom noted. "In fact, working with a swarm of gridiron types would be enough to make most people pull their hair out."

We both laughed.

"I'm impressed with the program you started," Tom got down to business. He opened a folder that included a pile of materials I had mailed weeks earlier. "Never have run into anything quite like it."

Coming from the man who directed Notre Dame's Master of Nonprofit Administration Program, I took his remark as a compliment. It was my first meeting with Tom, although I had heard his name many times in the past when he was CEO of Catholic Charities USA. I had been invited to Notre Dame to explore if/how a new nonprofit management program I had launched in 2011 could or should be brought to Notre Dame.

"Just want to be sure I have this straight," Tom leaned forward. "The way this program works is businesses select nonprofits to attend what you call New Strategies. Companies pay all the expenses for each nonprofit to show up in Charleston, South Carolina for four days of training. And they pay you a fee on top of that."

I nodded. "That's sort of right. Technically, since we vet each nonprofit recommended to us and sometimes end up rejecting an organization here or there, we own the responsibility for the final selections."

"And your program deals *exclusively* with how nonprofits can and should raise money," Tom went on.

"Which makes New Strategies unique," I said. "There are a lot of other programs that help nonprofits wrestle with general management and leadership issues. Indiana, Berkeley, Boston College, and many more universities including Notre Dame compete for that space. We hammer revenue generation and that's all we do."

"This might be a good fit for the Mendoza School," Tom mused. "How much do you know about Notre Dame's business school?"

I listened as Tom served up an abbreviated history. The school had been part of Notre Dame since the early 1920s. Then in 2000, Tom Mendoza, president of the cloud-based data services company NetApp headquartered in Sunnyvale, California, awarded the university a "naming gift." Mendoza's undergraduate and MBA programs moved up the rankings into the top tier of U.S. and global business schools.

"The university has had a pretty influential role in the nonprofit field," Tom said. "In1954 when the IRS coined the term 'nonprofit', Notre Dame's president at the time, Reverend Theodore Hesburgh established an MBA program. Back then, it was limited to executives who administered Catholic hospitals in the U.S."

How Notre Dame became an early and prominent leader in the nonprofit education field became clear as Tom continued his story. In 1967, the university made its MBA program more inclusive and was soon playing a major role in providing advanced management education to nonprofit leaders in all fields. "Today, our Executive Master of Nonprofit Administration Program is open to all," Tom finished his brief overview.

"I didn't realize how much of an impact Notre Dame had on the sector," I confessed.

"A big footprint," Tom nodded. "Let's get back to New Strategies. How many nonprofits are going through the program this year?"

"Sixty," I answered, knowing Tom already had the information in the packet of materials he was scanning. "But we're only in our second year. We should hit 100 next year."

"And the growth potential?"

"Between 250 to 500 nonprofits a year but only if we have the staff and venue capacity to handle those kinds of numbers."

"Which is why you are here," Tom noted.

"Yes."

"*And* why you're talking to Georgetown University," mumbled Tom.

"Yes." Tom was correct. Georgetown's McDonough School of Business also had a strong interest in New Strategies.

"When this New Strategies hits its stride, what's the revenue forecast?" Tom kept up the questioning.

"Between $2.5 million and $4 million a year," I said without hesitation. "Could be more depending on event sponsorship support, regional spin-off programs, and so on."

The projections certainly weren't eye-popping for a university with annual revenues topping $1 billion and an endowment well in excess of $10 billion. But I speculated Notre Dame was interested in New Strategies for another reason – the program would link the university with numerous businesses that were not currently donors. Our conversation continued as Tom took me to dinner in a nearby restaurant. He was as gracious a host as he was a gentleman. "Do you have any concerns about marrying your program with Notre Dame?" Tom asked over dessert. The way the question was posed, he knew I had reservations.

"Location," I replied truthfully. "Getting to South Bend is a bear, Tom. Not just for me but for most nonprofit executives."

Tom held up a hand. "Not to worry. I've thought about that. We have a new executive education center in Chicago. Close to the Palmer House where program attendees can stay."

I was impressed. I had stayed at the Palmer House. It was reputed to be the longest continuously operated hotel in the country, a legacy that would be appealing to many. And getting to/from Chicago would be easier than plane hopping to Notre Dame's main campus in northern Indiana. Still, with most New Strategies training sessions being held in fall, winter, and late spring, the thought of battling Chicago's often brutal weather gave me pause. Tom clearly read my apprehension.

"Quick question before we go," Tom said making his statement sound like an afterthought, but I was sure it was not. "You left

ACCP in late 2008 and started New Strategies in 2011. What did you do in between?"

I gave Tom an honest but incomplete answer. As soon as I was out the ACCP door, I was back in the philanthropy consulting business. Novartis, the Swiss-based pharmaceutical corporation, Blue Cross Blue Shield, and a few other firms booked most of my time. I deliberately avoided telling Tom about one client that pushed me off course; that led me to violate one of my earlier lessons learned – "pursue purpose; deflect distraction." Instead of staying on track to generate more money for the nonprofit world, I was sidetracked. It started with a phone call from a Chinese American medical doctor turned researcher turned entrepreneur. His name was John Dong.

A not-so-pleasant memory suddenly interrupted my dinner with Tom Harvey.

"You know many people in business," John had said, injecting the compliment shortly after our phone conversation began. He spoke in broken English. "You come work with GenPhar."

"Do we know each other?" I remember asking, completely befuddled by the call.

"We do background check," John informed me. "Know all about you."

That alone should have sent up a warning flag. But my curiosity ruled and I let the man talk. He asked for a face-to-face meeting in his office that happened to be in the same town where I lived, Mount Pleasant, South Carolina.

"We the only research lab developing vaccine to prevent Ebola, Marburg, and other bad viruses," John explained a week later when we were together. "Funded by Department of Defense and National Institutes of Health. But we want business partners to go commercial. You will make that happen."

"I will?"

"Make you consultant now and maybe senior vice president for business development later," John said.

I was hesitant but knew enough about Ebola and Marburg to give the offer consideration. John elaborated in detail about the effects of a hemorrhagic fever that Ebola inflicted on its victims. Patients bled profusely on the inside and outside, with death the usual outcome. The Marburg virus was nearly as deadly as its cousin, Ebola.

"Does your vaccine work?" I asked the logical question.

"Early testing all good," John replied, not elaborating. I should have extracted much more information. I didn't. "Defense Department want quick development and approval. Vaccine needed for military and first responders. All about biowarfare."

There were subsequent meetings and I agreed to sign a consulting and confidentiality agreement. Then, I made a few calls to contacts I had in the pharm industry. I was met with skepticism ("Know how many times we hear about a magic bullet vaccine that's going to save the world?") but did manage to connect John with a couple of possible private sector partners.

"You do good work," Jon praised me. "Make you senior vice president and give you corner office."

"Corner office?" I asked. GenPhar was operating out of rental space in a nondescript office barely large enough for his existing small staff. "What corner office?"

"In new headquarters." John rolled out the blueprints for a 50,000 square-foot building to be constructed on 2.6 acres in another part of town and included high-tech biolabs capable of storing the most dangerous viruses on the planet, GenPhar's home office would have a property value north of $30 million, John bragged.

It was another red flag that flew right by me. How could a struggling start-up find the capital needed to pay for such expensive real estate? I was familiar enough with government grants and contracts to know it was unlikely the feds were willing to underwrite the building. This was nothing more than a pie-in-the-sky dream, I thought, until GenPhar began construction on its new office.

"He got into a fight with one of the contractors," a GenPhar researcher confided during a phone call months after my first meeting with John.

"What kind of fight?"

GenPhar Headquarters

"Physical fight," the researcher revealed and went on to tell me about John's sometimes violent temper. John was shipping materials from China for the new building that the contractor said didn't meet code specifications. It wasn't the first time John Dong exploded, the researcher said. It wouldn't be the last.

With a lot of undisclosed maneuvering, the headquarters construction moved ahead and was near completion when John asked me to join him and his wife, Danher, for lunch at a local restaurant. Danher, like her husband, held both a M.D. and Ph.D. degree. She was also GenPhar's vice president for research & development.

"Need help," John said at the close of lunch. Danher looked uncomfortable which caused me to be on edge. "Want you to take $10,000."

"$10,000?"

"Keep $1,000 and make donation of $9,000."

"I don't understand."

"Donate to Lindsey Graham's political action committee," John said, as if this was all standard fare. He explained South Carolina's Senator Graham was critical in keeping money flowing from the federal government to GenPhar. By finding ways of funneling donations to the senator's PAC, odds were much higher there would be no slowdown in financial assistance for John's business.

For a few tense seconds, I was silent. Then remembering the insider leak about John's temper, I carefully explained this was something I couldn't and wouldn't do. When we left the restaurant, it was clear I wasn't getting the corner office.

I immediately pulled back from GenPhar but wasn't sure if divorcing myself completely from the business was a good idea. What if John Dong really *was* on the verge of developing the only vaccine effective against Ebola and Marburg? Could I help put him on a more ethical track so he could get to the finish line?

I stopped second guessing myself when John was indicted for illegal campaign contributions and fraud in 2011. The charges detailed how John donated money to Senator Graham through conduits including his wife, daughter, GenPhar employees, and even a German shareholder. In 2015, John and GenPhar (along with another side-company, Vaxima) were convicted of fraud following a five-day trial. A jury found John guilty of securing federal money for biodefense research and diverting those funds to construct a commercial office building and to pay lobbyists. The sprawling GenPhar headquarters went into foreclosure. In a follow-up proceeding held in 2017, GenPhar and Vaxima were fined $12.8 million. John Dong was sentenced to 70 months in prison for theft of government property, making false statements, and 22 counts of wire fraud. Senator Graham denied any knowledge of John's PAC donations.

The short but tumultuous experience taught me another **life lesson: deception's contorted path is littered with too much risk to warrant the journey.**

"Curt?" Tom Harvey called out.

"Sorry," I apologized and shook off the troubling GenPhar memory. "Momentary distraction."

"So, what do you think about Mendoza?" Tom asked.

"Well, Mendoza is a terrific business school that's lucky to have you on its team."

"Thank you," Tom responded. "But what about New Strategies? Is it a right fit for Mendoza?"

"I don't know. Is it?"

Tom smiled. "Let's both take some time to think this through."

"Okay."

"And I suppose in the meantime you'll take another look at Georgetown."

"I need to, Tom," I said.

And I did. As soon as I returned to Charleston, I set up another meeting with Bill Novelli, Georgetown's distinguished professor of the practice at Georgetown's McDonough School of Business. I not only knew Bill, I had enormous respect for the man. He was best known for a position he held just prior to moving to Georgetown – an eight-year run as CEO of AARP, an organization with 30 million-plus members. Earlier, he had served as president of the Campaign for Tobacco-Free Kids and executive vice president of CARE, the world's largest relief organization. Bill began his career by co-founding the public relations firm, Porter Novelli which became a highly regarded PR business. The firm was acquired by Omnicom Group, the massive media and marketing holding company.

"How do we stack up against Notre Dame?" Bill asked when we next met. He often got right to the point.

"They have a lot to offer."

"We have more," Bill shot back. "We have a state-of-the-art business school building that's practically brand new. There's quality staff everywhere you look on the campus. We've got a hotel next to the business school where nonprofit people can stay. And maybe most important, we can easily bring in people from the Capitol Hill and the administration to talk about government support for nonprofits."

A hard sell wasn't necessary. I had already decided if the right terms could be worked out, New Strategies would move from Charleston to Georgetown. The university was only an hour plane ride from my home. And Bill was certainly right about the value of being close to the federal government. A surprisingly large number of nonprofits were heavily dependent on public support from various government agencies. Then there was Bill himself. It would be enjoyable working with him on building New Strategies.

Before I could call Notre Dame about my decision, I received an email from Tom Harvey. He explained the Mendoza Business

School dean and Tom's team had given the New Strategies opportunity careful consideration. The university decided to pass.

"The decision in no way reflects on New Strategies," Tom wrote. "Rather it focused more on our own growth and ongoing commitments that are moving in a positive direction." Of all the rejections that had and would come my way, this one was most welcomed. I had been struggling with how to say "no" to Notre Dame and to Tom Harvey, two giants in the nonprofit world.

In late March 2015, the first New Strategies forum was held at Georgetown's McDonough School of Business. Bill Novelli assigned Ladan Manteghi, head of the school's Global Social Enterprise Institute (since changed to Business for Impact) along with a talented project coordinator, Bich Le, to be the on-site program supervisors. I enlisted Dana Frazeur, a South Carolina consultant who had worked with me on numerous ventures over the years, to work with the Georgetown crew. It was a masterful team.

Georgetown University   *Professor Bill Novelli*

American Express led the transition to Georgetown by sending eight nonprofits to Washington. The financial services organization, Thrivent Financial, added a half dozen more participants. Target, Rockwell Automation, Novartis, ConAgra, and Toyota USA filled the rest of the 29 seats. The New Strategies' Georgetown liftoff was the start of a rapid expansion of the program. By 2019, New Strategies was at capacity with four forums providing revenue-generating training to 240 nonprofit organizations, all of them sent to Georgetown by sponsoring corporations. In just eight years, New Strategies provided advanced management education to nearly 1,000 nonprofit executives (see appendix B for a partial listing of participating nonprofits).

New Strategies' effectiveness was linked to the caliber of instructors brought to each four-day forum. In recent years, four program faculty members have been particularly helpful to participants. Joe Waters, widely known for his blog, *Selfish Giving,* and recognized as the nation's top cause marketing specialist, works with nonprofits to design new ways to partner with businesses. Tanya Smith-Evans is a senior consultant for Community Wealth Partners who helps nonprofits leaders identify different types of non-charitable giving (e.g. fee-for-service) revenue options. Steve MacLaughlin, the data and analytics vice president at the technology firm, Blackbaud, shows attendees how to increase revenue from individuals with tips extracted from his book, *Data Driven Nonprofits.* Chris Gates, the former National Civic League president, advises nonprofit executives on where federal, state, and local government support for nonprofits is heading.

Perhaps most important to New Strategies is a group of businesses with strong corporate responsibility reputations that are represented on the program's advisory council. These businesses annually send most of the nonprofits that take part in New Strategies' forums. In addition, the council meets each year as a unique kind of think tank addressing developments and trends impacting how corporations, nonprofits, and government agencies intersect. The council includes:

* Aetna
* American Express
* BD
* Bristol-Myers Squibb Fdn
* Comcast NBCUniversal
* Ford Motor Company Fund
* Horizon Blue Cross BlueShield of NJ
* JPMorgan Chase & Co.
* Nike

* Alliant Energy Fdn
* Bank of America
* Best Buy
* The Coca-Cola Company
* Corning Inc. Fdn
* Johnson & Johnson
* Medtronic Fdn
* Merck Fdn
* Nordson Corp.
* PIMCO

* Northwestern Mutual Fdn
* Procter & Gamble
* PwC US
* Rockwell Fdn
* 3M
* Thrivent Financial Fdn
* Publix Super Markets
* Wells Fargo
* The Rite Aid Fdn
* Target
* MUFG Union Bank
* United Healthcare

Each New Strategies forum was updated and refreshed based on input from council members and evaluations from nonprofit leaders who completed earlier programs. There would be changes in administration (e.g. Ladan Manteghi would be replaced by social change expert and author, Leslie Crutchfield) with the most significant being the addition of two program directors:

* Ernest "Chico" Rosemond, a lawyer and formerly interim vice president for strategic alliances at AARP, and
* Bernard Boudreaux, a long-time Target Corporation executive prominent in the corporate responsibility field.

New Strategies forums all end with a guest speaker addressing nonprofit leaders at a closing dinner. No one delivered more eye-opening remarks to forum participants than my old Johnson & Johnson friend, Russ Deyo.

After winning Congressional approval to serve as undersecretary for management at the Department of Homeland Security, Russ spent much of his time in Washington. He volunteered to be the finishing speaker at numerous New Strategies events. In blunt terms, he disclosed how extremist groups used social media and other methods to recruit vulnerable young people. Russ also presented forum attendees with explicit details about human trafficking operations inside the U.S. He then outlined ways the nonprofit sector could play a much stronger role in addressing both these deeply troubling developments.

"Deputy Director Deyo recognizes the important role we play in this country and how we can do even more," one participant wrote after listening to Russ. In different words, that comment was echoed over and over by other nonprofit executives.

Four years after moving to Georgetown, New Strategies had become a fully integrated part of the university's business school. To ensure the program was meeting quality standards, nonprofit executives were asked to evaluate their experiences after each forum. These "outcome reactions" were consistently superior, which prompted sponsoring businesses to continue sending a new (and usually larger) batch of nonprofits to the program. New Strategies was delivering information and helping organization design revenue plans unlike any other institution or management training workshop. Although this was all very good news, I was left with one nagging question:

So what?

Yes, participants gave their Georgetown experience high marks. But were nonprofits applying New Strategies information in a way that made a difference to their overall revenue status? I had concluded long ago that outcome ratings don't always equate to the kind of impact programs usually aspire to achieve. That observation had led me to another **life lesson: outcomes are inches on impact's yardstick.** Outcomes are useful data points helpful in tweaking a program or making more notable course corrections. But it takes a credible impact assessment – a carefully designed yardstick – to answer the more important question: did the program affect measurable change? Regarding New Strategies, we needed to find out.

During the summer of 2018, over 500 New Strategies program graduates were asked to take part in an impact analysis which took months to complete. They reported the percentage increase in revenue achieved from fiscal years 2017 to 2018. That information was then matched against the average revenue growth for all nonprofits nationwide during that same period. The results:

Organizations that had participated in New Strategies reported revenue increases five times the national average.

Georgetown appropriately added a footnote that this extraordinary difference could not be fully attributed to New Strategies alone. Other factors came into play such as some New Strategies organizations receiving very large and atypical bequests. Nevertheless, unaided comments collected as part of the study made it clear that in most cases, it was New Strategies that directly or indirectly influenced revenue growth. The program was clearly making an impact.

Early in 2019, Bill Novelli and I met for dinner. As had become our tradition, we ordered sushi to go with a second round of adult beverages. "I think it's time, Bill," I said as a waiter brought a mix of mahi and shrimp tempura rolls to the table.

Bill didn't need a more detailed explanation. He knew exactly what I was saying.

"Wait a minute," Bill reacted strongly. "New Strategies is your baby. You can't just walk away."

"I want to move to the sidelines," I said. "Georgetown has a competent team in place and the program is on the right trajectory."

"You know what this is?" Bill noted. "It's ACCP all over again."

He was correct, of course. I had hatched ACCP and its forerunner, the Contributions Academy. Then when it was on solid ground, I turned it over to a talented, energetic management group that could take the organization to the next level.

Bill knew it was pointless to argue for a change of mind. Instead, we shifted to a discussion about a workable transition. Target's Bernard Boudreaux would replace me as program co-director. Chico Rosemond and a support team would remain in place. Bill would continue to provide general oversight.

"So, what are you going to do next?" Bill inquired. "Given how bad you are at golf, you're certainly not going to be spending a lot of time on the links."

"Not sure, Bill," I answered.

"I bet you have some thoughts."

Yes, I had thoughts. A lot of them. My career had been driven by a need to help the nation's million-plus nonprofits become more instrumental in improving the quality of life; in defusing conditions that were too often the seeds of conflict and war. In my view, that journey had not taken me very far. A line Bill would frequently fold into many of his public speaking appearances floated into my head: "We may not be able to change the world but we can at least try to make a dent." Being fully aware that nonprofit organizations were still operating far below their potential largely because of a lack of funding, my dent was an incredibly small one. Maybe I could do more. Maybe.

I leaned forward and said to Bill, "Suppose nonprofit organizations, businesses and government agencies could …"

Chapter 15

Reflections

Georgetown's Bulldog Tavern was crowded and noisy. It was after 10 pm and a few nonprofit executives had migrated to the basement bar not far from the university campus to wind down after a long day of New Strategies plenary and breakout sessions.

"I'm curious," said the CEO of a West Coast social service agency. "We all deal with issues we think are super-serious problems. Mine are homelessness, food insecurity, and mental illness. But if we were to rank order all the problems this country faces, would my issues be anywhere close to the top of the list?"

The question provoked an animated conversation fueled by draft beer and mediocre wine. The discussion led to this question: "What's the most serious challenge this country faces?" The responses were predictable: climate change; immigration; abortion; gun rights; religious and racial intolerance; white supremacy; health care access; gerrymandering; unchecked reproduction rates.

"We'll always be faced with high-priority problems," I chimed in. "The challenge is how we go about trying to tackle them."

"Any suggestions?" a woman asked. She was the development vice president for a disaster response organization.

"A couple," I replied. "We need the right kind of leaders working on solutions."

"And your definition of 'right kind of leader'?" The question came from a community health center executive.

"Character-centered," I answered. "People who bring the right attributes to the table."

"Attributes such as…?" another woman pressed.

I rattled off a small number of qualities that I argued added up to a definition of good character:

- Honesty. Every human is subject to making misstatements based on faulty information passed along by others. People make errors because of forgetfulness or a temporary inability to state facts correctly. But when falsehoods are knowingly made – and worse, repeated – a leader's character is seriously flawed. Deliberate deception and cheating fall in the same category.
- Respect. Putting others down by word or action sullies a leader's character. In addition to being tolerant of individual differences, positive leadership should include the capacity to "respectfully disagree" in a manner that excludes name calling or similar affronts.
- Responsibility. Taking ownership of problems when they fall under a leader's umbrella is a dimension of good character. Passing blame does nothing to enhance a leader's credibility.
- Empathy. An ability to understand someone else's concerns, misfortunes, pain, and suffering as well as their successes and achievements puts a leader in a different place when making decisions.

"Okay – what we're *really* talking about is how leaders here in Washington are falling short on character," noted the executive director of a Midwest community development nonprofit.

"Well not exclusively," I said. "Businesses don't always pay enough attention to character when picking leaders either. And, unfortunately, there are nonprofit leaders who wouldn't make the cut when it comes to passing a character test."

The group concurred that character flaws seemed to be more evident especially among government office holders. But the public seemed less concerned about character deficiencies if leaders "got things done," the group concluded.

"For sure, leaders need to accomplish tasks," I said. "But in doing so, they influence an organization's culture and can have a big impact on the behavior of those reporting to them. Even if a leader is a high achiever but is known as a liar, cheater, or has an arrogant disrespect for others, the institution or organization could pay a price in the long term."

"So, you'd like anyone running for public office or applying for a managerial job to make a kind of character pledge," the disaster response lady said. The group chuckled.

"I know that's a bit Pollyanna-ish," I said. "But at the very least, those of us already in leadership positions can use a character litmus test when selecting other managers."

"*And* we probably could do more to make it clear to our members and volunteers they should be making the right character-centered choices at the voting booth or in other situations where leadership comes into play," the health center executive added. Given that this small cluster of nonprofits at the Bulldog Tavern accounted for over a half million volunteers, this idea underscored the power of the nonprofit sector.

"For me," I said, "this is another **life lesson: a leader's character casts a wide shadow.** We sometimes forget just how much of an impact a leader's *character* has on others – whether the leader is running the country or managing an organization's accounts receivable department."

The group moved on to less serious topics until the social service executive reminded me I claimed to have a "couple" of thoughts about how to deal with society's big issues. "You have another life lesson up your sleeve?" she asked.

"Last one," I said. "This may sound over the top, but here goes – **life lesson: civility is an elixir for resolving political, social, and organizational differences.**"

Confused looks all around.

"Civility is good medicine," I explained. "It can make for really effective decision-making. And it can be a learned behavior."

"If you define civility as courteousness, that horse left the barn a long time ago," the community health leader pointed out. "Now it's who can shout the loudest."

I shook my head. "Doesn't have to be that way. Rules of behavior and discourse can be made clear for every event or meeting. It works in a courtroom and it can work in a classroom, corporate shareholder's meeting, or a legislative chamber. The more civil the proceedings, the better the odds for the best possible outcomes."

That was enough for a late evening. The group left the Bulldog and began the short walk to the Georgetown University Hotel where New Strategies participants and staff were housed.

"You've certainly been taught a lot of lessons over the years!" someone called out as we strolled toward the campus.

"Yes, but what was taught was not necessarily learned," I confessed. "And I suspect there is still so much more to know. So much more."

Epilogue

The 6 Pathways to Leadership & Organizational Success

"It was *very* hard to narrow the list of 50 pathway options," wrote Pamela Martin Turner, president & CEO of Vanguard Community Development in Detroit. "But for those I did select, experience has taught me they are true and important."

Pamela was one of 175 nonprofit leaders and 25 business executives asked to identify which of 50 principles, practices, and beliefs were the most relevant in guiding themselves and others toward professional and personal success. Many struggled with the sorting process. This was especially the case for nonprofit leaders whose agencies and institutions have broad mandates reflective of a range of social and economic concerns nationwide. Keeping in mind that the 175 nonprofits included in the pathways survey raise *$13.5 billion* in annual revenues and engage over *2.8 million* volunteers each year, feedback from leaders in these organizations proved very relevant. (Note: overall, the million-plus public

charities in the U.S. collect nearly $400 billion a year in dona-
tions and provide volunteer opportunities to more than 60 million
Americans).

No less essential to our pathways study were reactions from man-
agement-level employees in the for-profit sector. The 25 business
executives included in our survey work for corporations (selected
from different industry categories) with combined revenues of *$1.1
trillion* and *1.6 million* employees. So, getting the views of this constituency was also clearly important in our effort to pinpoint the
6 Pathways to Leadership and Organizational Success.

Using a process called the "Pathways Compass," the sorting exercise extracted what respondents considered highly valued
leadership behaviors and principles. Understandably, in assessing which few of the 50 options were priority concerns, the 200
leaders included in the study were influenced by the mission and
objectives of their respective organizations. But the Compass also
extricated numerous personal views and beliefs. "I gravitated to
those items on the list I found most important for my own children," said Stephanie Tolk, who is responsible for external relations
at Portland Children's Museum in Oregon. Several others echoed
Stephanie's reaction.

As taxing as it was for some, the Compass exercise yielded
conclusive and surprisingly similar results. The six top pathway
choices among nonprofit and business respondents were identical
(although with slight differences in the rank order of the top selections). Here are the *6 Pathways to Leadership Success*:

- **In your own way, be insatiably curious.**
- **Intellect, skill and wisdom are not exclusive to those with
  a formal education.**
- **Use positive thinking as a lens to look for an opportunity
  almost always hidden in a problem.**
- **Many errors are starting blocks for improved performance.**
- **Creating can be hard; sustaining can be harder.**
- **A leader's character casts a wide shadow.**

Why leaders in two different sectors picked the same set of six practices, beliefs, and principles can be better understood by examining respondent comments. These unsolicited statements helped make possible a deeper insight into each of the following top selections:

Pathway 1. In your own way, be insatiably curious. (Nonprofit rank: 1; Business rank: 1)

"Never stop learning and asking questions," advised Jennifer Pash, an executive with Habitat for Humanity of Collier County in Naples, Florida. Her words rang true with most other respondents who singled out "insatiable curiosity" as the number one preferred and important behavioral quality – more so than 49 other options.

This strong endorsement for irrepressible inquisitiveness sparked these questions:

- When counseling others either inside or outside an organization, does curiosity get enough attention as perhaps *the* most significant pathway to success?
- In hiring employees and/or promoting employees, how much emphasis is given to curiosity in making those important decisions?
- Should kids be informed about the importance of curiosity as part of their K-12 education experience? Can curiosity skills be taught?

Incorporating curiosity into an education curriculum could be a personal and occupational game changer. Turn curiosity into a subject or at least a topic of discussion for young people and the result might have life-long implications. "This is what inquisitive thinking actually means," is not a typical schoolroom take-away. Yet giving kids opportunities to develop their curiosity capacity could bolster their chances for success in school and long after they graduate. Plus, getting young people to understand how important employers consider curiosity could be a valuable career-development steppingstone.

In the workplace, as important as nonprofit and business leaders view curiosity, it is a factor that doesn't appear to get a lot of attention in the hiring process. There are easily accessible (and free) online questionnaires that would give employers an insight into an individual's curiosity level. Or, a job interview might include just a few telling questions:

* Do you think about creative ways to solve work problems even when you're not at work?
* Do you ever use social media to learn more about a subject?
* If you had the time and opportunity to take an adult education class, what would it be?
* Are you interested in learning how things work?

Answers will help uncover a candidate's penchant for acquiring new knowledge and skills. As for succession planning, a "curiosity check-up" might be added to the usual performance review as a way to earmark employees with the best potential for taking on added responsibilities.

Individuals demonstrating a strong interest in seeking out new information through exploration and investigation exhibit the single most important high-value indicator of leadership success.

Interestingly, the Pathways Compass exercise found senior managers were not at all concerned about the old proverb "curiosity killed the cat." That maxim is a warning against getting bogged down with unnecessary inquiry and experimentation. Respondents were not worried about curiosity going so far off the rails that it morphed into a detriment instead of an asset. Rather, leaders are much more in line with Thomas Hobbes' belief that "curiosity is the lust of the mind." Finding ways to recognize and satisfy that lust are a good way to move forward via this top-rated pathway to success.

Pathway 2. Intellect, skill, and wisdom are not exclusive to those with a formal education. (Nonprofit rank: 2; Business rank: 5)

This pathway selection prompted a lot of reaction. Nonprofit and business executives alike cautioned that "diploma fixation" can lead to serious organizational myopia. It makes sense to listen to those with impressive academic credentials who often can be a source of good ideas and concepts. But it is shortsighted to ignore others who have less notable education backgrounds – individuals with experience and innate capabilities that make them of high value.

Our 200 life lesson analysts also expressed concern that certain kinds of formal education can, at times, stifle creative thought. This was Albert Einstein's lament when he said: "it is a miracle that curiosity survives formal education."

Traveling along this pathway means being open to views and recommendations even from those who could easily be dismissed because they went to the "wrong school" or didn't finish their formal education. "If we listen, wisdom often comes from the places and people we least expect," wrote one nonprofit executive.

This pathway choice evoked other comments very much in line with a growing national concern about whether the benefits of a traditional higher education justify the high cost. Some respondents joined the chorus of Americans who question whether undergraduate and graduate education institutions are "delivering the goods" especially considering the long-term student debt often required to secure a degree. A few of our life lesson reviewers contended that intellect and wisdom may be an outgrowth of apprenticeships, skill-based long-term training, and community college education programs in the years ahead.

Pathway 3. Use positive thinking as a lens to look for an opportunity almost always hidden in a problem. (Nonprofit rank: 3; Business rank: 2)

The reaction by nonprofit and business executives alike to this life lesson made it clear there is little room for negativism when it comes to problem-solving. Giving up or conceding to failure is not acceptable to senior leaders. Their advice: To stay on the pathway to professional success, find a way to extract a positive from what on the surface might seem to be an unmitigated disaster.

"It's how you look at a problem from the get-go," was a comment passed along by one respondent. Obsessing on what went wrong or who was to blame puts a nonproductive spin on the process. Searching for bits and pieces that went right and learning how to avoid repeating mistakes is far more productive.

Pathway #3 is not relegated only to the march toward occupational success. On the personal front, individuals who strive to uncover something of value in a sticky family or domestic situation will generally travel a path to a better place than those who dwell on the problem itself.

There will be occasional wreckage blocking every pathway in life. Plucking out nuggets of value and then moving on will keep one pointed in the right direction according to most of the executives who took part in our pathways survey.

Pathway 4. Many errors are starting blocks for improved performance. (Nonprofit rank: 4; Business rank: 6)

Check any roster of quotable quotes, and you will find a statement from James Burke, the former Johnson & Johnson CEO. "Any successful company is riddled with failures," Burke contended. He added that even faced with that reality, "we don't grow unless we take risks."

Burke didn't shy away from risk-taking even when fully aware failure was lurking around the corner (see chapter 12 for more on

Burke's business approach). On those occasions when projects or efforts faltered because of errors, he ordered a rigorous autopsy. For sure, Burke wanted to identify the root cause of a problem to prevent it from reoccurring. But beyond that, he also wanted a full understanding of the component parts of a problem, convinced that amidst the ruins there would be reusable pieces that could be patched together for a new (and most often successful) undertaking.

While most of our 200 executive analysts concurred that many (although not all) errors could be fashioned into performance-enhancing building blocks, it seems nonprofit leaders more so than business executives view this pathway as especially important – in effect, an extension of pathway #3: using positive thinking to unlock value from a problem. Perhaps this is because in certain corners of the nonprofit world (e.g. organizations that work with at-risk youth, homeless clients, ex-offenders looking for employment, etc.), nonprofits are often confronted with situations where mistakes and missteps are more frequently encountered than in the private sector. But in any setting, the underlying principle of this life lesson is the same: when possible, don't let an error clog a pathway to success but rather use it to make a course correction.

Pathway 5. Creating can be hard; sustaining can be harder. (Nonprofit rank: 5; Business rank: 4)

"New programs are often darlings in the eyes of a funder – asking for help to continue an effective program is one of *the* hardest sells," commented Kit Rains, an executive with Habitat for Humanity in Asheville, North Carolina. Several other nonprofit leaders – particularly those charged with raising revenue – agreed. A new and different project can have a kind of glitter that attracts individual, business, or private foundation donors like a shiny lure. Tried and true programs – even those backed with solid impact assessments that prove they are meeting expectations – too often are considered ho-hum and are left to struggle for ongoing financial help.

For different reasons, business executives also concluded that anyone attempting to navigate a pathway to success needed to confront this life lesson. In fact, those in the corporate world viewed this life lesson as more challenging than nonprofit leaders. Business managers responsible for sustaining ongoing programs are less likely to get the visibility, accolades, and even promotion opportunities than those fellow employees engaged in widely acknowledged new corporate ventures. While the upsides tied to program sustainment are few, the downsides can be perilous if existing business operations don't meet company forecasts.

"The trick is to put some sparkle on what's already in place," was one suggestion. "Make what's old look new."

Respondents concurred that while the risks and effort needed to get a new project or program off the ground can be daunting, assuming it is easier to manage what's already in place can be a serious error in judgment. Sustainment needs constant attention and much more recognition than the responsibility usually gets.

Pathway 6. A leader's character casts a wide shadow. (Nonprofit rank: 6; Business rank: 3)

Political rhetoric and partisan behavior might explain why this life lesson received such strong attention. Elected officials acting badly have provided the public with consistent examples of how character can have negative effects on vast numbers of people. Even in the face of that reality, most of our list reviewers put emphasis on the positives that can and should be associated with character – e.g. how decency and respect can be accelerants that move one along the pathway to success.

Several business and nonprofit respondents made the point that undertaking a task and achieving a goal should not be the only measure of truly successful leadership. *How* an individual carries out responsibilities is also important. Here are a few observations that propelled this life lesson into one of the 6 pathways:

- A leader's behavior ...*matters*
- The words a leader uses ... *matter*
- Respect for others ... *matters*

Judge character before giving an individual a leadership role, many respondents recommended. Concluding that a person can "get the job done" is not enough. How an individual acts (or is likely to act) in carrying out "the job" should be of great concern to any organization, were among the comments made about this pathway.

"Too often, we underestimate how wide a shadow a leader does cast," noted one nonprofit leader. "So many people can be affected by just one person."

Character can be an amorphous term with a lot of latitude given to its meaning. An Iowa-based nonprofit called Character Counts! (housed at Drake University's Ray Center) gives us a widely applicable definition folded into what the organization calls "The Six Pillars of Character" which are:

- Trustworthiness
- Respect
- Responsibility
- Fairness
- Caring
- Citizenship

Our pathways survey suggests these are the kinds of desirable qualities that can and should define effective leadership. Sending executives consistent reminders about what constitutes good character should help leaders stay on track – and ensure whatever shadow they cast is for the betterment of their organizations.

Other Pathways

Several life lessons not included in the top six pathways list sparked strong responses from more than a few nonprofit and business respondents. Rebecca Justin of the Minnesota-North Dakota office of the Alzheimer's Association singled out **Gray power is America's most unexploited energy source.** "I think we will see a time when the retirement age will either not exist or will be raised by 10 years," she predicts.

Some problems cannot be resolved in full; all problems can be mitigated in part reminded Jessica Graham of advice passed along by her father. Jessica is an executive with the Children's Literacy Initiative (headquartered in Philadelphia). After retiring from his 40-year teaching career at Booker T. Washington High School in Houston, Jessica's dad said, "Do good and mitigate what you can."

"In my shop," Michelle Murphy notes, "**check the prize before running the race** gets put into different words." Michelle, the executive director of Malta House of Care in Hartford, Connecticut adds: "We ask 'is the juice worth the squeeze.'"

Luck trumps everything caught the attention of Eduardo Cetlin, president of the Amgen Foundation in Thousand Oaks, California. At a recent Social Innovation Summit, Eduardo recalled a keynote speaker making the point that "50 percent of life is pure luck."

Another foundation president, Michael Dominowski, who heads the Minneapolis-based Thrivent Foundation wrote "simple, clear communications will always win the day" as an endorsement for **a strong delivery with light content is usually more effective than a tepid delivery with strong content.**

These and many other observations about life lessons that didn't make the cluster of six leadership-related principles and practices point out how the Pathways Compass can be used in other ways to strengthen an organization. The Compass process is not designed to extract "right" or "wrong" responses – only information about deep-seated attitudes and beliefs that are the basis for how people really feel about the mission and purpose of an organization.

Pathways Compass: A Leadership Development Resource

Corporations and nonprofits invest millions of dollars annually to develop leadership skills of emerging executives. Some universities charge $50,000 (or more) for individuals to take part in leadership development programs. In short, bolstering leadership competency is serious business for most organizations.

Strengthening core competencies in team building, negotiations, and other aspects of effective leadership can be worthwhile take-aways from well-run executive education programs. However, without incurring any costs other than a small investment of staff time, organizations have an easy way to address two topics commonly included in most leadership training curricula: (a) how to build staff alignment; and (b) ways to motivate team performance.

While there are *formal* aspects to leadership (e.g. the authority to make organizational decisions), the *informal* role leaders can and should play (team building, collaboration encouragement, etc.) is often equally consequential. The Pathways Compass addresses these informal leadership dynamics by identifying subordinate, board member, or other audience values and beliefs that can influence organizational cohesiveness.

A Gallup study (*2017 State of the American Workplace*) is a reminder that only 21 percent of employees feel they are being managed in a way that motivates them to do a better job. What can a leader do to improve this perception? The Pathways Compass allows a leader to dig deeper into team attitudes and beliefs that are at the root of opinions about leadership. Here's an example ...

A cohort asked to take part in a Pathways Compass exercise chooses the following life lesson as one of six high priority statements related to organization leadership: **talk and promises are easy; deliverables are not.** A follow-up discussion vents frustration among most team members who feel leaders are quick to make unreasonable promises and then dump the responsibility for fulfillment on those lower in the organization. The Compass process uncovered a concern that has festered for quite some time leading to negative feelings about team leaders. Through group facilitation, an agreement is reached giving team members much more input before any future pledge is made about organization deliverables.

Pathways Compass: A Mission Appraisal Resource

A statement of purpose or behavior should not be static. This particular life lesson hit home for many business and nonprofit executives who felt their mission statements were outdated and increasingly irrelevant. But finding ways to amend or even replace an organization's publicly stated principal reason for being can be incredibly challenging – and even professionally risky for those who push too hard for change.

Enter the Pathways Compass. The exercise presents a way to gauge how priority beliefs of those working for – or impacted by – an organization line up with its principal goals and objectives. For nonprofits, the Compass can be a very effective way to probe board member values with that information used to reinforce or refine the organization's priorities. Here's an example:

A nonprofit mission statement says, in part ... "in carrying out our programs, we shall strive to achieve measurable outcomes ..." The organization conducts a Pathways Compass exercise, with each board member asked to pick six statements from the list of 50 life lessons that best relate to the nonprofit's programs and practices. Most board members select **outcomes are inches on impact's yardstick** as their top choice. Once results have been tabulated, the board meets to discuss findings.

While specific nonprofit programs and activities have led to successful outcomes, the organization has had little *impact* on social issues it was set up to address. The mission statement is edited to read "...we shall strive to achieve measurable impact..." and the organization is retooled and refocused as a result.

For a nonprofit or a business, the Pathways Compass exercise (Appendix II) is an easy and non-intimidating way to uncover expectations and motivations of all those affected in one way or another by an organization. Those asked to participate in the exercise become genuinely curious as to priority selections made by other team or board members. This heightened level of interest sets the stage for a stimulating – and usually very productive – follow-up discussion.

A Multitude of Pathways – and Why They Matter

"The 50 life lessons made me stop and think about how all of them apply to my life," said Amanda Kamman Robertson, an executive with Project Lead The Way in Indianapolis. In asking 175 non-profit and 25 for-profit executives to choose just six life lessons as pathways to leadership success, the exercise required thinking more broadly and necessitated a lot of introspection.

If the train is moving in the wrong direction, get off is a life lesson that struck a chord with some and demonstrated how the Pathways Compass exercise is a kind of "time out" enabling individuals to take a hard look at where they are heading both professionally and personally. If they are being pulled in a direction inconsistent with their values or best interests, it could be time for a career or interpersonal "reset."

There was consensus among business and nonprofit leaders that **civility is an elixir for resolving political, social, and organizational differences.** Respondents worried that more visible role models – especially those in public office – were not showcasing the kind of civil behavior that should be the norm for government, businesses, nonprofit organizations, and society as a whole. "From the schoolroom to the board room, maybe it's time for an enforceable civility code," was one suggestion.

Linked to a call for more civility is the life lesson, **hubris may bring attention but humility will win respect.** Some nonprofit leaders pointed out how the media (particularly social media) can be manipulated by those with the loudest voices and an excess of self-adulation. "Far more should be done to celebrate leaders known for their humility," was a respondent comment.

One life lesson, **green is discrimination's color of choice,** drew attention to income inequality in America. According to the U.S. government's *The World Factbook,* 70 percent of all countries on the planet have more equal income distribution than our nation. More troublesome to many is evidence that U.S. income inequality has grown significantly since the 1970s after several decades of relative stability. Nonprofit leaders in the social services sector cite numerous examples of how discrimination largely based on economic status affects millions of citizens throughout the country.

Reactions to the Pathways Compass made it clear that while there are six preferred pathways to leadership success, these are not the only avenues worth traveling. No pathway should be overlooked or dismissed, respondents insisted. There are, indeed, a multitude of routes that lead to personal and organizational success. And those avenues are certainly not limited to just the 50 options included in the Pathways Compass. We *all* encounter or engage in experiences that become teachable moments. But these lessons lack value unless they are recognized, chronicled, and (most importantly) *learned.*

Life is a classroom for all of us and – as I have discovered – school is always in session.

Ranking Chart: 50 Life Lessons

The list below is a ranking of 50 principles, practices & beliefs (life lessons) as determined by 175 nonprofit organization executives. Shown in parentheses are the highest ranked life lessons selected by the panel of 25 business executives. Without conferring with one another, both groups gave highest priority to the same six selections – the *6 Pathways to Leadership and Organizational Success.*

6 Pathways

1. In your own way, be insatiably curious. (1)
2. Intellect, skill, and wisdom are not exclusive to those with a formal education. (5)
3. Use positive thinking as a lens to look for an opportunity almost always hidden in a problem. (2)
4. Many errors are starting blocks for improved performance. (6)
5. Creating can be hard; sustaining can be harder. (4)
6. A leader's character casts a wide shadow. (3)

Additional Life lessons

7. Bad news is best delivered directly and honestly, but with empathy.
8. A strong delivery with light content is usually more effective than a tepid delivery with strong content.
9. Talk and promises are easy; deliverables are not.
10. Hubris may bring attention but humility will win respect.
11. Everyone's a salesperson – some better than others.
12 - tie. If the train is moving in the wrong direction, get off.
12 – tie. Pursue purpose; deflect distraction.
14 - tie. Civility is an elixir for resolving political, social, and organizational differences.
14 - tie. Check the prize before running the race.
14 – tie. Faith fosters hope; confrontation fosters change.
17. Green is discrimination's color of choice.
18. When you only want to see what you want to see – you will see what you want to see.
19. Those who have no regard for respect and dignity should not be respected or dignified.
20 – tie. Compassion elevates forgiveness to its highest level.
20 – tie. To get to a good place begin the journey headed in the right direction.
20. – tie. The past can be a guidepost for the future or a headwind to progress.
23 – tie. Value those the most who are the least indifferent.
23 – tie. Enough is rarely enough.
23 – tie. Some problems cannot be resolved in full; all problems can be mitigated in part.
26. The classroom is democracy's nursery.
27 – tie. A partner should bring as much or more to you as you bring to a partner.
27 – tie. Principles are more meaningful and actionable when translated into responsibilities.
29. A statement of purpose or behavior should not be static.

30 – tie. Luck trumps everything.

30 – tie. Build your brand when you can.

30 – tie Outcomes are inches on impact's yardstick.

33 – tie Wounding the rich is more consequential than ravaging the poor.

33 – tie. Verify first; trust later.

33 – tie. Reality is perfection's flaw.

33 – tie. Gray power is America's most unexploited energy source.

37. Prejudice permits exceptions.

38. Be wary of titles that sap ambition and foster grandiose delusions.

39 – tie. Visions that are possible are not always probable.

39 – tie. The two most consequential words in any language are yes and no.

41 – tie. There is honor in duty and service if conscience is uncompromised.

41 – tie. Time boils away fabrication and exaggeration to leave a residue called truth.

41 - tie. Caution – manufactured public images can mask arrogance and disrespect.

41– tie. Deception's contorted path is littered with too much risk to warrant the journey.

45 – tie. For rousing the masses, use a homily; for achieving real transformational change, get personal.

45 – tie. Marriage is a kind of interpersonal battery that is powered up at the start but likely to weaken or die if not periodically recharged.

47– tie. What you say can be as important as what you do.

47– tie. Accepted authoritarianism puts truth in jeopardy.

49. Let whom and what you know best be the compass for your charity.

50. Caution is a speedbump to progress and a magnifying glass to progress.

Appendix 2

The Pathways Leadership & Mission Analysis Compass

The Pathways Compass is a helpful resource for identifying and developing institutional leaders. It is also a productive way to collect valuable feedback regarding an organization's mission and purpose. The "Pathways Leadership & Mission Analysis Compass" (detailed in this appendix) can be used to address either or both issues.

For leadership development ...
The Pathways Compass can determine how aligned team members are (or are not) in regard to the underlying principles and practices of a leader's department, division, or general organization. With only a small commitment of time, differences of views (if any) can be determined. That information can be the starting point for a team discussion aimed at creating a more cohesive alignment around commonly accepted statements drawn from the Compass

list. The exercise leads to more widely accepted organization objectives that will prove advantageous to a leader.

For an Organization Mission Analysis...
Whether used with a business department/division or a nonprofit board of directors, the Pathways Compass can help address this question:

Is an organization's current stated mission in sync with the values and beliefs of those most directly affected by the organization (senior staff, boards of directors)?

The Compass appraisal process yields information useful in determining whether or not an organization's mission is consistent with the values and priorities of those asked to take part in the appraisal process. If there are significant disparities, the appraisal results are a starting point for making mission modifications.

The Pathways Leadership & Mission Analysis Compass Process ...
A. Determine those individuals to be included in the appraisal cohort (e.g. nonprofit board members; employees with supervisory responsibilities in a business department or division; association trustees; etc.)
B. Copy the list of 50 statements below and distribute one copy to each individual in the cohort.
C – 1. For a Pathways leadership analysis, instruct individuals in the cohort to circle 6 statements they consider high priority principles and practices for the leadership of the organization. (If the Pathways appraisal is used with a department within a larger corporation or organization, the 6 selections should apply to that department and not the business in general).
C – 2. For a Pathways organization mission analysis, instruct individuals in the cohort to circle 6 statements that are considered the most important to the organization's mission and purpose.

D. Collect and tally results.

E. Set aside time (from an hour to a full-day retreat) to report findings. Provide an opportunity for cohort participants to explain selection choices – particularly those that may be inconsistent with views expressed by most respondents.

F. Based on the pathway appraisal findings and subsequent discussions, determine if/how the leadership and/or mission adjustment should be made.

Pathways Leadership and Mission Analysis Compass List

1. Intellect, skill, and wisdom are not exclusive to those with a formal education.
2. Prejudice permits exceptions.
3. Wounding the rich is more consequential than ravaging the poor.
4. Compassion elevates forgiveness to its highest level.
5. Luck trumps everything.
6. Green is discrimination's color of choice.
7. Everyone's a salesperson – some better than others.
8. Verify first, trust later.
9. Let who and what you know best be the compass for your charity.
10. In your own way, be insatiably curious.
11. Enough is rarely enough.
12. Check the prize before running the race.
13. The classroom is democracy's nursery.
14. There is honor in duty and service if conscience is uncompromised.
15. Time boils away fabrication and exaggeration to leave a residue called truth.
16. Marriage is a kind of interpersonal battery, powered up at the start; likely to weaken or die if not periodically recharged.
17. To get to a good place begin the journey headed in the right direction.

18. A strong delivery with light content is usually more effective than a tepid delivery with strong content.
19. Those who have no regard for respect and dignity should not be respected or dignified.
20. Caution – manufactured public images can mask arrogance and disrespect.
21. Many errors are starting blocks for improved performance.
22. Hubris may bring attention but humility will win respect.
23. Use positive thinking as a lens to look for an opportunity almost always hidden in a problem.
24. Bad news is best delivered directly and honestly, but with empathy.
25. Talk and promises are easy; deliverables are not.
26. Value those the most who are the least indifferent.
27. When you only want to see what you only want to see – you will see what you want to see.
28. Reality is perfection's flaw.
29. Build your brand when you can.
30. Be wary of titles that sap ambition and foster grandiose delusions.
31. Some problems cannot be resolved in full; all problems can be mitigated in part.
32. A partner should bring as much or more to you as you bring to a partner.
33. Pursue purpose; deflect distraction.
34. Visions that are possible are not always probable.
35. If the train is moving in the wrong direction, get off.
36. The two most consequential words in any language: yes and no.
37. Creating can be hard; sustaining can be harder.
38. Caution is a speedbump to progress and a magnifying glass to outcomes.
39. Principles are more meaningful and actionable when translated into responsibilities.
40. A statement of purpose or behavior should not be static.

41. For rousing the masses, use a homily; for achieving transformational change, get personal.
42. What you say can be as important as what you do.
43. Faith fosters hope; confrontation fosters change.
44. Accepted authoritarianism puts truth in jeopardy.
45. Gray power is America's most unexploited energy source.
46. The past can be a guidepost for the future or a headwind to progress.
47. Deception's contorted path is littered with too much risk to warrant the journey.
48. Outcomes are inches on impact's yardstick.
49. A leader's character casts a wide shadow.
50. Civility is an elixir for resolving political, social, and organizational differences.

Appendix 3

ACCP Member Companies

Abbott
AbbVie
Accenture AdventHealth
Aetna
AIG
Alliant Energy Fdn
Allstate Insurance
Altria
AMD
American Family Insurance
Amgen
Amway International
Anthem
Aon
Archer-Daniels-Midland
Arizona Public Service
Assurant
Astellas
AstraZeneca Avery Dennison
   Fdn

BAE Systems
Bank of America
Bausch Fdn
Baxter International
Bayer
BBVA Compass
BD
Bendix
Benjamin Moore
Best Buy Co
Biogen
Blackbaud.
Blue Cross & Blue Shield of
   Louisiana
Blue Shield of California
BNSF Railway
Boeing
Booz Allen Hamilton
Burger King McLamore Fdn
C&S Wholesale Grocers

Cambia Health Solutions
Capital One
Cargill
Caterpillar Foundation
CDW
Charter
  Communications
Chick-fil-A
Cisco
City National Bank
Clif Bar & Company
CNH Industrial
Collette
Comcast
Con Edison
Conagra Brands
ConocoPhillips
Corning Inc. Fdn
Cracker Barrel Old Country
  Store
CSAA Insurance Group
CSX
CTIA Wireless Fdn
CUNA Mutual Group
  Fdn
Darden Restaurants
Deloitte Services
Dominion Energy
Duke Energy
DuPont Pioneer
Eaton
eBay
Ecolab
Edwards Life-sciences
FedEx

Ferguson Enterprises
Fidelity Investments
First Tech
  Federal Credit Union
FirstEnergy
Florida Blue/Florida Blue Fdn
Ford Motor Company
Georgia-Pacific
GoDaddy
Grainger
GSK
Guardian Life Insurance Co.
  of Am.
Gulfstream Aerospace
Hasbro
HCA Healthcare
HCR ManorCare
Henry Schein
Hilton
Hilton Grand Vacations
Horizon Blue Cross Blue
  Shield of NJ
Hyland
Illumina
Ingersoll Rand
Intel
JCPenney
Johnson & Johnson
JPMorgan Chase
KCP&L
Kilpatrick Townsend &
  Stockton
Kohl's Department Stores
KPMG
Lamb Weston

Lenovo Fdn
Liberty Mutual Insurance
Live Oak Bank
Lockheed Martin Corporation
LPL Financial
MassMutual
McKesson Corporation
McMaster-Carr Supply
  Company
Medtronic Fdn
Merck & Co.
MGM Resorts International
Micron Technology Fdn
Microsoft
Mondelez International
Morgan Stanley
MUFG Union Bank
Mutual of Omaha
NetApp
New York Life Insurance
Newport News Shipbuilding
Nordson
Norfolk Southern
Northrop Grumman
Northwestern Mutual
Novartis
Novo Nordisk
NV Energy
NVent
O'Melveny & Myers
Oportun
Orange Lake Resorts
Orlando Health
Owens Corning
Pacific Gas & Electric

Parker Hannifin
Paul Hastings
PayPal
PIMCO
Pitney Bowes
Portland General Electric
Premera Blue Cross
PSEG Services
Publix Super Markets
PVH
PwC
Regions Bank
Rockwell Automation
Rockwell Collins
Sage Fdn
Samsonite
Sanofi US
Sealed Air
Sempra Energy
Sodexo
Sony Corporation of America
Southern Company
Southwest Airlines
Starbucks Coffee Company
Strada Education Network
SUEZ SunTrust Fdn
Swinerton
Symantec Corporation
Synopsys Inc.
T. Rowe Price Fdn
Target
TD Ameritrade
Textron
The Coca-Cola Company
The Dow Chemical Company

The Goodyear
  Tire & Rubber Company
The Hartford
The Home Depot Fdn
The James S. Kemper Fdn
The Lubrizol Corporation
The Northern Trust Company
The Prudential Fdn
The Sherwin-Williams
  Company
The Walt Disney Company
Thrivent Financial
Toyota Motor
  North America
TripAdvisor Charitable Fdn
Tupperware Brands
Turner Construction
Union Pacific Railroad
United Airlines

United Technologies
  Corporation
UnitedHealthcare
UPS
US Foods
Venable
Viacom
Viasat
Visa
Voya Financial
Walmart
WEC Energy Group
WellCare Community Fdn
Wells Fargo
Weyerhaeuser
William Blair and Company
Workday Fdn
WWE
Xcel Energy

Appendix 4

New Strategies Nonprofit Organizations

100 Black Men of Am.
171 Cedar Arts
  Center
180 Degrees Inc.
A Better Chance
A Breath of Hope
  Lung Fdn
A World Fit for Kids!
AAMA
AARP Foundation
ACCESS
Access Living of Metro
  Chicago
Access Plus Capital
Accion East
AchieveMpls
ACS Cancer
Action Network

Action for Healthy
  Kids
Acumen Fund
African-American
  Board Leadership
  Institute
African-American
  Chamber of
  Commerce
Africare
After-School
All-Stars
Alex's Lemonade Stand
All Hands Raised
Allergy &
Asthma Network
Alliance for
  Independence

Alliance for Patient
  Access
Alliance for Aging
  Research
Alvin Ailey Dance
  Fnd.
Alzheimer's Assoc.
  MN/ND
America Needs You
Am. Indian OIC
Am. Warrior
  Partnership
Assc. Heart Failure
  Nurses
American Cancer
  Society
Am. Council on
  Education

American Heart Assoc.

Am. Heart Assoc LA

Am. Indian College
Fund

American Lung Assoc.

Am. Lung Assoc. Wisc.

Am. Med. Assoc.
Fdn

Am. Red Cross Finger
Lakes

Am. Red Cross Greater
Cincinnati-Dayton
Region

Am. Society of
Transplantation

AmeriCares

AnewAmerica Comm.
Corp.

Anne Arundel Med.
Center

APIC

Asian & Pacific
Islander

Am. Health Forum

Asian Services in
Action

AZ Hispanic Chamber
of Commerce

AZ Partnership for
Immunization

AZ Science Center

Arthur Ashe Inst.
Urban Health

Arthur Ashe Learning
Ctr

ARTS Coun. S. Finger
Lakes

Ashoka

Asian Am. Advancing
Justice

AAJC

Assc. AZ Food Banks

Assc. of Black
Cardiologists

Assc. Comm. Cancer
Ctrs

Assc. Univ. Centers on
Disability

Assc. Women's
Business Ctrs

Athletes for Hope

Atlanta Comm. Food
Bank

Atlas Service Corps.

Audubon California

Audubon Nature
Institute

Autism Speaks

AVANCE-Dallas

Avenues for Homeless
Youth

AVID

Avivo

Bartram's Garden

BCL of Texas

Bergen Volunteer Med.

Bergen Volunteers

Berkeley Repertory
Theatre

Best Buddies Texas

BestPrep

Better Futures
Minnesota

Bridges Outreach

Brighter Way Institute

Brinn's Children's
Museum

BB/BS Hampden Co.

BB/BS Metro
Milwaukee

Billings Forge Comm
Works

BIO Ventures for
Global Health

Black History Museum

Blue Star Families

Boardstar

Boys & Girls Clubs

Boys & Girls Clubs Gr
Milwaukee

Brewers Comm.
Fdn

Bright Horizons
Foundation for
Children

Brooklyn Academy
Music

Brooklyn Museum

Bronx Museum of the
Arts

BSD Industries L3C

Byrd Barr Place

C-STEM Teacher and
Student Support
Services

Café Reconcile

Cal Ripken Sr. Fdn

CA Coalition of Rural Housing

Campaign Grade Level Reading

Campaign for Tobacco Free Kids

Cancer Care

Capital Roots

CARE USA

Carolina Small Bus. Development Fund

CASA of Oregon

Cascade AIDS Project

Cass Community Social Services

CDC Foundation

Center for Arts Education

Ctr for Creative Leadership

Center for Health Law & Policy Innovation

Center for NYC Neighborhoods

Central Detroit Christian

Central Park Conservancy

Central PA Food Bank

Centro Hispano Dane Co.

Challenged Athletes Fdn

ChangeLab Solutions

Charity Water

Charles Drew Health Ctr

Chicago Foundation for Women

Chicago Neighborhood Initiatives

Chicago State Univeristy

Chicanos Por La Causa

Child First Inc.

Child's World America

ChildFund International

Children's Clinic

Children's Developmental Center

Children's Diagnostic & Treatment Center

Children's Literacy Init.

Children's Museum Atlanta

Children's Mus. Houston

Child's Music Thtr San Jose

Children's Health Fund

Children's Spec. Hosp. Fnd.

Childsplay

CincySmiles Fdn

Cities of Service

Citizens Committee for NYC

City Harvest

City Lore

City Parks Fdn

City Year

City Year Milwaukee

Civil Liberties/ Public Policy

Clemens Center

CMMB

COA Youth/ Family Services

Coalition of Communities of Color

Code of Support Fdn

Colorado Open Lands

College Possible Milw

Common Hope

Communities in Schools Richmond

Communities in Schools Dallas

Community Catalyst

Community Dev. Alliance

Comm. Dev. for all People

Comm. ER Assist. Program

Comm. Food Bank of Central AL

Comm. Food Bank of NJ

Comm. Health Charities

Community Hope

COMPAS

Comunidades Latinas Unidas en Servicio (CLUES)

Congreso of Latinos Unidos

Conservation Fund

Convoy of Hope

Cooper's Ferry Partnership

Copper Beech Inst.

Cornerstone Family Programs

Corning Museum of Glass

Corp. to Develop Communities of Tampa

Credit Builders Alliance

Crispus Attucks Association

Dallas Black Dance Theatre

Daughters of Charity Health Centers

DevelopSpringfield

Diabetes Foundation Inc.

Dignity U Wear

Direct Relief

Disability Opportunity Fund

Discovery World

Disparities Solutions Ctr at Mass General

Dress for Success-Charlotte

Dress for Success West East Bay Comm. Fdn

Eastside Comm. Network

El Centro de la Raza

El Museo del Barrio

Elegba Folklore Society

EMERGE Comm. Dev.

Enactus

EnCorps Teachers Program

Endometriosis Found. Am.

Enterprise Comm. Partners

Entrepreneurial Center & Women's Business Center

Erie Neighborhood House

Fair Chance

Fairleigh Dickinson Univ.

Families in Schools

Family First

Family First Health

Farm Worker Justice

Feeding America

Feeding America E. Wisc.

Feeding Am. SW VA

Feeding South Florida

Feeding Tampa Bay

Fernbank Museum

Fidelco Guide Dog Foundation

Figure Skating in Harlem

Financial Info & Svcs Center

FIRST

First Book

First Focus

Five Rivers Co., BSA

FLIPANY

FL Comm. Loan Fund

Food Bank of the Rockies

Food Bank of So. Jersey

Food Bank of the So. Tier

Food Lifelife

Food Research &
  Action Ctr

FOOD Share Inc.

Ford's Theatre Society

Forum Youth
  Investment

Frazer Center

Freestore Food Bank

Fresno Area Hispanic
  Fdn

Friends of St. Paul
  College Fdn

Fund for Ed.
  Excellence

Games for Change

Gaston & Porter
  Health Improvement
  Center

George Street
  Playhouse

GA Cancer Ctr for
  Excellence at
  Grady Health
  System

Girl Be Heard

Girl Scouts of
  Wisconsin

Girl Scouts of Wisc.
  SE

Girls Inc.

Girls on the Run
  Int'l

Girls Who Invest

Give An Hour

GBC
  Health

Global Citizen

Global Health Corps

Golden Gate Nat'l
  Parks Conservancy

Good Shepherd
  Services

Goodwill Easter Seals
  MN

Grtr Houston Black
  Chamber

Grt Lakes Science
  Center

Grtr Metro Housing
  Corp.

Grt Milw Committee
  for Community
  Development

Grtr Newark
  Conservancy

Grtr Ohio Policy
  Center

Groundwork Denver

Gulf of Mexico
  Foundation

Habitat for
  Humanity

Habitat Wake Co.

Habitat Asheville

Habitat Austin

Habitat Beaches

Habitat Beaumont

Habitat Bergen Co.

Habitat Central AZ

Habitat Charlotte

Habitat Collier Co.

Habitat Dallas

Habitat Dane Co.

Habitat Durham

Habitat East Bay/
  Silicon

Habitat Flower City

Habitat Greeley-Weld

Habitat Grtr
  Birmingham

Habitat Grtr Des
  Moines

Habitat Greater
  Memphis

Habitat Greater Pitt

Habitat Grtr Sioux
  Falls

Habitat Highlands
  Co. FL

Habitat Hillsborough
  Co. FL

Habitat Houston

Habitat Kent Co.

Habitat Lakeshore

Habitat Lee/Hednry
  Co.

Habitat Lexington

Habitat Lincoln

Habitat Fox Cities

Habitat Greater
  Cincinnati

Habitat Greater Miami

Habitat Greater
  Orlando

Habitat Philadelphia
Habitat Grtr
  Sacramento
Habitat Hartford
Habitat Huron Valley
Habitat Indianapolis
Habitat International
Habitat Jacksonville
Habitat Metro
  Denver
Habitat Metro
  Louisville
Habitat Nashville
Habitat Omaha
Habitat Palm Beach
  Co.
Habitat Portland
  Metro
Habitat San Diego
Habitat SE Ohio
Habitat Trinity
Habitat Twin Cities
Habitat York Co.
HandsOn Richmond
HAP (Hmong
  American
  Partnership)
Harbor House
  Domestic Abuse
  Programs
Harlem Children's
  Zone
Harlem
  Commonwealth
  Council

Harlem Congregations
  for Community
  Improvement
Harlem Grown
Hartford Performs
Harvesters
Health Leads
Healthy Places by
  Design
HealthyWomen.org
Heart Failure Society
  of America
Heart of America
Heart to
  Heart Int'l
Helen Keller Int'l
Help at Your Door
Henry Ford
  Learning Institute
Henry Street
  Settlement
HIRED
Hispanic Alliance for
  Career Enhancement
  (HACE)
Hispanic Family Ctr
  So. NJ
Hispanic Federation
Hispanic
  Heritage Fdn
Hispanic Unity of
  Florida
History Theatre
Hole in the Wall Camp
HomeFree USA

Homeless Connections
Hopeworks 'N
  Camden
House of Charity
Housing Partnership
  Fox Cities
Housing Works
Houston Food Bank
ICA Food Shelf
Imagine Milwaukee
IMPACCT Brooklyn
Independent College
  Fund
IngenuityNE
Institute of Women &
  Ethnic Studies
Interact Ctr for the
  Visual & Perf. Arts
Interfaith Action of
  Greater St. Paul
Interfaith Ministries
  Grtr Houston
Institute of Minnesota
Int'l Racing Research
  Ctr
Int'l Rescue
  Committee
Invest Detroit Found.
Japanese Am. Citizens
  League
Jefferson East
Jeremiah Program
Jersey Battered
  Women's Service
Jersey Cares

Joint Comm. Center
for Transforming
Healthcare
Jordan Valley Comm.
Health Ctr
Joshua Group
Junior Achievement
JA Greater Clevelenad
JA W. Mass.
JA Wisconsin
Jungle Theater
Juxtaposition Arts
KaBOOM!
Keep America
Beautiful
Kids in Need
Fdn
Knox Inc.
La Casa de Don
Pedro
La Clinicia del Pueblo
LA Regional Food
Bank
LA Urban League
Land Trust Alliance
Las Vegas Urban
League
Last Mile Health
Latin Ballet of
Virginia
Latino Comm. Found.
Latino Health Access
Latino Memphis
Lawndale Christian
Dev. Corporation

Lawyer's Comm. For
Civil Rts under the
Law
Leadership Conf on
Civil & Human
Rights
Leadership Educ. for
Asian Pacifics
Leadership Enterprise
for a Diverse America
Learning Forward
Leg Up Farm
Liberty Science Center
Lions Club
International
LISC Milwaukee
Literacy Inc.
Live6 Alliance
Loft
Literary Center
Longwood University
Lowcountry Food
Bank
LA Philharmonic
LA Regional Food
Bank
LA Urban
League
Lower East Side
Tenement Museum
LULAC
Lung Cancer Alliance
LUNGevity
Maine Medical
Center

Make A Wish
Foundation
Malta House of Care
Fnd.
Mama Hope
Manhattan Inst. For
Policy Research
Manna Food Center
MAP International
Marathon Kids
Mark Morris Dance
Group
Marshall Heights
Comm.
Development Org.
Martha's Table
Matthew 25:Ministries
Mayor's Fund to
Advance NYC
Meals on Wheels
America
Medical Teams Int'l
Mended Hearts
MENTOR: Nat'l
Mentoring
Partnership
Mercy Corps
Northwest
Mercy Ships
Mi Casa Resource
Center
Miami Children's
Museum
Miami Homes for
All

MidAm. Nazarene
  Univ.
Migrant Clinicians
  Nwk
Mile High United Way
Milwaukee Public
  Museum
Milw Repertory
  Theater
Milw Symph.
  Orchestra
MIND Research
  Institute
MN College
  Foundation
MN Community Care
Mississippi First
Monroe Comm.
  College Fd.
MORTAR
MS Public Health Inst.
MoneyThink
More Than Wheels
Morristown
  Med. Ctr Fdn
Mtn Region Speech &
  Hearing
MS Society of America
Muliticultural
  Media, Telecom &
  Internet Co.
Museum of Discovery
  & Science
Museum of Science
  & Ind.

Museum of the City of
  NY
NACME
Nat'l Assoc. for Latino
  Community Asset
  Builders
Natl' Assoc. of
  Community Health
  Centers
Nat'l Assoc. of Free &
  Charitable Clinics
National Audubon
  Society
National Black Arts
  Festival
National Black Justice
  Coalition
Nat'l Ctr for Families
  Learning
Nat'l Ctr for Med/
  Legal Partnership at
  GWU
National Civil Rights
  Museum
Nat'l Conf. for
  Community &
  Justice
Nat'l Consumers
  League
Nat'l Council
  for Behavioral
  Healthcare
Nat'l Council of
  Juvenile & Family
  Court Justices

Nat'l Council of
  Negro Women
Nat'l Diaper Bank
  Network
Nat'l Disability Inst.
Nat'l Enviro. Ed Fnd.
Nat'l Fair Housing
  Alliance
Nat'l Guild Comm.
  Arts Ed.
Nat'l Head Start Assoc.
National Health
  Council
Nat'l Hispanic Caucus
  of State Legislators
Nat'l League of Cities
National MS Society
Nat'l Network
  of Public Health
  Institutes
Nat'l Park Foundation
Nat'l Parks
  Conservation Assoc
Nat'l Parks & Rec
  Association
Nat'l Safe Place
  Network
Nat'l Trust for Historic
  Preservation
National Urban
  Fellows
National Urban
  League
National Women's Law
  Center

NatureServe

Neighbors Inc.

Neighborhood
Housing Services of
S. Florida

Network of Executive
Women

NJ Performing Arts
Center

NJ YMCA State
Alliance

New York Cares

New York Common
Pantry

NY Hall of Science

NY Historical
Society

Newark Museum

Nextdoor Foundation

NJCU

Nomi Network

Nonprofit Center of
NE Florida

NC A&T St
Univ Center for
Alzheimer's, Aging &
Comm. Health

NC Alliance for
School Leadership
Development

NC New Schools

North Point Health &
Wellness Center

North TX Food
Bank

Northside
Achievement Zone

Notah Begay III
Fdn

Nurse-Family
Partnerships

NYC Leadership
Academy

NYC Outward Bound
School

One Mind

Operation
Outreach USA

Opportunity Fund

Opp. Resource Fund

OCAPICA (Orange
Co. Asian Pacific
Islander Community
Alliance)

Our Military
Kids Inc.

Overtown Youth
Center

Pacesetter

Pangea World Theatre

Park Avenue Armory

Park Square Theatre

Partners for Self-
Employment Inc

Partners in Food
Solutions

Partners in Health

Partnership for After
School Education
(PASE)

Partnership for a
Drug-Free NJ

Partnership for a
Healthier America

Pathfinders

Patient Advocate
Fdn

PAVE + Schools That
Can Milwaukee

PCYC

Peace Players Int'l

PEARLS for Teen
Girls

Peer Health Exchange

Penumbra Theatre

PeopleFund

People Reaching Out
to Other People

Peter Paul Develop.
Ctr

Philanthropy W. VA

Pillsbury United
Communities

Playworks

Playworks So. CA

Population Services
Int'l

Portland Children
Museum

Potlatch Fund

PowerPlay NYC

PPL

Prepare + Prosper

Project for Pride in
Living

Project GRAD
Houston
Project HOPE
Project Lead the Way
Project Success
Project Sunshine
Prospera
Prosperity Now
Provide Inc.
P.S. Arts
Public Allies-
Milwaukee
Pueblo a
Pueblo
Quality Care for
Children
Rails-to-Trails
Conservancy
Raising A
Reader
Re:Gender
Reach Out and
Read
Reading Partners
Rebuild Foundation
Recycling Partnership
Red Cross of Greater
NY
Red Sox Fdn
Renaissance
Entrepreneurship
Center
Renaissance Youth
Center
Resource Fdn

RespectAbility
Resurrection Project
Robert Russa
Moton Museum
Robin Hood
Foundation
Ronald McDonald
House E. Wisconsin
Sabathani Community
Ctr
Sacramento Comm.
Clinics
Safe Kids Worldwide
Sandy Hook Promise
Sant La Haitian
Neighborhood Ctr.
Save the Children
Science & Discovery
Ctr of NW Florida
Seattle Art Museum
Second Harvest Food
Bank
Second Harvest
Central Florida
Second Harvest
Greater New Orleans
& Acadiana
Second Harvest
Mid-TN
Second Harvest
Heartland
Second State
Theater
Self-Enhancement
Inc.

SER-Jobs for Progress
Nat'l
Serve Minnesota
Sesame Workshop
Share Our Strength
SHE-CAN
SkillsUSA Inc.
Smithsonian
Institute
Soccer Without
Borders
Society for
Science & the Public
Society Women
Engineers
Sojourners Family
Center
Spark Program
Special Olympics
St. Ann's Warehouse
St. Mary's Food Bank
Alliance
St. Mary's Health
Wagon
St. Phillip's School &
Community Center
St. Sabina
Employment
Resource Center
Starfish Family
Services
StriveTogether
Student Conserv.
Assoc.
Students Run LA

Studio Museum
Harlem

Summit Academy OIC

Sunshine Gospel
Ministries

Susan G Komen NYC

Swords to Plowshares

Symphony Silicon
Valley

Tragedy Assistance
Program for
Survivors

TAPS

Teach for America
Milw

Teach for America NJ

Teach for America NY

Team Red White Blue

Team Rubicon

Tech Goes Home

Tennyson Ctr for
Children ALS Assoc.
MN, ND, SD

The Clubhouse
Network

The Diaper Bank CT

The Edible
Schoolyard

The Enterprise Center

The Field Museum

The Food Group

The Food Trust

The Global
Foodbanking
Network

The Greening of
Detroit

The Greenlining
Institute

The Health Wagon

The Literacy Lab

The Mind Trust

The Mission
Continues

The NY Academy of
Med.

The Newark School
Dist.

The Ron Clark
Academy

The Salvation Army

The Salvation Army
Arkansas/Oklahoma
Div.

The Salvation Army
E. MI

The Schwartz Center

Trust for Public Land

The Urban Institute

The Women's Business
Center at First St.
Community Loan
Fund

Three Square

TreeHouse Inc.

Trenton Health
Team

Trust for National
Mall

Twin Cities Rise

Ujamma Place

UK Markey Cancer
Found.

UNCF

UNICEF
USA

UnidosUS

United Community
Ctr

UN Foundation

United Network for
Organ Sharing

United Performing
Arts Fund

United Spinal Assoc.

US Capitol Hist.
Society

US Hispanic Chamber

United Through
Reading

United Way

United Way-Cape Fear
Area

United Way Delaware

United Way Gr.
Cleveland

United Way Gr. Milw

United Way Gr. Milw
& Waukesha Co.

United Way No. NJ

United Way So. Tier

United Way SE Mich.

United Way Gtr
Union Co.

Univ. N. IA Fdn

Univ. MI Depression
Ctr
Urban Affairs
Coalition
Urban Ecology Center
Urban Initiatives
Urban League – Austin
Area
Urban League Milw
Urban League Broward
Co.
Urban League Buffalo
UL Central Carolinas
Urban League
Chicago
UL Detroit & SE
Michigan
UL Eastern Mass.
UL Essex County
Urban League Gr.
Atlanta
UL Greater Cleveland
Urban League Gr.
Pittsb
Urban League Gr. SW
OH
Urban League Greater
Chattanooga
UL Greater
Sacramento
Urban League
Houston
Urban League
Jacksonville

Urban League Los
Angeles
Urban League
Louisiana
Urban League
Louisville
UL Metro St. Louis
UL Metro Seattle
Urban League New
York
UL Philadelphia
UL San Diego County
Urban League
Rochester
Urban Promise
Ministry
U of SC School of
Nursing
Utah Food Bank
UTEC
Vanguar Comm. Dev.
Venture for America
Verde
Vizcaya Museum &
Gardens Trust
Volunteers Enlisted to
Assist People
Volunteers of America
Way to Grow LLC
W. Maryland Health
System
Wesley Comm. Service
Whitman Walker
Wildlife Con. Society

Williamson Health &
Wellness
Women & Girls Fund
Waukesha Co.
WomenHeart
Woodruff Arts Center
World Food Program
USA
World Monuments
Fund
World Vision US
World Vision Int'l
World Wildlife Fund
WSKG
WVU Cancer Institute
Xerces Society
for Invertebrate
Conservation
Year Up
Year Up – National
Capital
YMCA
YMCA Greater
Rochester
YMCA Metro
Milwaukee
YMCA Metro WA
YMCA USA
Yosemite Conservancy
Young Women's
Leadership Network
Youth Service
America
Youthlink

YWCA Greater Los
  Angeles
YWCA SE Wisconsin

Zoological Society
  Milw.
Zufall Health

Zuni Youth
  Enrichment
  Program

Photograph & Image Credits

Chapter 1
* **Map** – Md Omur F (Cozy Action Pro)
* **White Church** – Creative Commons
* **Red Church** – Creative Commons

Chapter 2
* **Map** – Md Omur F (Cozy Action Pro)
* **Wharf Tavern** – WharfTavern.com
* **American Tourister factory** – Shaun C. Williams
* **Jamiel's Shoe World** – bing file

Chapter 3
* **Map** – Md Omur F (Cozy Action Pro)
* **Prudential Building** – Creative Commons
* **Anna Sleslers** – *Boston Globe*
* **Suffolk Downs** – Wikipedia
* **Gillette Stadium** – Wikipedia
* **Foxborough** – Foxborough Historical Society
* **Northeastern University** – Wikimedia
* **Everett Marston** – Northeastern University Library
* **Evening Institute** – Springfield College Archives and Special Collections

Chapter 4
* **Map** – Md Omur F (Cozy Action Pro)
* **Bristol Phoenix** – East BayRI.com
* **Linotype** – Creative Commons
* **Graflex Press Camera** – National Museum of American History – Behring Center
* **Mount Hope Bridge** – Civitello Project Management
* **Coggeshall Farm** – Coggeshall Farm Museum
* **Herreshoff Marine Museum** – Creative Commons

Chapter 5
* **Map** – Md Omur F (Cozy Action Pro)
* **Manhattan View from NJ** – Bill Gracey – Creative Commons
* **A Train** – Metro US
* **Precious** – Ivaj Aicrag – Creative Commons
* **Albert Shanker** – Wikipedia
* **UFT/NEA** – www.uft.org; www.nea.org
* **Grasslands Hospital** – Cardcow.com

Chapter 6
* **Map** – Md Omur F (Cozy Action Pro)
* **New Jersey State Capitol** – Wikipedia
* **NJEA Headquarters** – hatzelandbuehlercom
* **NJEA Convention** – NJSpotlight.com
* **F. Lee Bailey** – Library of Congress
* **Lucy the Elephant** – Creative Commons
* **Marvin Reed** – Princeton Future
* **NJEA Review** – NJEA
* **Ball Four** – Wikipedia
* **NJN** – Wikipedia

Chapter 7
* **Map** – Md Omur F (Cozy Action Pro)
* **AFS** – Wikipedia

* **Dr. Stephen Rhinesmith** – by permission – Stephen Rhinesmith
* **Helen Hayes** – Wikipedia
* **One of Our Dinosaurs Is Missing** – Amazon
* **English Mastiff** – Creative Commons
* **Ford Foundation** – Creative Commons
* **AFS Headquarters** – AFS Virtual Museum
* **Salvador Allende** – Creative Commons
* **Augusto Pinochet** – The Red Phoenix
* **Aviendo Balboa** – TripAdvisor.com
* **Panama Canal** – Wikimedia

Chapter 8
* **Map** – Md Omur F (Cozy Action Pro)
* **Haydn Williams** – The Asia Foundation
* **Tudor City** – Creative Commons
* **Sausalito Ferry** – James MacIndoe – Creative Commons
* **Mount Tamalpais** – Nelson-Atkins Museum of Art
* **Keidanren** – Keidanren Kaikan – Creative Commons
* **Carabao Water Buffalo** – Creative Commons
* **Dog Meat** – Rob Sheridan – Creative Commons
* **Soju** – Creative Commons
* **Pacific-Union Club** – Carol Highsmith

Chapter 9
* **Map** – Md Omur F (Cozy Action Pro)
* **Donald M. Kendall Sculpture Garden** – Wikimedia Commons
* **Thomas Donohue** – Commonwealth Club – Creative Commons
* **River blindness map** – BlankMap-World6.svg
* **Lloyd Huck** – Creative Commons
* **GM logo** – Wikimedia Commons

Chapter 10
* **Map** – Md Omur F (Cozy Action Pro)
* **Walmart Headquarters** – flickr
* **IBM and P&G Logos** – Creative Commons

* **Bethlehem Steel Sparrows Point** – Wikipedia
* **Doughnuts** – BrokenSphere - Wikimedia Commons.
* **Focus group meeting room** – fuelinggreatbusiness.com
* **Raman Noodles Wikimedia commons** – Wikimedia Commons
* **Raman Noodle Commercial Machine** – Creative Commons

Chapter 11
* **Map** – Md Omur F (Cozy Action Pro)
* **Jasna Polana** – Creative Commons
* **Harbor Branch** – Dr. Dwayne Meadows, NOAA/NMFS/OPR, Courtesy: National Oceanic and Atmospheric Administration
* **Herb & Joy Kaiser** – Roger Crawford: Kaiser family photos
* **Penn State Nittany Lion** – Wikimedia Commons
* **Splenda®** – Creative Commons
* **Tate & Lyle** – F H K Henrion - Creative Commons
* **New Brunswick View** – Forevaclevah at English Wikipedia
* **Johnson & Johnson Headquarters** – Ekem – Creative Commons
* **The Old Shepherd's Chief Mourner** – Wikimedia Commons
* **Heldrich Hotel** – Atanasentchev – Creative Commons

Chapter 12
* **Map** – Md Omur F (Cozy Action Pro)
* **Project HOPE** – Project HOPE (Millwood, VA)
* **START Program** – William Dearstyne
* **Ponce, Puerto Rico** – Jose Oquendo – Creative Commons
* **Presidential Medal of Freedom** – Wikipedia Commons
* **Gulfstream** – Creative Commons
* **NACHC Logo** – Courtesy: National Association of Community Health Centers
* **Nanyang Technological University** – Creative Commons
* **Alfred E. Osborne, Jr.**- by permission – Dean Alfred E. Osborne

Chapter 13
* **Map** – Md Omur F (Cozy Action Pro)
* **Hyatt Regency Savannah** – Chris Gent – Creative Commons

* **Corporate Social Investing** – by permission – Curt Weeden
* **Confederate flag** – Wikipedia
* **Georgia State flag** – Wikipedia
* **ACCP** – Association of Corporate Contribution Professionals (archive)
* **Orlando Amway Center** – Creative Commons
* **Mark Shamley** – Courtesy of Mark Shamley

Chapter 14
* **Map** – Md Omur F (Cozy Action Pro)
* **Notre Dame Stadium** – Creative Commons
* **Lou Holtz Statue** – Flickr
* **GenPhar Building** – Brad Nettles – *Post and Courier* (*Charleston, SC*)
* **Georgetown University** – Creative Commons
* **William Novelli** – Creative Commons

CPSIA information can be obtained
at www.ICGtesting.com
Printed in the USA
LVHW052159131121
703162LV00005B/7

9 780974 371429